McGinness

INNER SPEECH AND THOUGHT

INNER SPEECH AND THOUGHT

A. N. Sokolov
Institute of Psychology
Moscow, USSR

Translated by George T. Onischenko

Translation edited by Donald B. Lindsley
Departments of Psychology and Physiology and
Member, Brain Research Institute
University of California
Los Angeles, California

A PLENUM/ROSETTA EDITION

Library of Congress Cataloging in Publication Data

Sokolov, Aleksandr Nikolaevich.
 Inner speech and thought.

 "A Plenum/Rosetta edition."
 Translation of Vnutrenniai̯a rech' i myshlenie.
 Bibliography: p.
 Includes indexes.
 1. Thought and thinking. 2. Speech. I. Title.
 BF455.S54513 1974   153.4'2   74-26701
 ISBN 0-306-20013-9

A Plenum/Rosetta Edition
Published by Plenum Publishing Corporation
227 West 17th Street, New York, N.Y. 10011

First paperback printing 1975

Inner Speech and Thought was first published as a volume in
Monographs in Psychology: An International Series

© 1972 Plenum Press, New York
A Division of Plenum Publishing Corporation

United Kingdom edition published by Plenum Press, London
A Division of Plenum Publishing Company, Ltd.
4a Lower John Street, London W1R 3PD, England

Printed in the United States of America

Editor's Preface

At a time when there is a recrudescence of interest in the higher cognitive functions of man and when a great deal of research is being initiated on problems of perception, concept formation, thinking, and the like, it is very appropriate and timely that A. N. Sokolov's "Inner Speech and Thought" has appeared. It is especially important for non-Russian-reading scholars in several disciplines to have this book available in English translation.

The book should prove to be stimulating and valuable to psychologists and neurophysiologists interested in information processing and some of the basic steps in problem solving. The behaviorist and physiological psychologist will be interested in some of the efforts made to externalize thought processes and measure objectively the activity of articulatory structures and speech musculature during problem-solving and thinking exercises. Speech pathologists, neurologists, psycholinguists and others should find the effects of articulatory interference on mental activity and the effects of articulatory conditions on processes of perception, memorization, and thought of special interest.

Sokolov very ably reviews some of the early history of theories and concepts concerning the interrelation of speech and thought, going back to the early Greek philosophers and the concept of *logos*. He traces the course of thinking about ideas and their role in language and thought from Descartes, Leibnitz, and Locke and the British empiricists and associationists to Külpe's Würzburg school of imageless thought, and finally to Piaget and to modern Gestalt and behaviorist psychologists, including some of his own countrymen. Chapters II and III are very important in reviewing modern psychological and physiological concepts of inner speech in psychology and in setting the stage for the experimental investigations of Sokolov and his students which follow in the next several chapters.

Sokolov and his collaborators have employed the electromyogram and the electroencephalogram, as well as some other special mechanical–electrical techniques, to reveal the state of the speech organs and musculature and the brain electrical activity during thinking, both with and without verbalization and the use of language. Although seemingly simple, these experiments tackle a very complex subject with which psychologists, linguists, and others are only beginning to come to grips. Sokolov and his group have succeeded admirably in splitting the subject apart by driving in the wedges of objective measurement and unique experimental formulations.

Chapter IX dips into the neurology and neurophysiology of motor speech and its feedback mechanisms and the dynamic localization and organization of the cerebral mechanisms responsible for symbolic formulation of speech and thought. The bibliography brings together a considerable number of Russian publications on this subject, as well as some of the pertinent American and European literature. This book is a welcome addition to an important field.

Donald B. Lindsley

Professor, Departments of Psychology,
Physiology, and Psychiatry, and
Member of the Brain Research Institute,
University of California, Los Angeles

Contents

Part Three
ELECTROMYOGRAPHIC STUDIES OF INNER SPEECH

Introduction

The subject of the present book is the psychological and physiological study of inner speech and its role in the thought processes of man.

In psychology, the term "inner speech" usually signifies soundless, mental speech, arising at the instant we think about something, plan or solve problems in our mind, recall books read or conversations heard, read and write silently. In all such instances, we think and remember with the aid of words which we articulate to ourselves. Inner speech is nothing but speech to oneself, or concealed verbalization, which is instrumental in the logical processing of sensory data, in their realization and comprehension within a definite system of concepts and judgments. The elements of inner speech are found in all our conscious perceptions, actions, and emotional experiences, where they manifest themselves as verbal sets, instructions to oneself, or as verbal interpretation of sensations and perceptions. This renders inner speech a rather important and universal mechanism in human consciousness and psychic activity.

The first investigations of inner speech carried out in the Soviet Union by L. S. Vygotskii (1934), P. P. Blonskii (1935), B. G. Anan'ev (1946), and the author (1941), made it clear, however, that despite its specificity (soundlessness and fragmentariness), inner speech, far from being an independent entity, is a secondary phenomenon derived from external speech—auditory perception of the speech of other persons and active mastery of all the forms of the spoken and written word. Seen from this viewpoint, inner speech represents a psychological transformation of external speech, its "internal projection," arising at first as a repetition (echo) of the speech being uttered and heard, but becoming later its increasingly abbreviated reproduction in the form of verbal designs, schemes, and semantic complexes operating not unlike "quanta" of thought. From these psychological descriptions, inner speech emerges as a rather intricate phenomenon, where thought and language are bound in a single, indissoluble complex acting as the speech mechanism of thinking.

1

This is also the determining factor in the great importance of inner speech to an explanation of the relationship between thought and speech—one of the oldest and most sharply debated problems, not only in psychology but in logic and linguistics as well. Two principal viewpoints have most often held sway in this field. The first of these claims thought and speech to be identical (thinking being soundless speech, "speech minus sound"); the second regards thought and speech to be interrelated in outward appearance only (speech being the external envelope of thought, a means of expressing ready-made ideas regardless of the form of words and sensory images). In modern psychology, the former view is reflected in the behaviorist interpretation of thinking as a motor speech habit. The latter view is found in the various theories of "pure" thought, generated by the Würzburg school of thought psychology. Sociohistorical analysis of the language-and-thought problem from the standpoint of dialectical materialism has revealed the unsoundness, scientifically speaking, of such ideas, their mechanistic and idealistic character. It has established an interrelationship between language and thought, their indissoluble unity within the process of human communication and cognitive activity. Having originated as a means of social intercourse and mutual understanding, language became at the same time a vehicle of thought, generalizing and fixating the social experience of man and mankind in concepts, judgments, and deductions. Hence the classical tenets of Marxism concerning the relation of thought to language: "*Language* is the immediate reality of thought" [1: 448]; "Ideas have no existence apart from language" [5: 99].*

The existence of a direct and inseparable connection between language and thought means that in contradistinction to the elementary thinking of animals, human thinking is, in its essence and its specificity, verbal thinking, where speech emerges not only as a means of expressing thought but, primarily, as a means of its formation and development, of analysis and synthesis, of abstraction and generalization.

A rather complex phonetic, lexical, and grammatical system, human speech is characterized by a sound envelope, its form, with which is associated a meaning, which comprises its objective content. Both become fixed in the course of the historical development of language, acquiring a relatively constant character, and are mastered by each individual in the process of his intercourse with other members of a given language community. In mastering the societally determined system of generalized and abstract signals of reality that is language, man masters all the logical forms and thought operations connected with it in its role as a (verbally) mediated reflection of real connections and relationships among objects.

---

* The first number in brackets is the reference number; the second, the page(s) of the source cited. Successive references are separated by a semicolon.

Speech also affects the intellectualization of sensations and perceptions (i.e., generalizes them not only according to apparent external attributes but also according to conceptual attributes), rendering them specifically human. This means that thinking is not only expressed by but also fulfilled in speech (L. S. Vygotskii), not only formulated by it but also formed in it (S. L. Rubinshtein). Early mastery of the verbal system of concepts ensures that virtually all other forms of thinking (objective-pictorial and objective-practical) will occur within the conceptual framework of language, i.e., on the basis of previously acquired concepts which are retained in memory and are subsequently actualized in the form of concealed, or inner, speech.

The above does not mean, however, that speech and thought are identical. Though inseparably interlinked, thought and speech at the same time retain their identities. The same thought can be expressed in different words and different grammatical forms (e.g., when translating or giving an account of ideas in one's own words). In some instances, words and sentences can be replaced by various conventional signs or symbols as, for example, in mathematics, the sciences, telegraphy, and cryptography. Such substitutions are more likely in inner speech, whose vocabulary frequently assumes a very individual, subjective significance and is complemented by graphic images. This indicates that the thought-language system is not as rigid as it would be if thinking and speech were identical; it is, on the contrary, labile and dynamic, allowing for the use in the thought process of the most diversified linguistic means and conventional signs for expressing concepts.

Hence, concepts are relatively free relative to the concrete forms for their expression, but still they cannot exist separate from their forms.

The neurophysiological aspect of the inner-speech-and-thought problem was treated by us on the basis of the reflex theory of I. M. Sechenov and I. P. Pavlov, taking into account current psychophysiological and clinical data. We shall deal briefly with the premises of this theory.

In Sechenov's famous books *Reflexes of the Brain* (1863) and *Elements of Thought* (1878), thinking is construed as a process of the formation, at first, of concrete (objective) associations which then gradually become ever more complex through "verbal symbolization" of impressions. Proceeding from the central inhibition of reflexes discovered by him, Sechenov applied this principle also to the analysis of thinking, believing that "*thought is the first two-thirds of the psychic reflex*" [141: 155]. In other words, thought is a reflex where its initial (receptor) and central (cerebral) components are present but its outward manifestation is inhibited. At the same time I. M. Sechenov stressed the enormous importance of the "muscle sense" (kinesthetic sensations) both in objective-pictorial and in verbal-abstract thinking; he pointed out that, owing to muscle sense, various sensory impressions are integrated into one complex whole impression of objects, a notion concerning the interrelationship between objects and phenomena in space and time comes into being, and finally, there arises the possibility of abstract thinking with the aid of an embryonic articulation of words (soundless or dumb speech).

Sechenov illustrates these propositions by the following example of thought development in the child. Initially the child learns to apprehend the surrounding world by means of various movements which in his mind become associated with various visual, tactile, auditory, and other impressions. As the child masters speech, he develops the capability to arrest his movements, and begins to express his thoughts in words (the reflex is now confined to the muscles of speech only). Subsequently, inhibition may spread to the external expression of words as well; what remains then is but dumb speech, accompanied by soundless movements of the tongue muscles within the oral cavity. This results in the sound image of words being replaced by kinesthetic sensations (speech kinesthesia). "It even seems to me," writes Sechenov, "that I never think directly in words, but always instead in muscular sensations which accompany my thought in the form of a conversation. At any rate, I am unable to sing to myself a song mentally in sounds alone; I always sing it with muscles, and then a memory of the sounds seems to appear" [141: 142].

Pavlov outlined his hypothesis of the physiological mechanisms of thinking in his concept of interaction between the first (objective) and second (verbal) signal systems. According to Pavlov, thought is either an objective or a verbal association, the latter being the more common since words make possible the abstraction and generalization characteristic of our "specifically human, higher thinking" [120: 490].

Pavlov originally related the second signal system chiefly to the frontal lobes of the brain, but later on he assigned to it all the speech segments of the brain whose impairment produces various forms of aphasia [123: 471-472].

Physiologically, following Sechenov, Pavlov assigned the greatest significance to the motor speech (kinesthetic) stimuli passing from the organs of speech to the cerebral cortex; he called them the "basis" or the "basal component" of the second signal system. Pavlov also took into account the auditory and visual verbal stimuli which arise when one listens to speech or reads and which are linked with kinesthetic speech impulses, forming with them the mechanism of the second signal system.

Thus, Pavlov planned to investigate the physiological mechanisms of the second signal system in relation to motor speech stimuli, whose function — following modern usage — consists in establishing feedback connections between the kinesthetic speech impulses and the central, cerebral mechanisms of speech. Although Pavlov's statements do not contain direct references to the functions of motor speech stimuli, definite conclusions about their roles may be drawn from Sechenov's research into the basis of muscle sensations: they organize and regulate movements on the basis of kinesthetic control, and they unify (integrate) separate sensory stimuli into a single functional system. In applying Sechenov's conception on the controlling and integrative functions of kinesthetic stimuli, it may be assumed that in the given case such control is executed not only over the correctness of word articulation but also over the correctness of word selection according to their semantic significance. Such control is likely to take place not only in human social intercourse but also in thinking "in private," when speech signalling takes on the form of inner speech, accompanied by an embryonic articulation of words.

It should be noted that the reflex theory of thought, developed by Pavlov and Sechenov, is radically different from the behaviorist "motor theory," though the latter too relates thinking to concealed speech reactions. The reflex approach differs from the behaviorist approach in its entirely different interpretation of the nature of speech reactions. According to the reflex theory, speech reactions are a manifestation of the acts of central, cerebral mechanisms, a result of integration of sense data by the brain's speech systems, in the process of which the feedback from the kinesthetic speech impulses to the brain is taken into account, the behaviorist theory—at least in the form propounded by Watson and his adherents—treats the speech reactions only as peripheral muscle processes in the larynx or other organs [173: 295; 279].

Though the extreme complexity of the brain structure has thus far prevented our acquisition of complete knowledge of the cerebral mechanisms of speech and thought, it is nevertheless evident that light can be shed on this problem, too, by investigating the role played by motor speech stimuli in cerebral activity. The book being offered to the reader's attention deals with an attempt to do precisely this.

The first two chapters offer a brief review of the history and current state of the problem of the interrelationship between speech and thought, and specifically the history of the inner speech problem. These chapters introduce the reader to a wide range of the philosophical, logical, and psychological problems related to inner speech, its development, and structure; they also describe the results of its investigations by various methods.

Chapter III deals with studies of the processes of verbal generalization and verbal reduction, and of the formation of abbreviated (generalized) associations and their semantic complexes during formation of mental acts. These processes were investigated by the method of thinking aloud—compulsory verbalization of thoughts at the moment of their inception. This made it possible to compare the logically surmised pattern (algorithm) of mental problem solving with the actual pattern revealed by the students of secondary schools. Certain physics problems were used as examples, and the results of comparisons between the logically-surmised and the actual courses of solution were represented in the form of charts demonstrating the processes of speech reduction during the formation of mental acts. The formation of abbreviated inferences is also exemplified by the results of a psychological analysis of the way foreign-language tests are understood by people with different degrees of mastery of a particular language. When the mastery is fair, the process of reading is considerably reduced—to a hurried grasping at the basic, key words which carry the general meaning of a sentence or text. In this connection, the hypothesis is advanced that semantic complexes (operators) of this kind are the main structural elements of inner speech, instrumental in the logical processing (differentiation and integration) of semantic information in the process of thinking.

The next step, bringing us closer to the direct study of inner speech, consisted in experiments elucidating the effect of various artificial speech (articulatory and auditory) interferences on various kinds of mental activity. Interferences of this sort made the internal articulation of words very difficult (by temporarily blocking inner speech), allowing it thereby to determine the role of inner speech in mental acts of various kinds. The results of these studies are reported in Chapters IV and V. They indicate that inner speech possesses both a function of semantic generalization and a function of semantic memorization, and both of them are very much disturbed whenever speech is interfered with.

Chapters VI-VIII give an account of the results of real-time electrophysiological investigation of inner speech during verbal and pictorial thinking. The most precise of our experiments, they enable us to make inferences about the neurodynamics of thought processes. Results indicate that the solving of all more or less complicated abstract problems, including the pictorial ones, is accompanied by distinct motor speech impulses either as an increase in the general tone of the speech musculature (tonic response) or as short-lived bursts of motor speech impulses arising at the moment of concealed articulation of words (phasic response). As the mental acts become automatized, however, the motor speech impulses grow progressively weaker and may even disappear altogether, arising only with the transition from one kind of mental act(s) to another. The electromyograms discussed in these chapters frequently demonstrate the discrete character of motor speech impulses, making it possible to regard inner speech as a "quantum" mechanism of thinking.

Finally, in Chapter IX we return to the clinical and neuroanatomical findings and discuss their application to our data on the dynamics and functions of inner speech.

Despite the fact that our inner speech studies have continued for quite sometime (they were initiated in 1940), they could not have possibly covered all the aspects of the problem because of its enormous complexity. We confined ourselves chiefly to the psychophysiological aspect; specifically, to the dynamics and functions of motor speech stimuli as the basal component of the second signal system. The rest of the issues involved are dealt with in outline only; they contain many lacunae which are only partially filled by a review of the work done by other researchers.*

My study owes much to my former scientific adviser, B. M. Teplov, with whom it was started and with whom I constantly consulted in my subsequent work. I am very grateful also to the scientific personnel of the Laboratory for Thought and Speech at the Institute of Psychology, Academy of Pedagogical Sciences of the USSR, for discussing my work with me and in many instances directly participating in it. The great help rendered to me by N. I. Balasheva in conducting the experiments and in the data processing deserves particular mention.

I should also like to express my gratitude to E. I. Boiko for valuable comment concerning the manuscript when it was being prepared for publication.

---

* Some important supplementary information bearing on this problem is furnished in the proceedings of a colloquium titled "Language and Thought" held in 1965 by the Department of Language and Literature, Department of Philosophy and Law, and the Institute of Linguistics, Academy of Sciences of the USSR (*Language and Thought,* "Nauka," Moscow, 1967). Unfortunately, we were unable to make use of these materials because they were published after the present book had been sent to press.

Part One

General Problems of Study

Chapter I

Theories of the Interrelation of Speech and Thought

The main questions forever arising when the problem of relationship between speech and thought comes up for discussion may be formulated as follows:

1. What is thinking and what is language (or speech)—are they the same or are they two different things?
2. Are thinking and speech always interrelated or is it possible to have thinking without speech and speech without thinking?
3. If thinking and speech are not identical, being only in some way related to each other, what is the role of speech in the thought process?

Ancient Greek philosophers created an interpretation of the term *logos* (λογος) which unified in one undifferentiated whole the categories of being, thinking, and language. The *logos* of the ancients was multivalued, signifying word (speech, language, statement) and thought (concept, reason, sense), as well as the universal law and the universe. Depending on whether matter or idea was held to be the initial principle, the concept of *logos* underwent radical changes, but always with the preservation of a unity or even identity of thought and word.

To Heraclitus of Ephesus, *logos* meant word, reasoning, intellect, a correlation, or, in a more general sense, the law of interpenetration of opposites and, at the same time, the understanding of this law whereby the cosmos is governed. "This order of things for everything in existence was made neither by any god nor by any man, but ever was, is, and will be: everliving fire, kindled according to measure and extinguished according to measure." Lenin thought this "a very good exposition of the principles of dialectical materialism" [6: 311]. The *logos* of Heraclitus reflected the dialectic of the universe and was itself the dialectic whereby it became known: everything is fleeting,

11

everything is in a constant state of coming into being and dissolving into nothingness; the only absolutes are strife, motion, and change.*

Plato's interpretation of *logos* was at the other end of the spectrum. To him, *logos* meant a mystical "pure idea" (εἰδος), the external world being but the outward appearance of ideas, their reflection. In reality, somewhere in a transcendental world, there existed the prototypes, or archetypes, of all things. Cognition consisted in the remembering by the immortal soul of this world of ideas, where it abode prior to its installation in the body. The remembering of ideas is effected by means of thinking or reasoning. By reasoning and talking with itself, the soul remembers the ideas associated with words, thus once more becoming cognate with them.†

Aristotle's concept of *logos* was contradictory and inconsistent, a mixture of materialist and idealist elements. He sharply criticized his teacher's theory of "ideas," and saw the basis of logical cognition to be a material, sensory world of things. He developed his logic ("analytics") as an instrument for demonstrating truth by establishing links between the premises of a syllogism, or by following the rules of induction, according to the existing facts. But the facts provide a knowledge of the individual and particular, while logic (thinking) has to establish that which is "universal," i.e., "that which is always and everywhere," since it is only the "universal" that reveals the essence of objects, their causes and patterns [11: 242].

The "universal" is expressed in concepts, and the concepts in words, or "nouns." By themselves, concepts and names comprise the "elements of thought," and out of their combination in speech (judgments) arises thought —statements, correct or erroneous, about objects. In the treatise *De Interpretatione* one finds:

> "For truth and falsity, both in thought and speech, imply a combination of the elements of thought, not their separation. By themselves, nouns and verbs are like thoughts without combination or separation; for instance, "man" and "white," provided nothing is added, are neither true nor false; yet they stand for something. For the word "goat-stag," too, has significance, but there is no truth or falsity about it, unless "is" or "is not" is added, either in the present or in some other sense" [14: 45].

Though combining thought and word into an inseparable whole, Aristotle does not identify them either with each other or with the objects of thought. He defines words as "symbols of thought" and letters as "symbols of words" [14: 12]. These symbols are not the same for all people, but the ideas

---

* A detailed exposition of the Logos concept is to be found in G. Thomson's book *The First Philosophers* [171: 262-267]. Heraclitus' excerpt concerning the "everliving fire" is quoted from M. A. Dynnik's translation [104: 44].

† The doctrine of reminiscence is expounded by Plato in his dialogues "Phaedrus" and "Phaedo"; the problem of speech and thought—in "Theaetetus" and "Cratylus."

and objects reflected by these ideas, are; by the same token, noun and concept cannot be identical: one and the same noun may signify different objects and imply different concepts. For instance, the word "creature" (ζῶον) may signify both man and a picture: the noun here is the same but the concepts are different. According to Aristotle, such things are named "equivocally." There are also cases when things are named "univocally" as, for instance, when the same word, "creature," refers to both a man and an ox; here, not only the name, but also the definition ("animal") are the same in both cases [12].

Aristotle thought it inadmissible to confuse thoughts and words with things ("For the essence of thought and the object of thought are not the same") [13: 215], believing that it is only in certain cases—in the realm of art and theoretical knowledge—the "logical definition [of a thing] and the thought [which cognizes it] are the same as the object of knowing. But even this coincidence of thought and thing is nothing but the product of logical abstraction. As for the source of thought, it derives, according to Aristotle, not from incorporeal abstractions, or "ideas," but from the perception of things. In *De Anima* he writes: "The soul never thinks without images," and, further on, "He who has no sensory perceptions will never learn anything and will never know anything by reason alone. Since man contemplates in his mind it is necessary that he at the same time contemplate in images. These are, as it were, sense observations, only without substance" [16: 100, 103].

However, Aristotle makes it quite clear that an image (imagining the particular) and a thought (common sensible) are not the same. He poses the question: "What are the attributes that distinguish primary concepts from images? Or [let] these concepts be not images but [at any rate, they cannot manifest themselves] without images" [16: 103]. He thus formulates a very important philosophical and psychophysiological problem of transition from particular to general, from sensual to logical, from sensation to thought; nevertheless, he was unable to resolve this problem in a materialistic way. In order to know the "general" he had to resort to a mystical source—a "reasonable soul," or "reason" which he calls the principle of all principles, or "the form of forms," and to which he ascribes the possibility of incorporeal existence.

This Aristotelian tribute to idealism for a long time retarded the scientific investigation into the study of speech and thought, tinting it for centuries with the mystical logos whose vestiges still survive whenever thinking, ideas, and concepts are considered by themselves, as if they were outside space, time and personality. To overcome idealism of this kind, it was necessary to expand the two-member "thought-word" relationship and include in it, as a material basis, the object world and the practical activity of men in which the logical processing of sense data takes place: their analysis, synthesis, and generalization by means of language. All of these elements were contained in Aristotle's philosophy and psychology, but in a contradictory form (inasmuch as they allowed for the intervention of nonmaterial factors ["rational soul" or "entelechy"], and it was these that prevented him from constructing a consistent materialistic theory of generalization.

It is interesting to note that, using as a point of departure notions about a relationship between thought and words and between words and breathing, ancient thinkers used to infer that thoughts and words originated in the lungs. Thus, in the *Iliad* restless thoughts are depicted as quick-moving creatures within the chest. In Plato's *Phaedrus*, Socrates says that "his chest is full of thoughts" [quoted in 258: 13, 67, 71]. Even for Aristotle, the substrate of thinking was the blood, as well as the Pneuma (air) and inborn heat, which imparted to the blood its higher functions. Hippocrates related all psychic functions to the brain, but even he regarded the air inhaled by man during respiration, as the substrate of apprehension [80: 233]. Generally speaking, these notions about the physiological substrate of thinking were not too far removed from the "primitive" introspection of Frazer and Max Müller, according to which thinking was supposed to be "speech in the stomach," [111: 43].

Medieval scholasticism, following in the footsteps of Platonic and Aristotelian philosophy, intensified the contradictions between sensory and logical cognition, making every effort to emancipate thought not only from sensory cognition but from language as well. Nowhere was this more evident than in the controversy between realists and nominalists apropos general concepts, or "universals," such as genus, species, difference, property, and accident. Extreme realists (Erigena, Anselm of Canterbury) believed these concepts to exist as metaphysical archetypes of things prior to things and irrespective of words, as assumed in Platonic mythology. Moderate realists (e.g., Thomas Aquinas) were not as rigid in their views and allowed for a triple mode of existence of the universals: before all things—in the thought of God; in the things themselves—in their finite form; and after things—in the thoughts of man. In contradistinction, nominalists held the universal concepts to be nothing but designations, or names (nomina), used by people to designate similar objects. Extreme nominalists (e.g., Roscellinus) asserted that a universal was not even a word as such but merely its acoustic shell—a mere "puff of sound" (*flatus vocis*), while moderate nominalists (Abelard *et al.*) saw the essence of the universal, on the contrary, only in the "significants" (*sermones*), or meaning, of words [75: 425, 431]. Abelard is also the author of the well-known dictum: "Language is generated by the intellect and generates it" ("*Sermo generatur ab intellectu, et generat intellectum*") [111: 31-32].

In modern philosophy, there has hardly been a thinker who in one way or another hasn't been interested in the problem of thought and speech and who hasn't left some statements about it. For the most part speculative, these are, nevertheless, of great interest since they continue to influence in one way or another the current attitude toward the problem of thought and speech. We shall consider briefly the more important contributions.

The first to continue the traditions of medieval nominalism in the philosophy of recent times were Bacon and Hobbes, who sharply criticized the medieval realism whose continued influence was making itself felt in philosophy and science. Bacon and Hobbes both were courageously paving the way for scientific knowledge, attacking theories, concepts, and statements which were out of accord with experience.

"People believe," wrote Bacon, "that their reason rules over their words, but sometimes it happens that the words turn their power against reason" [36: 124], for the majority of words take their origin in common opinion, unverified either by systematic experience or scientific induction. Because of this, words easily give birth to belief in nonexistent things and superficial abstractions. This Baconian critique of words and unverified opinions was continued by Descartes, Spinoza, Locke, and Leibnitz. Goethe, almost two centuries after Bacon, had Mephistopheles mouth it with bitter sarcasm:

> "Denn eben, wo Begriffe fehlen,
> Da stellt ein Wort zur rechten Zeit sich ein."

Hobbes was the first of the modern materialists to believe the thought process to be nothing more than combination and separation or, in other words, addition and subtraction—a principle which nowadays is being utilized with such success in cybernetics. This mathematical mechanism of thinking rests on sensations—in part ongoing, in part present in the memory, retained there by virtue of signs (words or nomina) which are used as a means for thought. Hobbes held, moreover, that the formation of thoughts is the first and natural purpose of language, its utilization for communication being next in importance he called the words used by us in thinking, notae (marks), as distinct from signa (signs)—the same words used during social intercourse. "*Names* are, therefore," wrote Hobbes, "in their essence first of all *marks* for strengthening memory. At the same time, secondarily, they also serve to designate and to give account of what we retain in our memory" [56: 62].

Opposed to Hobbes (who quite clearly restricted thinking to the combinative activity of the mind) were the 17th century rationalists, who defined "thinking" very broadly, including in it the entire content of human consciousness, not excluding the emotions or will. Descartes writes in *Principia philosophiae*: "By the word 'thought' [*cogitatio*] I mean all that which, when we are conscious, takes place in us, in so far as there is in us consciousness of these things. And accordingly, not only to understand, to will, to imagine, but even to feel, is the same here as to think" [62: 429]. These components of thinking also enter into the Cartesian formula "I think, therefore I am."

The term "thinking" is as broadly defined by Spinoza who, like Descartes, relegates to the modes of thinking not only "ideas" (images and concepts) but also various affects of the soul, such as love, desire, and so on [163: 403]. With such an all-encompassing definition, it is rather difficult to determine the relation of thinking to language, for the participation of language in the processes of reasoning and comprehension is one thing, and in the processes of imagination, desire, and feeling—quite another. It is for this reason perhaps, that neither Descartes' nor Spinoza's writings contain any special discussion of this topic. It is only from study of isolated passages that one may conclude that "general ideas" (or "universals," as Descartes continues to call them) must be linked with words (names of things).

Despite the breadth of approach which unites Descartes and Spinoza, however, there is a fundamental difference between them. Descartes was a dualist, believing man to be a union of two independent entities—body and soul (or, in other words, "extended" and "thinking" substance) and, as such, man in his behavior manifested duality, "involuntary" movements being of a reflex nature, whereas thought—an act of "higher reason." As for Spinoza, his was the stand of materialistic monism; all human actions, including thinking, he explained in a strictly deterministic way, believing that "the order and connection of ideas is the same as the order and connection of things." Proceeding from this, Spinoza gives a strictly materialistic formulation to the principle of association of ideas (without using this term, introduced later by Locke): "If the human body has at any time been simultaneously affected by two or more bodies, whenever the mind afterwards imagines one of them, it will also remember the others" [163: 423].

We should like to emphasize here that Spinoza uses this principle to explain not only memory (as formulated by him in Proposition XVIII quoted above) but also language and thought. In the note to this proposition he writes: "Hence we can also clearly understand how it is that the mind from the thought of one thing at once turns to the thought of another thing which is not in any way like the first. For example, from the thought of the word *pomum* [apple] a Roman immediately turns to the thought of the fruit which has no resemblance to the articulate sound *pomum*, nor anything common with it, except that the body of that man was often affected by the thing and the sound; that is to say, he often heard the word *pomum* when he saw the fruit. In this manner each person will turn from one thought to another according to the manner in which the habit of each has arranged the images of things in the body. The soldier, for instance, if he sees the footsteps of a horse in the sand, will immediately turn from the thought of a horse to the thought of a horseman, and so to the thought of war. The countryman, on the other hand, from the thought of a horse will turn to the thought of his plough, his field, etc.; and thus each person will turn from one thought to this or that thought, according to the manner in which he has been accustomed to connect and bind together the images of things in his mind [163: 424-425].

The tendency toward ever greater differentiation in discussion of the relationship between speech and thought becomes more and more pronounced after Descartes and Spinoza, invoking dependence on the psychological elements making up thought: "simple" and "complex" ideas, "singular" and "generic" images, etc., nothing but the "higher" forms of thinking being linked to words (abstraction and generalization of concepts). This tendency is already quite noticeable in Locke, becoming more pronounced in subsequent associationists (especially in J. S. Mill and, later, in Ribot).

In Locke we encounter both a broad and a narrow conception of thought. In the former case, he subsumes under thinking all forms of cognition (sensations, perceptions, memory, imagination, concepts), as well as various volitional and emotional states, designating it all by the Cartesian term "idea" [100: 240, 317]. Thinking in the narrow sense means "operation of the mind with respect to its ideas, where the mind is active, contemplating everything with a certain degree of voluntary attention" [100: 162-163]. In this case Locke makes a distinction between thought and perception, characterizing the latter as a more passive state of the mind. In connection with this dichotomy in the definition of thinking, Locke seems not to have had any firm opinion about the necessity of language for thinking. On the one hand he acknowledged the immense importance of language in cognition; language makes it possible for the mind to penetrate into the mysteries of nature, to unify and fix the results of thinking by means of common terms. On the other hand, Locke allowed for a society where man already possessed a "great multitude of ideas," useful not only for him but for others as well, for whose transmission he had to invent language. It seems to follow that he considered it possible for thoughts to be generated without language. The possibility of such "speechless" thoughts is also admitted by Locke for people possessing speech who find it necessary to compose a "mental sentence" (bringing together and separation of ideas) about things directly, bypassing words, although he concedes that "it is very difficult to discourse on mental sentences" [100: 559-560].

In spite of these contradictory statements, Locke must be given credit for his detailed treatment of many philosophical-psychological problems of language and thought, to which he devoted the entire third chapter of his *Essay Concerning Human Understanding*, as well as for formulating the principle of "association of ideas," which he also uses to explain the formation of connections between names and objects.

Leibnitz had more definite statements to make about the necessity of language in thinking. Of particular interest are his remarks about the role played by language in the process of mental reasoning "in private." In *New Essays Concerning Human Understanding* he writes: "Having been created, language serves man also as a tool for reasoning in private with himself both because words help him remember abstract thoughts, and because of the benefit he derives by having recourse to signs and silent thoughts while reasoning. And indeed, too much time would be needed if everything had to be explained and if definitions had to be substituted for terms" [97: 239].

From this quotation it may be concluded that Leibnitz already suspected the existence of some structural differences between external and internal speech, believing that thinking in private language is used in a somewhat different form (without logical definition of terms) than when it is used for communicating thoughts to others. This difference between the thought language and communicative language was fixed by Leibnitz terminologically as well; like Hobbes before him, he called the words used in thinking, notes for one's own use (*notae*), and the words used to communicate thoughts to others, signs (*signa*). He pointed out, moreover, that besides words, numerals and algebraic signs, too, could be used as *notae* [97: 294].

Post-Lockean associationism developed in the materialistic and in the idealistic directions. The first was represented by Hartley and the French materialists; the second, by Berkeley, Hume, and their followers in logic and psychology (James Mill, J. S. Mill, A. Bain, and others).

Hartley's viewpoint is of interest, primarily, as the first attempt at a physiological explanation of associations by "nervous vibrations," the agitation of the medullary substance under the influence of extraneous stimuli acting on the sense organs. Too, Hartley included in the associative process the "muscular vibrations," whose attenuated effect he thought explained images of movements (ideomotor acts), association of ideas with movements and words being responsible for volitional acts (the possibility of a voluntary control over movements with the aid of words) [239: 52-58].

Although Hartley's ideas on the nervous and muscular vibrations were of a rather speculative nature, they nevertheless strongly influenced the subsequent development of physiological concepts of psychic activity, providing as they did a materialistic explanation not only for the automatic acts of animals (as was done by Descartes) but also for the higher mental functions of man.

As for idealistic associationism, words possessed for it purely symbolic "reality," with actually nothing behind it. This viewpoint is most pronounced in Berkeley and Hume. For Berkeley, objects do not exist "outside the mind," they are but "collections of ideas," and matter is a "nonentity."

Declaring matter to be an empty abstraction, Berkeley held that the mind could not contain any abstract ideas at all, that which is called "universal ideas" being but particular ideas (individual images) connected with general terms, whose use does nothing but damage to thinking. The question even occurred to him whether "speech was not more of a hindrance than an aid in the advancement of science" [25: 55-56].

To divorce thought from language obviously verged on the absurd and this philosophy was completely rejected by Kant, Hegel, and the linguists who followed them, Humboldt and Steinthal, for whom language was the principal actor of the "spirit," no thought being able to exist without language. Kant considered language necessary for understanding not only others but oneself as well. "To think means to *speak* to oneself [Tahiti Indians (*sic*) call thinking 'speech in the stomach'], hence to *hear* oneself inwardly (through reproductive imagination)" [78: 430].

Hegel, too, believed that we think in names and that it is impossible to think without words [50: 273]. However, both Kant and Hegel interpreted the connection between thought and language in a purely idealistic way: for Kant, it was based on the *a priori* categories of "pure reason"; for Hegel, on the activity of "the absolute spirit."

Of greater interest are the views of Hegel, for whom thinking is the "grasping and joining together of the diversity into a unity" [51: 96]. In this sense his interpretation of thought is similar to the Greeks' *logos* (the collecting and joining together; word and reason). The influence of the ancients is also felt in Hegel's almost verbatim reiteration of the Aristotelian thesis on the relationship between thought and sensations: "When we grasp sensory diversity, we do not think yet; thought is only when we bring it together (*das Beziehen*)" [51: 96].

According to Hegel, the joining of contemplations and notions takes place by means of the memory, a sign. The highest creation of productive memory is language–an abstract sign of memory, with the aid of which a concrete notion becomes "something imageless, identical to the sign" [51: 180]. What may be new here, as compared to Aristotle, is that sense experience becomes absorbed by the abstract sign, whereas for Aristotle thinking seemed impossible without images, though it was not reduced to them. The emphasis on the role of language as the abstract sign of memory is an important factor in Hegel's psychology of thought, but since thought and memory (even if "productive") still are not identical, the indication of its mnemonic function alone does not exhaust all its significance in thinking, leaving obscure other aspects of their relationships.

Nowhere was this circumstance manifested as distinctly as in the well-known Hamiltonian analogy comparing thinking to the digging of a tunnel on a sandy shore–an analogy which stems precisely from attributing to language only a fixing function. Hamilton points out that when digging a tunnel in sand one cannot advance without securing every inch of the tunnel with an arch of bricks, and that the same occurs in thinking: each step of the thought process has to be fixated with words, so that no forward movement of thought is possible without words. This entirely correct proposition is followed, however, by a second, questionable, part of the analogy, where it is asserted that, similar to the fact that the intensity of tunnel digging is independent of the bricklaying work, the intensity of thinking does not depend on language, whence it should be evident that thoughts as such arise prior to and independent of the words that fixate them [109].

This conclusion has its adherents, but if it is assumed that there is organic unity of thought and language, so that language acts not only as an external support but also as an internal mechanism of the thought act itself, then the Hamiltonian analogy is clearly insufficient, clearing a path for various dubious ventures into "speechless thought."

Thus, Schopenhauer, while acknowledging the extreme importance of language for intellectual development and regarding words as "valuable material wherein the treasure-house of thought can be expressed and preserved" [198: 857], also asserted that "thought lives the true, full life only so long as it does not transgress the boundary where words begin; here it becomes petrified and is henceforth dead" [198: 817]. Similarly, Jessen held that "thoughts occur in us not through words; they exist in us prior to any generation of words, only later on presenting themselves to us in the shape of words" [247: 116-117].

Düring, Bergson, Husserl, and the psychologists of the Würzburg school (Külpe, Bühler, and others) expressed similar views. Moreover, it was not just the elementary forms of abstraction and generalization commonly ascribed to animals (e.g., by J. S. Mill, Ribot, and many contemporary scholars, including Pavlov) that were in all cases relegated to "wordless thinking," but the highest and most abstract forms of philosophical thought. Düring had precisely this type of philosophical thought in mind when he wrote: "He who is capable of thinking with the aid of language alone, has not yet experienced *abstract* and *genuine* thinking." Quoting this statement, Engels remarks with irony: "If this is so, animals turn out to be the most abstract and genuine thinkers, since their thinking is never obscured by the importunate meddling of language" [3: 85]. At the end of the last century, Max Müller urged against such divorcement of thought from language. Arguing from the ideas of Humboldt and Steinthal, he asserted: "There is no reason without language. There is no language without reason." He chose these words as the epigraph for his book *Science of Thought,* where he adduces a large amount of linguistic material on this problem and analyzes critically the views of various philosophers, logicians, and linguists. By the word "thought" Müller understands an act of thinking; and "thinking" means for him mental combinations (joining and separation) of things. Each thought is inseparably bound up with sensations, notions, conceptions, and names. To the latter he assigns not only words but all the signs useful in human intercourse (gestures, symbols, hieroglyphs, etc.); in the case of silent thinking he includes here also the muscular reproduction of words in a very curt, compact form, which owing to practice, forms an "algebra of signs" of a sort and is being mistaken for wordless thoughts [111: 43].

Müller's propositions are interesting and fruitful. Most characteristic is, however, his persistent tendency to equate thought with words. For him, "Language is thought, and thought is language" [111: 61]; "Language and intellect are identical" [111: 63]. But if language and thought are indeed identical, then it is obvious that the very problem of their interrelation ceases to exist, and differentiation of any kind among logic, psychology, and linguistics is completely unnecessary (which shows Müller's conception to have been rather naive). Müller's greatest contribution was the lively interest aroused by his polemics in later psychologists and psychoneurologists and which directed them toward genetic and experimental investigations in the subject.

* * * * *

Of great importance to an understanding of the current theories of the interrelation between speech and thought is its discussion in the works of many Russian philosophers, psychologists, and linguists of the 19th century, especially in those of A. I. Herzen, A. A. Potebnya, and K. D. Ushinskii.

A. I. Herzen's opinions on this subject have been discussed comprehensively and eloquently by B. M. Teplov in his article "Herzen's psychological viewpoint" [169], from which we shall cite several excerpts. Herzen's distinguishing characteristic as a psychologist is his attempt to overcome dualism, including that present in discussion of the relationship of thought to words. Herzen perceived no antagonism between thought and speech, although he was well aware of their rather complex interrelations in the over-all "drama of knowledge."

To Herzen, a word was a form of thought sufficient to communicate one's thoughts to other people, and to make them clear to oneself. "A thought becomes clear to me when I write it down" [54: 27]. "There is no thought which could not be expressed simply and clearly, particularly in its dialectical developments" [52: 64]. So-called "inexpressibility in words" occurs, according to Herzen, because the thought-contents inexpressible in words are of an exceptionally "private," or "casual" nature which becomes lost in verbal communication.

At the same time Herzen points out that a word devoid of concrete content may well be not only useless but deleterious by retarding the movement of thought, creating an illusion of knowledge where in actuality there is none. In cases like this, "In uttering a word, we are under the illusion that we know its meaning, that we are pin-pointing the very cause, while *all we are doing is naming it*" [53: 133]. Hence Herzen's demand that a thought be terse, simple, and clearly stated—qualities which only a profound knowledge of life, a combination of theory and practice, can provide.

The views of A. A. Potebnya, found in his *Thought and Language* (1862), had largely been formed under the influence of the revolutionary democrats A. I. Herzen, N. G. Chernyshevskii, and N. A. Dobrolyubov, which had enabled him to part Humboldt's and Steinthal's notions of language as creative activity of the spirit.

As a result of his analysis of the relationship between thought and word, Potebnya concluded that: "Language is not a means of expressing an already formulated thought but a means of creating it ... It is not a reflection of an established world outlook but the activity which leads to its establishment. In order to become aware of his emotional states, to apprehend his external perceptions, man has to objectify each of them in a word and to relate this word to other words" [135: 130]. The word taken as a whole, i.e., as a combination of meaning and sound, appears also as a means of understanding the speaker's thought, as a means of apperceiving the content of his thought.

Although Potebnya notes the organic unity of language and thought, he does not equate word and thought. He points out that the sphere of language is far from being coincident with that of thought; he believes elementary, sensual generalizations to be possible without words, just as it can be observed in animals and in children who do not yet speak. In these cases, Potebnya believes, a sensory image unconsciously becomes assimilated into a single common image or "schematic notion" which in children is later joined by the word.

Mastery over words brings to the child's psychology something fundamentally new—the possibility to form concepts instrumental to the creation of an internal unity between an object and its attributes—objects become systematized. Potebnya states that the "transition from the image of an object to a notion about an object" takes place through the word alone, although the mechanism of this transition remains for him obscure. He believed that "Like many other things in personal and national life, the concept will forever remain for us an entity generated, so to speak, by multiplying known conditions by unknown, and *probably* unexplorable, forces" [135: 49].

Potebnya is of the opinion that thinking without words can only occur, in speaking people, on the basis of a previous knowledge of language or, at any rate, when words are more or less clearly referred to (as, for instance, in the use of scientific formulae). "One should not forget, however, that the faculty of thinking in a human manner but without words comes only through words, and that without speaking people, or teachers taught by speaking people, a deaf-mute would for ages remain almost an animal" [135: 49].

Potebnya also sees a link between language and the more complex forms of man's creative activity. "The creative thought of the painter, sculptor, or musician is inexpressible in words and occurs without them, although it presupposes a considerable degree of development, obtainable only through language" [135: 127].

Potebnya regarded as quite felicitous Goethe's simile, wherein the poet likens the process of thought formation to the manufacture of cloth with a loom, if to the word, as Steinthal assumes [270: 197-201], is assigned the role of the shuttle whose single stroke "weaves a hundred loops and makes a thousand knots."* This simile conveys the relationship between thought and word much more precisely than does the Hamiltonian analogy between thinking and tunneling, where the word is merely assigned the role of a mechanical support for thought, whereas the comparison of the word to a loom points to the actual inseparability of the thought-word process, where the word acts as the internal mechanism of the thought act itself.

The little that has been said is sufficient to show how careful and thorough Potebnya was in his approach, contrasting speech and thought and demonstrating by way of numerous examples that they cannot be equated. The idea of the complex and contradictory nature of the relation of thought to speech brings, in many respects, Potebnya's conception close to the current notions about them, and, though over a hundred years have passed since the publication of *Thought and Language,* it still retains its scientific value.

Research into the relation of thought to speech was furthered by K. D. Ushinskii for whom it was not only of theoretical but also of considerable practical, educational interest.

With the data furnished by psychology, logic, and linguistics as his starting point, Ushinskii asserted that the transition to abstract concepts could be implemented only through the intermediary of the word, or language. The word enables man to embrace at once many individual notions, to unify them into a single concept. "The entire process of thinking ... is accomplished through words" [177: 633].

The high value Ushinskii placed upon the mother tongue is well known. For him the mother tongue was "the spiritual garment every kind of knowledge should clothe itself in to become the true possession of human consciousness" [179: 356].

However, Ushinskii emphasized that language, though a powerful tool for the education of man, cannot replace knowledge derived directly from observations and experiments. "True, language accelerates and facilitates the acquisition of such knowledge, but it also may hinder it if man's attention has too early and primarily been centered not on the content but the form of thought, and somebody else's thought at that, which the pupil is perhaps not even old enough to understand" [177: 35].

The educator should never forget, in this respect, the difference between the thought processes of the adult and that of the child. "In pursuit of science," wrote Ushinskii, "we gradually get into the habit of abstracting ourselves from the materials we use, without ever, be it even in the case of a single word, being able to divorce ourselves from them. But the child, if one may put it that way, thinks in terms of forms, colors, sounds, and sensations

---

* *"Ein Schlag tausend Verbindungen schlägt." (Faust).*

in general; and he who would have the child think in a different way would wrongfully, and in vain, violate the child's nature" [180: 266].

Hence Ushinskii's requirement that visual methods of teaching be used and that transition from the concrete to the abstract, from a notion to a thought, be gradual and handled with great caution. Just imagine the amount of pedagogical talent expanded on "The Grammar" (*Rodnoe Slovo*, 3rd year of publication). The pupil was acquainted by means of a gradual and most detailed analysis of Pushkin's "The Tale of the Fisherman and the Golden Fish," with the concepts of "noun," "adjective," "numeral," etc. Ushinskii achieved, through analysis of the graphic pictures painted by the poet, the utmost clarity in the explanation of abstract grammatical categories. In examining, further, the teaching of arithmetic, he noted that failure in arithmetical studies usually is due to the fact that children start solving problems without having become used to arithmetical language. He advised teachers to pay special attention to this facet of the pupils' studies so much so as to train children in the writing down and reading of problems already solved, and only then to pass on to the actual solution of written problems.

The preceding demonstrates Ushinskii's conviction that the transition to abstract concepts in the elementary school was one of the most crucial factors in teaching, a factor which to a considerable degree determines the subsequent course of the child's intellectual development. It is not at all a matter of indifference to the teacher whether the child will understand or not some grammatical or arithmetical rule or another, whether or not he will master a concept, the indifference not only in a narrow "grammatical" or "arithmetical" but also in a much broader respect—in the sense of the child's over-all intellectual development, in the sense of the development of abstract thinking, upon which school and life place ever increasing demands every succeeding year of school and every succeeding year of life.

Having discussed the processes of concept formation, Ushinskii subsequently demonstrates their dependence on the emotions, will, and ideas (world outlook) of man.

Many past philosophers, such as Bacon, Descartes, Spinoza, and Kant, are known to have regarded feelings (emotions) as a hindrance to "pure," impassive thought, i.e., unencumbered by passion. Thus, Bacon authored the well-known aphorism, ". . . his feelings imbue and corrupt his understanding in innumerable and sometimes imperceptible ways" [36: Aphorism XLIX].

Ushinskii was well aware that feelings and desires may sometimes lead man into error. "For instance, a man may develop an aversion to something—a vocation, object, or science, or a dislike for a person as a result of a misconception concerning these things, resulting, in turn, from faulty observations which, again, were due to various causes. This feeling of aversion and the desires and disinclinations will from now on enter into any new decision as a finished result" [178: 421], thereby distorting the truth.

While admitting that everyone may be prone to many such erroneous results, Ushinskii nonetheless could in no way agree to regard "pure," impassive thinking as the ideal of education. He considered it to be absolutely impossible and contrary to the nature of man. Man cannot be deprived of his feelings and desires. "Even Kant himself, whom none other than the cold Hegel accuses of coldness, was, it seems to us, one of the most passionate of men, except that the objects of his passion were metaphysical and logical investigations" [178: 257]. Ushinskii believed that the emotions should be cultivated in such a manner as to mold them into a powerful stimulus to be applied to the search for truth, rather than to allow them to act as a source of error.

Among the great diversity of sensations involved in intellectual activity, Ushinskii assigns a special place to "intellectual" or "mental" sensations (e.g., the sensation of difference and similarity, sensations of mental tension, astonishment, and the like).

Starting from the fact of constant interaction not only of sensations and desires but also of the latter with the notions and concepts, Ushinskii established a principle quite important to psychology—that of the formation of stable notions imbued with feelings and desires, which, as the sum total of previous thought and experience, enter into almost all the decisions and beliefs of man. Ushinskii called such stable concepts, imbued with feelings and desires, general, main concepts and attached vital importance to them, as, being a part of the process of deliberation, they may predetermine human decisions.

* * * * *

Of particular interest to a discussion of recent theory on the relation of thought to speech are the views of West European and American scholars, particularly as reflected in the pages of *Acta Psychologica* (Amsterdam, 1954). The discussion was initiated by the editor, Professor G. Révész, who enlisted the cooperation of a number of prominent scholars in this field. Among them were representatives of the various schools of psychology—J. Piaget (Geneva-Paris), F. Kainz (Berlin), W. Eliasberg (New York), J. Cohen (Manchester), Révész himself (Amsterdam); a philosopher, J. Jorgensen (Copenhagen), a linguist, E. Buyssens (Brussels), a mathematician, B. Van der Waerden (Zurich), and two psychoneurologists, K. Goldstein (New York) and H. Gruhle (Bonn).

It was the editor's desire that a selection of specialists from such diverse fields would ensure the greatest possible breadth of discussion and would, perhaps, facilitate the adoption of general propositions enabling the creation of a unified theory of speech and thought. This project has not been successfully concluded, however, due to the extreme disparity of the opinions expressed.

The two main questions posed were: 1) Is thinking possible without speech? and 2) Is speech possible without thought? Answers to these questions presupposed the existence of a definition of the functions of thought and speech (language), of the extent of their interrelation, as well as of their relation(s) to graphic-image cognition, practical activities, and nonverbal forms of social intercourse.

On the whole, Révész [263], Kainz [249], and Goldstein [231] championed the unity and interrelation of thought and language, though differentiating certain of their structural and functional features; thinking carries out a cognitive function in conformity to the laws of logic, and language (words and other signs and symbols) has a symbolic function according to the grammatical rules of a given language. At the same time, language and thought are equivalent in content, existing only as a "dualistic unity" (Révész) or as a "functional symbiosis" (Kainz) whereby the cognitive purpose of thought is achieved.

Goldstein supplements these propositions by noting the importance of the symbolic function of language and thought not only for cognitive processes but also in formation of the main structural characteristic of personality —the capacity to look at the world from the position of an "abstract set" which, according to his observations, is constantly disturbed in the presence of the speech disorders accompanying aphasias.

Though recognizing the impossibility of separating thought from language in all types of human intellectual activity (including those which are usually classed as belonging to nonverbal activity—architecture, painting, chess playing, etc.), Révész at the same time admits the existence of "wordless thought," to which category he relegates quiet (silent) thinking as well as unconscious and intuitive thinking. True, he emphasizes that these forms of thought, too, only become possible on the basis of antecedent verbal thinking and are of but limited duration, constantly switching over to verbal thinking, without which they cannot exist. As proof of the "wordlessness" of these forms of thought, Révész cites the self-observations of competent researchers (G. Müller, K. Koffka, K. Bühler, O. Selz, J. Dewey, M. Wertheimer, J. Piaget, and others) and the opinions of poets and mathematicians who frequently report that creative thoughts occur to them without words and that much effort is required to put them into verbal form.

One should not forget, however, that introspection may be rather imprecise and subjective in spite of the psychological competence of the researchers. It is very likely that in many cases, especially those involving creative activity on the part of natural scientists and technicians, as well as of poets and writers in search of imagery, the thought-process is not concentrated predominantly on verbal objects (words and sentences) but on real objects or on images, in which case the arising verbal generalizations of images readily escape the focus of attention and are ignored.

This is the more likely, for in an attempt to explain wordless thought, Révész himself resorts to the latent effect of language, which manifests itself particularly clearly in a "provisional" and fragmentary formulation of ideas, i.e., when out of what is thought, very little is formulated, the rest being implied as something known, that is, stored in our memory, or, according to Révész's hypothesis, in the sphere of the unconscious.

But if this be so, if wordless thinking is based on language and cannot exist without it, and, accompanied moreover, by provisional formulation of some of the ideas, then the term "wordless thinking" is very imprecise as applied to these cases, since it fails completely to reflect the role of language in it. This kind of thinking would more appropriately be called "mixed" or "verbal-pictorial," in which, besides the predominant imaging elements, words or their fragments operate, or, at least, signs or symbols replacing the words. This comment also applies to Kainz's interpretation of wordless thought as a preform or prestage of thought (Vorformen des Denkens). It would be more correct if it referred only to the very first stages of sensory (Pavlov's "first-signal") analysis and synthesis, prior to the activation of vocal ("second-signal") connections, not, to the most creative and richest aspects of activity, as assumed by Kainz.

Piaget's [259] view on the problem of the relation between thought and speech has developed little since he first enunciated it in his *The Language and Thought of the Child* (1923). Guided by his research in child psychology, he notes that in the development of thought and speech there are elements of "divergence" and "convergence" and that genetically thought is antecedent to speech. The beginning of thought he sees in the symbolic play which may be observed at the end of the first year of life, and later on, in the delayed imitation by the child of speech heard. Speech is at this time, according to Piaget, of no significance for the development of thought in the child, and subsequently it comes into play only after mental actions have been formed on the basis of practical operations. Piaget reduces the role of speech at all stages of mental development to little more than the formation of thought structures and their integration into synchronous systems, or ensembles.

In this theory, thought has priority in all cases, as if it could arise spontaneously from the sensorimotor acts as such, without the cooperation of language, whose services Piaget enlists only for completing the "structurization" of the created thought-acts and their "socialization." It is true that thoughts cannot arise *ex nihilo* and that they presuppose manipulation of objects to be based on. But it is also quite evident that sensorimotor acts in themselves, without the simultaneous cooperation and formation in them of verbal acts (naming, classification, generalizations, etc.), would never be able to lead the child past the stage of the "sensorimotor intellect." All that precedes makes the theory of genetic asynchronism of thought and speech rather artificial.

Along with the adherents of the rather narrow interpretation of thinking as a "conscious differentiation, comparison, and categorical ordering" (Révész) or as an "abstract set" of personality (Goldstein), inherent in man alone, there were also representatives of a broader definition of thinking. From their point of view, thinking embraces all the problem-solving processes, from object manipulation to abstract philosophical reasoning. In defending this viewpoint, the Danish philosopher, J. Jorgensen [248] points out that in all cases thought operates with symbols, the role of which can be played not only by words but also by drawings, concrete images, as well as by indicatory movements of various kinds (turning of the head, eye and hand movements, shrugging the shoulders, etc.). Correspondingly, he distinguishes between two groups of symbols: verbal (or "nondepictive") and "depictive." Interpreted narrowly, as operations on abstract forms, thinking is impossible without language. Without a broader definition of thought, when it is made to contain all types of problem-solving processes, it is possible without language, with the aid of the "depictive" symbols alone. In this connection, Jorgensen, like Kainz, believes in the existence of various kinds of thinking: the abstract type, based on words, and the empirical, or technical, type, based on images and movements. This typology does not take into account, however, the constant interaction of the "depictive" and "nondepictive" symbols, which makes thinking with the aid of the "depictive" symbols alone or thinking in words alone very unlikely in people who use speech.

The greatest predilection for wordless thinking was shown in this discussion by the mathematician Van der Waerden and the linguist E. Buyssens. Van der Waerden [277] held that for an understanding of geometrical concepts, such as "circle," "straight line," "equality," "Pascal's helix," etc., only graphic-pictorial and motor representations associated with the construction of geometric figures were necessary, the words and formulae used only facilitating mental activity. In support of his thesis, Van der Waerden cites as examples the ancient, pre-Christian scholars, who founded the theory of mathematics without any knowledge of formulae. But can this be considered an argument against the thesis that language is necessary for thought?The Greeks were satisfied to formulate their mathematical investigation in words, and so they did not doubt that their thinking, too, was done in words; otherwise they would not have combined thought and word in their "logos."

Buyssens went even further in this direction. He held that in principle, language, by its very nature, could be neither an instrument of thoughts nor a means of their expression; in his opinion, words always have only a general, abstract meaning, whereas thoughts are individual and concrete. "Words only refer to meaning, not to thought, still less to facts" [211: 164]. As proof, he notes that one and the same phrase, for instance, "My father is ill," may have different thought contents (in one instance, for example, it may refer to a robust eighty-year-old, in another, it may refer to a younger man, slight in stature, etc. The same is found when several artists are commissioned to illustrate the same novel. For the same page of the work their interpretations of what is written will differ, and their illustrations will reflect the differences [211: 142-143].

These examples are adduced by Buyssens to convince the reader that language is not to be regarded as the embodiment of thought and that, therefore, "we think not in a certain language but outside our language" [211: 157].

Psychologically, Buyssens' interpretation contains much that is in error. Buyssens' tendency toward reducing thought to concrete representations, or individual images comes immediately to mind. It was clear even to Aristotle that, though interconnected, thought and image were not the same. The thought contains the universal (a number of relationships forming a concept), and it is precisely for this reason that the word, possessing a common meaning, is the most adequate form for expressing thought or a reference to thought if the latter is represented by a concrete image. Equally erroneous is Buyssens' denial that the concrete content of thoughts can be expressed in words. His argumentation here is the same as that of the Socratics who held that "language expresses, essentially, only the universal; but that which is thought is special, particular. Language therefore cannot express what is thought." Lenin, quoting Hegel, notes in the margin, "NB: language has only the universal," writes at the same time, "Why not name the particular? One of the objects of a given kind (tables) differs from the rest in precisely such and such features" [6: 249]. And indeed, why cannot the phrase "My father is ill" be supplemented (if necessary) by the information that the father is already eighty years old, that he is robust, etc.? For Buyssens did just that, and he did it through language.

Nor were the views of psychoneurologists united. Whereas for Goldstein the functional unity and interrelation of thought and speech was an undeniable fact, for Gruhle, a colleague of his, this was more than questionable. Disturbances of reasoning activity in aphasia Gruhle regards as secondary phenomena, produced not by the speech disturbances as such but by the depressed emotional state ("inferiority complex") of aphasic patients [237]. However, Eliasberg reports that his long-term observations of aphasic patients show no evidence whatever of any mental disturbances [225].

* * * * *

In view of the fact that many of the participants based their arguments in favor of the existence of "wordless thought" on the statements of mathematicians and physicists (Einstein's in particular), these statements should be considered in some detail. The material concerning this issue has in the main been collated by the French mathematician J. Hadamard, who has made an inquiry among his colleagues on the form and method of their mathematical reasoning [238]. His correspondents included many prominent mathematicians, among them Birkhoff, Wiener, Douglas, Pólya, and Einstein.

In a number of cases the mathematicians reported that in their thought process they used mental words, algebraic signs and various vague images. Hadamard himself insists that when he is engaged in thought, words are absent from his consciousness. Even he, however, retains a shadow of doubt, and he writes in a footnote: "It is quite possible, and rather probable, that words are present in fringe-consciousness. Such is the case, I imagine, for me, as concerns words used in mathematics. I doubt, however, that it is so for some other kinds of thoughts because, if it were, I should have less difficulty in finding them" [238: 75].

Not all mathematicians gave such answers, however. Some of them were quite certain that in one form or other, words and algebraic signs are of great importance in their mathematical investigations. Birkhoff reported that he visualized algebraic signs; Wiener answered that he happened to think both in words and without them; Douglas emphasized not the significance of words as such, as much as the rhythm of their enunciation, with an emphasis on separate syllables, similar to the tapping out of the Morse code. Pólya has characterized his thinking as verbal. "I believe," he writes, "that the decisive idea which brings the solution of a problem is rather often connnected with a well-turned word or sentence. The word or the sentence enlightens the situation, gives things, as you say, physiognomy." He further notes that the word can be preceded by little but the decisive idea, and that, in general, he often makes use of letters to denote a mathematical quantity, along with diagrams and mathematical symbols which enable him to denote mathematical ideas more precisely.*

Of particular interest are the answers received from Einstein. He noted, however, that he was not satisfied with them and that he would like to be asked more questions if it would be of any advantage for the very interesting and difficult work undertaken by Hadamard. Einstein then goes on to make the following statement about himself: "The words or the language, as they are written or spoken, do not seem to play any role in my mechanism of thought. The psychical entities which seem to serve as elements in thought are certain signs and more or less clear images which can be "voluntarily" reproduced and combined.

There is, of course, a connection between those elements and relevant logical concepts. It is also clear that the desire to arrive finally at logically

---

* Pólya expresses similar thoughts in his book *How to Solve It*, emphasizing that, given some experience in mathematical work, the latter can be carried out without recourse to words, using nothing but algebraic symbols and figures; he holds that, instead of the usual thesis "There is no thinking without words," it would be more appropriate to say, "There is no thought without symbols" [132: 116].

connected concepts is the emotional basis of this rather vague play with the above-mentioned elements. But, taken from a psychological viewpoint, this combinatory play seems to be the essential feature in productive thought— before there is any connection with logical construction in words or other kinds of signs which can be communicated to others."*

To the question "What internal or mental images, what kind of "internal word"–motor, auditory, visual, or mixed–do mathematicians use?," Einstein answered: "The above-mentioned elements are, in my case, of visual and, some, of muscular type. Conventional words or other signs have to be sought for laboriously only in a secondary stage, when the mentioned associative play is sufficiently established and can be reproduced at will.

Thus, the play with the mentioned elements is aimed to be analogous to certain logical connections one is searching for."

In reply to the same question, only this time concerning not mathematical but ordinary thought, Einstein answered that in this case, too, his images were visual and motor; as for words, when they intervened at all, they were "purely auditive."

Einstein's statements about his thought mechanism comprise a document of extreme interest to psychology, attesting to the great importance of images in the process of creative thought. During the first stage of problem solving, the essential feature for Einstein is the "combinatory play with images," directed by the desire to arrive at logically connected concepts which are formulated in words after the associative play, in the second stage of thinking, "when words intervene at all," and the thinker hears them inwardly. The fact that the words intervene only in a secondary stage has, as we have seen, been confirmed by many investigators, yet whether words are completely absent in the first stage (during the associative play) remains obscure. At any rate, the points of a problem must in some way be realized and retained in the mind in the first stage of problem solving as well, otherwise the combinatory play becomes senseless and cannot lead to a solution of the problem. But then, strictly speaking, even this first stage can no longer be regarded as wordless and unconscious.

Very interesting comments are also contained in Einstein's "Creative Autobiography," especially as regards the formation of wordless, or graphic-image, concepts, arising as a result of usual perceptions of causal connections and relationships. The effect of these concepts is particularly evident when, in our perceptions, we encounter something out of tune with the already established concrete notions, and when, as described by Einstein, we conceive feelings of wonder or "marvel." As an example of such a marvel he adduces an episode of his childhood, when he, a child of 4-5, was shown a compass by

---

* Einstein's letter is reproduced in full in [283].

his father. The boy was amazed by the compass needle, which functioned without being touched, and he experienced this as a "marvel." The conclusion Einstein draws from this reminiscence is that his feeling of amazement was due to the fact that in his "unconscious world of concepts" action was associated with touch, and since it was absent in the case of the compass, it produced the feeling of amazement which he terms an important stimulus for human intellectual development [200: 133].

That graphic generalizations of this type do exist is questioned neither on philosophical nor on psychological grounds. Engels, who is known to have believed wordless higher (theoretical) thought to be impossible, nevertheless pointed out that our reasoning activity is analogous to that of animals (empirical analysis, synthesis, etc.).

Primary, or lower, forms of generalization, which precede the appearance of words, have been described in detail by T. Ribot who termed them "generic" images (*image générique*) [137]. Pavlov, observing similar generalizations during the elaboration of conditioned reflexes to the "ratio of stimuli," interpreted them as "analogs" in the animal kingdom of our concepts—a "form of concrete thinking, animal thinking without words" [120: 7-8]. Numerous instances of such generalized concepts can also be provided from child psychology. Their formation is much more complicated, however, in adults who have mastered speech and who can designate verbally the objects of their perceptions. It is difficult to imagine how, in this case, purely motor or purely visual generalizations could have formed without the participation of verbal symbolization.

Psychological studies indeed show that as soon as the child masters speech, he accumulates verbal generalizations of the shape, size, and color of objects (N. Kh. Shvachkin [193]; Z. I. Istomina [73; 74] at an ever-accelerating rate, although verbal differentiation of individual characteristics (e.g., various hues) may not always be precise even in adults (F. N. Shemyakin [197]).

On the other hand, there exists a clear-cut distinction between graphic generalizations and logical verbal concepts, which makes it impossible to unify them terminologically, and in this sense application of the term "concept" to graphic-image and motor generalizations can result in nothing but confusion. Both psychologically and logically, it would be much more precise to call the latter graphic or image-bearing generalizations instead of concepts, or preconcepts, reserving the term concepts proper only for the verbal forms of generalizations.

In view of all the preceding, we regard as more correct the definition of the relation between thought and speech contained in Einstein's address "The Common Language of Science," in which he stated:

> "What is it that brings about such an intimate connection between language and thought? Is there no thinking without the use of language, that is, in concepts and concept-combinations for which words need not

necessarily come to mind? Has not every one of us struggled for words although the connection between "things" was already clear?

We might be inclined to attribute to the act of thinking complete independence from language if the individual formed or were able to form his concepts without the verbal guidance of his environment. Yet most likely the mental status of an individual growing up under such conditions would be very poor. Thus we may conclude that the mental development of the individual and his way of forming concepts depend to a high degree upon language. This makes us realize to what extent the same language means the same mentality. In this sense thinking and language are linked together" [222: 336].

In an even more definite way, however, the relation between language and thought has been expressed by Bohr, Einstein's opponent in the field of atomic physics: ". . . no proper human thinking is imaginable without the use of concepts framed in some language which every generation has to learn anew" [32: 45].

Finally, of great interest in this respect is the opinion of one of the most prominent Soviet mathematicians, A. N. Kolmogorov. "Perhaps," he writes, "one of the most interesting studies (in which, of course, the ideas of cybernetics, the new mathematical apparatus, and modern logic may be combined) is that of word formation as the second signal system. . . Prior to proper, formal-logical thinking, thoughts arose without being formalized into concepts—as combinations of words entailing other words, as attempts to fix directly the stream of images passing before our consciousness, and so forth. To trace the mechanism of the transformation of words into signals containing a complex of images, and of the creation, on the basis of this transformation, of early logic, is a very gratifying field of research" [82: 26].

The discussion thus far makes it quite evident that the relation of language to thought is as yet unresolved. It is also evident that further discussion may be made more fruitful if it is put on the basis of as precise psychological and physiological investigations as are possible, especially with respect to the latent (potential) operation of that speech usually described as "internal," or "mental." It is this problem which we shall discuss in the next chapter.

Chapter II

The Problem of Inner Speech in Psychology

1. EARLY INVESTIGATIONS OF INNER SPEECH

Inner speech has been little studied, either theoretically or experimentally. Yet it is of great importance to psychology as a whole, chiefly because of its close connection to thought. In thinking over silently some question, in comparing and generalizing the data of the problem being solved, we often notice that we utter to ourselves separate words and occasionally fragmentary phrases. At times, moreover, especially in solving difficult problems, we enter into a kind of discussion with ourselves: we formulate mentally a number of propositions, criticize them from various points of view, and finally select one of them, rejecting the rest. We then say that we "think in words." The speech arising in such cases usually is in the form of soundless, "mental" talking, but sometimes it is accompanied by overt articulation, thus making its individual components perceptible for another observer as well.

Plato's *Theaetetus* contains a very picturesque description of inner speech and its role in the thought process. Plato defines thinking as "the conversation which the soul holds with itself in considering anything." He remarks that "The soul when thinking appears to me to be just talking—asking questions of itself and answering them, affirming and denying. And when it has arrived at a decision, either gradually or on sudden impulse, and has at last agreed, and does not doubt, this is called its opinion. I say, then, that to form an opinion is to speak, and opinion is a word spoken—I mean, to oneself and in silence, not aloud or to another" [129: 118-119].

The Platonic definition of thinking as a "word spoken . . . in silence" emphasizes the significance of inner speech to thinking. However, this definition also contains grounds for equating thought with inner speech and speech in general. The latter circumstance was particularly stressed in the last century by Max Müller, a linguist, who asserted strongly the unequivocally identical nature of thought and speech. As seen from this point of view, subsequently

34

supported by American behaviorism, thinking is silent speech, "speech less sound."

Müller's opinions gave birth to a strong controversy, leading some scholars to make quite a few subtle observations on the relation of thought to speech, but the problem as a whole was not solved.

The first investigators of the problem of inner speech–V. Egger [221] and G. Ballet [205] –noted that inner speech, though always accompanying our thinking, is far from being identical with it. Relying on their introspective observations, they believed that inner speech does not enter the thought process until the moment of almost complete formation of a thought. They noted the almost perceptible time interval present between the instant of appearance of a thought and the onset of inner speech, particularly in those cases when something new and difficult is the object of thought. Eventually both investigators arrived at the conclusion that inner speech is nothing but the carrier of thought.

Subsequently, representatives of the Würzburg school (K. Bühler, O. Külpe, and others) attempted to establish experimentally the independence of thinking from pictorial images, including the "independence of thoughts from the signs by which we express them" [94: 59], i.e., from words and language in general.

The experiments underlying these conclusions consisted in the solution by psychologists versed in introspection of tasks which usually involved attempts to unravel the meanings of aphorisms or paradoxes. Having heard a question, the subjects answered "yes" or "no" and reported on their mental states during problem solving. They were, for instance, asked "Can our thinking be instrumental in understanding the essence of thinking?"; "Do you understand the sentence, To fertilize the past and to beget the future–this is the task of the present?" The subjects' answers usually indicated that no pictorial images of any kind arose in answering these questions. When, however, such images did arise, the subjects considered them to be casual and sporadic. On these grounds the psychologists of the Würzburg school denied the necessity of the presence of images as a foundation for thought.

They also denied the necessity of inner speech to thought, e.g., as defined by Bühler, of "optical, acoustic or motor representations of words." Yet inner speech was frequently very much in evidence in their experiments. Let it be exemplified by at least these two experiments of Bühler's:

1. The subject is asked: "Do you understand the sentence: Thinking is so extremely difficult that some people merely prefer to make inferences?" After 17 seconds the following answer is given: "Yes. I got the point the moment the sentence ended. But the idea was not yet quite clear. To achieve clarity, I repeated the sentence slowly, and after I had finished, the idea too was ready, and I said yes. The complete thought was an awareness which I now can put this way: to make an inference means here to state something

without meditating on it, to have a ready conclusion, as opposed to independent conclusions based on reasoning. Apart from those words of the sentence, which I had heard and then reproduced, no other ideas whatever were present in my consciousness" [212, Chap. IX: 321].

2. The subject is asked: "Do you understand the sentence: You ask how the apple got to be on the tree, and in the meantime somebody else has silently removed it?" The answer, given after ten seconds: "Yes. After thinking it over for a bit (where word fragments served for differentiation), the thought occurred to me about theoretical and practical behavior ("theoretical" and "practical" as words). By that I knew that I understood. This thought also contained something about the theoretician being tricked by the practical worker" [212, Chap. XII: 13-14].

In both cases Bühler describes the process of understanding abstract ideas by means of inner speech. This circumstance, very significant for the psychology of thought, has, however, been kept in the background by the Würzburg school. The preconceived notion—the emancipation of thought from everything sensory—seems to have compelled these investigators to ignore the significance of inner speech to thinking and understanding even if this meant to contradict their own experiments.

In divorcing thinking from images and sensations, the researchers of the Würzburg school thus arrived at the idealistic doctrine of "pure thought," later adopted by some American psychologists as well (Woodworth [281], and others).

Even at that time, however, the introspection of the Würzburg psychologists gave rise to grave doubts since it was not confirmed by other psychologists who though performing analogous experiments, detected no trace of any "pure" states of consciousness, finding instead, consistent references in their subjects' reports to the appearance, at the moment of thought, of various visual, auditory or kinesthetic images linked with the objects of thought or with the internal enunciation of words. The chief critic of the Würzburg researchers was Titchener (1909, 1910) who arranged a verification of their experiments in the psychology laboratory at Cornell.

The most interesting of the experiments were those of E. Jacobson (1911) which at first were based on an analysis of the subjects' verbal reports, a methodology later (in the Thirties) replaced by electrophysiological recording of muscular tension during mental activity. Let us first consider his experimentally-based findings on the perception of individual letters and on the comprehension of words and sentences [242].

Stimuli (a letter, word or phrase) were presented to the subject in written or printed form. In response to a signal, the subject opened his eyes, examined the paper lying in front of him, and, having completed a certain task (e.g., grasping the meaning of a letter, word or phrase), reported the consciously perceived events. The objective of the first test series was to determine accurately just what does occur in the consciousness during the perception of a single letter.

The visual sensations evoked by the stimulus were for the most part found in themselves insufficient to generate the perception of a single letter; some additional process or processes had to come into play, their purpose being to designate the object of perception—Jacobson's "designatory processes." Usually they consist of kinesthetic or auditory sensations, or of images of the pronounciation or hearing of words, or of combinations of both. If the "designatory processes" are absent, so is usually the visual perception of the letter: in this case the subject is faced with senseless lines and spots, without grasping the meaning of the letter.

The following report of one of the subjects is characteristic*:

Subject F. Stimulus—the letter Z.

"As soon as I opened my eyes, sensations of black, white, and greyish became clear (paper, ink, the letter, and background served as stimuli). The visual field was like this [the subject shows approximately the circular outlines of the field on the table]. This state does not last long. (All of this represented perception [of a letter] on white paper against a black background) [242: 558].

Later on, there appeared an auditory image of Z, accompanied by perception (Z). [As specified by the subject, on the whole it was just the letter that has been replaced at first.]"

The understanding of the meaning of words was investigated in the next test series. Here too the chief role was played by the "designatory processes." This is demonstrated clearly by the extract quoted below.

Subject G. Stimulus—the word "cutting."

"The meaning is perceived as a vague visual image of a knife blade and a kinesthetic tendency to press it downward. [Wherein does this tendency consist?] In the first three fingers of the right hand it was accompanied by eye movements toward a spot on the right-hand side" [242: 564].

Subject J. Stimulus—the word "botany."

". . . Recollection that I have to concentrate on meaning [has not been analyzed]. Then a visual image of green plants and a greenhouse seen recently. This went away, leaving only the sounds of articulation. Then there was again an attempt to follow instructions [not analyzed], accompanied by motor articulation of the words "study of plants," followed still later by "study of plants and flowers," and these phrases were often repeated, despite the simultaneous articulation of the word "botany" [242: 564].

The carriers of the meaning of word stimuli were thus visual, auditory, and kinesthetic processes. If we were to use the term "association," the

---

* The report utilizes the brackets method: outside brackets, report on the "processes"; in parentheses, report on "objective meanings"; within brackets, experimenter's comments.

author comments, "in its broadest sense, which would include both the peripheral kinesthetic processes and the processes of representation, we would be able to state that meanings accrue to words in the form of associations" [242: 564]. This was particularly evident when the subjects suppressed voluntarily their kinesthetic and other associations: words then became "lifeless" and "senseless."

Of interest in these experiments is the indication that the associations of a given word do not remain constant; thus, a visual image of a plant and hothouse, associated with the word "botany," an instant later makes way for verbal-motor articulation of the phrase "study of plants." It seems to follow that, since they are apprehended, the meanings of words undergo changes similar to those of associations.

This circumstance must be especially stressed because it points to a distinction between the logical meaning of a word as expressed in a formal definition, and its psychological meaning as experienced at a given moment. The logical meaning, the author points out, remains a constant and perfect one, while that which appears in a person's concrete experience represents rather a phase of meaning, or partial meaning, inherent in certain processes. "From the logical point of view, such a representation of meaning is inadequate; psychologically it is adequate to the requirements of this particular case. We may add that, particularly at the outset, the subjects often displayed a tendency to verbalize certain word stimuli, thus resolving the situation with both logical and psychological adequacy" [242: 569].

Similar phenomena were also observed in the test series devoted to the understanding of sentences. Representation processes occasionally arose here together with the initial perception of a sentence and, at times, somewhat later; in some cases they seem to be absent, but this is the result of their extreme fleetness and the subjects' inattention toward them.

It was also found in these experiments that one and the same meaning may be represented by different processes. For instance, in comparing the processes representing the meaning of an individual word and the meaning of the same word in the context of a sentence, it may be seen that it is only in very rare instances that the same processes repeat themselves. Due to the fact that a word in a sentence partially embodies the meaning of the whole, the character of the representation processes changes completely in the overwhelming majority of cases. In one experiment involving the word stimulus "heavily," the subject reports that "the meaning was primarily kinesthetic and secondarily organic," and in the experiments with the sentence-stimulus "the iron cube fell heavily on the floor" this meaning of the word "heavily" disappeared, its effect manifesting itself only in a weak auditory image designating a very loud sound. Particularly noticeable in this respect were the results of experiments involving prepositions: taken individually, the prepositions tended to form their own context—verbal or mimic—as gesticulation;

encountered in a sentence, they just colored the meaning of the sentence as a whole [242: 573].

The experiments described enable us to draw several important conclusions concerning the psychological nature of meaning.

First, they indicate that even introspective analysis, provided it is as thorough and cautious as possible, establishes the presence of various sensory and motor processes during the perception of the meaning of letters, words, and sentences. If these processes are absent, the meaning too is absent. Hence the assumption of "pure meaning" can only result from erroneous introspection or bias on the part of investigators.

Second, the relations between meaning and the sensorimotor processes which represent them are determined not only by the object of perception but also by the subject's set, in virtue of which the psychological meaning usually corresponds to the peculiarities of the moment, without always coinciding with the stable logical meaning of words and sentences, and are thus but a phase of meaning, or partial meaning.

Third, there exist no strictly fixed relationships between meanings and processes: one and the same meaning may be represented by different sensorimotor processes.

Finally, the principal point: since the introspective reports of subjects may be questioned as being subjective and intrinsically inaccurate, the final say in the polemics with the Würzburg school rests with the more objective methods of study, initiated by the electrophysiological work of Jacobson, applied to this problem twenty years after its introspective investigation. We shall return to this work later on.

Of some interest also is, a later attempt to verify Bühler's hypothesis on the possibility of nonsensory (imageless and speechless) recall of thoughts, carried out by H. Friedlander [228], a British psychologist, in 1947. He used to read short stories (each thrice), trying to reproduce them after a brief pause of five minutes. He was particularly interested in the question of how thoughts are recalled in those cases when we no longer remember their original formulation and communicate the thought content "in our own words," i.e., by means of new expressions similar in meaning. In analyzing his experiments, the author notes that in our memory we may be referred to a thought without being able to express it. This does not mean, however, that the thought is already present at this moment or that we are recalling it in some nonsensory way. In reality, the thought is in this case recalled by means of various auxiliary images or ideas with which it had been associated at the moment of reading (for example, by recalling the place on top of the preceding page, or the person who had expressed this thought, or the occasion on which it had been expressed, and so on). The author calls such auxiliary images "indicatory" since they do not represent the object as such, pointing to it but indirectly, thus setting in motion the mechanism of thought recollection in verbal form. The latter may vary to a considerable extent, particularly in bilingual people, whose thoughts are retained by memory in their mother tongue but are expressed in a foreign one.

This psychological description of the process of thought recall makes it quite clear that thoughts are always associated with words, i.e., in the absence of words there are no thoughts. That this may involve a great variety of the verbal forms of thought expression indicates not the possibility of separating thoughts from words but a greater degree of generalization and synonymity (equivalent meaning) of many verbal expressions, which explains the dynamic nature of verbal memory mentioned above.

The identification of thinking with speech on the one hand, and their complete divorcement on the other, became the two extreme viewpoints concerning the relation of speech to thought. In pointing to these extreme views, one should not, however, oversimplify the situation and assert, as is usually done, that every and each investigation has always run around a vicious circle. Psychology has known quite a few attempts at leaving this circle and solving the problem of thought and speech in a more meaningful way.

One such attempt was undertaken by A. Binet in his book *L'étude expérimentale de l'intelligence* (1903). To Binet it was evident that words not only express but also develop, direct, and organize thought. Demonstrating convincingly that the "mind is not a colony of polyps-images" and that "to think is not the same as to contemplate a colored painting" [210: 104], Binet wrote that "to understand, compare, correlate, assert, and negate are, in fact, intellectual acts, not images; it is always the internal language which expresses so well the ways of our thought" [210: 105].

Binet arrived at this conclusion as a result of his experiments with his two daughters. He would ask one of the girls to read a statement and then ask her: "Did you understand? What have you experienced? What mental representations did you have?", etc. In the girls' answers Binet often found traces of inner speech, e.g., the phrase, "I said to myself." Eventually, Binet points out, both children realized that they were thinking in words. "Hence," Binet concludes, "it may be assumed that where thought is devoid of images, it consists essentially of internal speech—it is a monologue."

However, Binet's subjects drew a certain distinction between thought and word. According to their reports, words occurred to them after a thought had already been caught by them. This has led Binet to the assumption that "verbal images are an expression of a thought which is already on the hook (*amorcé*), i.e., that thought precedes words" [210: 106].

But what might it be—a "thought which precedes words"? Without claiming to have found any precise solution for this problem, Binet all the same tried to investigate it experimentally. He asked his subjects to read aloud, to count, whistle, or repeat some phrase or verse while a question was being asked. Their task was to understand the question and find an answer to it.

Some of these "tricks," Binet points out, hampered internal speech at first, but the subjects were quick to adapt themselves to situations of this kind and, after repeated trials, reached the stage of inner speech automatically despite the fact that their organs of articulation were busy.

The most interesting were, of course, cases where it was possible to inhibit inner speech. In such cases one of the girls—Marguerite—used to test some "feeling" or other; for instance, the feeling that the person mentioned in the sentence was close to her, or the feeling that she had to answer "no" to the question asked. She asserted, moreover, that this feeling was there before she uttered the word "no." Armande—Binet's other daughter—in reply to the question as to where her hat was, asked under similar conditions, answered: "The one which we took today is in the cabinet by the lamp." This sentence, the subject claimed, was assembled from many thoughts which came to her suddenly, without words, as a sentiment of some kind [210: 107].

A wordless thought, a thought in embryo, is thus, according to Binet, a feeling, an emotional attitude. But this is where we begin to doubt: is this really a thought? Is it not perhaps merely a recognition of something out of previous experience, which is stored in our emotional memory?

The Würzburg school denied completely not only the imaginal but also the emotional basis of thought. Bühler, in principle, separated thought both from representations and emotions, believing each act of thinking to be pure thought (*der Gedanke*). At the other pole, Binet attempted to discover the emotional aspect of thought. Just how lawful is this approximation of thought at the moment of its inception to emotional states is a question which cannot be resolved *a priori* without special theoretical and experimental investigations.

For the time being, it is important merely to note that the posing of this question is, in itself, undoubtedly a major step forward compared to the usual treatment of the problem of thought and speech.

On one point Binet's findings are in agreement with the conclusions reached by the Würzburg school—that thinking and understanding may run their course without direct recourse to images. But, in contradistinction to Würzburg, Binet did not exclude the operation of fragmentary internal speech which he detected in his subjects even in those cases where the organs of articulation were enunciating phrases or verses of some kind, etc. There arises a question which is very important for an understanding of the problem of inner speech: What kind of inner speech was taking place when speech movements were inhibited? Binet does not provide an answer to this question. In approximating thought to feelings, he shows little interest in this "residual" inner speech, noticed by his subjects.

What, then, might be the real significance of this phenomenon of inner speech which takes place when speech movements are inhibited? Might it not mean that inner speech is not always associated with speech movements and motor mechanisms in general?

Psychiatrists who have studied inner speech in relation to aphasic phenomena believe inner speech to be images of words, reproduction of words
from memory. This leads one to question which memory images are involved
in thinking—auditory, visual, or motor.

S. Stricker [272] advanced the hypothesis that "speech representations
are motor representations," and, in fact, asserted that he was unable to
imagine any sound without sensing a muscular effort of some kind. Thus, in
thinking of the sound of the letter *b* he tried to compress his lips, being aware
of distinct tension in both lips; with the sound of the letter *d* he felt the
involuntary movement of the tip of the tongue. While thinking the Latin
words *pater* and *mater*, he felt a very clear distinction between the initial
sounds of these words, but his sensation of movement when thinking about
the subsequent combinations of sounds were less clear. Stricker questioned
more than one hundred persons whether they talked to themselves while
thinking or while reciting mentally familiar verses. All those questioned
answered "yes."

It is for this reason that Stricker believed inner speech to be based on
motor phenomena.

In contradistinction, V. Egger believed inner speech to exist separate
from motor phenomena. He insisted that inner speech was based not on
motor but on auditory representations of speech. "My inner speech (*ma
parole intérieure*)," he wrote, "is a reproduction of my voice" [221: 67] or "of
the voice of other people" [221: 72].

The contemporaries of these authors tried to reconcile their views, believing the question as to the motor or auditory representation of words to be
an issue of individual differences. Thus G. Ballet, noting the obvious contradictions of their views, wrote: "Egger's and Stricker's mistake consisted in
generalizing that which related to them personally. That which Egger asserted
is valid to him since it is peculiar to him to think with the aid of auditory
images; to Stricker, however, who thinks in motor images, Egger's proposition
turns out to be incorrect" [205: 58].

Even so, the question arises whether a "purely" motor or "purely"
auditory representation of words is possible at all, even if the degree of
predominance of one or the other of these elements is variable with the
individual? Might not auditory representations be in all cases connected with
motor processes, and the so-called motor representations with the auditory or
visual ones?

According to K. Goldstein (1908), "the psychological basis of speech is
a unity. Psychologically the distinction between the auditory and motor
images of words should be rejected and substituted by a single representation
of the word, which is, on the one hand, evoked by acoustic lingual perceptions in principle no different from all the rest of perceptions, and which, on

the other hand, gives rise to speech movements (*die Sprachbewegungen*) which in principle are not different from other movements" [230: 416].

This viewpoint is supported by investigations of Bärwald who, based on the vast amount of factual material collected by him, arrived at the conclusion that, on the one hand, "no one could be found among healthy people who wouldn't have, at least potentially, auditory representations" and, on the other hand, there are no people who in fact use no motor images, although in some these images remain completely unconscious and unnoticed [208: 74-75].

The issue becomes more complicated, however, because of the extremely uncertain nature of our knowledge about the nature of motor representations. When the auditory or visual representations of words are mentioned, we know what one talks about: people who possess them, as it were, hear words or sounds or see them in print or in writing, without the words being pronounced intentionally. But is it possible to have motor images of words without actually uttering them? One can, of course, visualize the motor structure of word enunciation by studying in advance the corresponding positions of the organs of articulation when words are pronounced, but in reality such an image turns out to be nothing but a visual image.

In analyzing this problem, the French psychiatrist Bernheim (1907) came to deny the existence of the motor images of words. "If we stop to think about what is called verbal images, we shall be unable to see in the auditory and visual images of words anything but varieties of the auditory and visual images in general; otherwise they cannot be visualized. As for the motor images of words, the more we try to visualize them mentally, the less able we are to do so" [209: 367].

Of interest in this connection are the views of B. M. Teplov [167: 135] who believes motor representations to be embryonic forms of real motor sensations, linked with the corresponding visual or motor representations. As seen from this standpoint, it would be very important to investigate experimentally the possibility of purely auditory (without participation of the motor apparatus) representations of verbal and vocal material, as well as the possibility of the existence of purely auditory (again, without participation of the motor apparatus) inner speech.

There have been numerous attempts to investigate experimentally the degree of participation of the motor processes in inner speech. As yet they have led to no definite conclusions. Here is a summary of the main experimental work done in this field.

1. R. Dodge (1898) anesthetized his own lips and tongue and found that the exclusion of these organs had no effect on inner speech [219]. Subsequently, instances of a reestablishment of speech following amputation of the entire tongue [230] and larynx [273] were described, with the conclusion that the speech function of these organs could, to a certain degree, be

replaced by the operation of other parts of the mouth or the esophagus. If replacement of this kind is possible for external, loud speech, they should be even more so in the case of internal, soundless speech which is usually accompanied only by embryonic articulatory movements.

2. H. Curtis (1899) recorded, with the aid of a pneumatic drum connected to a kymograph, laryngeal movements while his subjects were mentally reciting verses learned by heart or reading silently. Of 20 subjects, 15 displayed laryngeal movements, whereas five subjects had none, even when whispering [217].

3. H. Courten (1902), using the same method applied to the tongues of subjects who were reciting or reading mentally, found that tongue movements were not always present and not in all the subjects, and that if present, their character depends on what is being read or thought, as well as on the degree of understanding [216].

4. A. Wyczoikowska (1913) placed the tongue in a tightly fitting glass balloon connected to the recording drum and kymograph. The subjects were instructed to enunciate mentally verses learned previously and the phrase "experimental psychology" or merely to listen to the words uttered by the experimenter. These experiments implied that every thought process was accompanied by tongue movements of some sort [283].

5. R. Pintner (1913) investigated the extent to which it was possible to exclude articulatory movements without hampering the understanding of a text and the speed of reading. He made his subjects pronounce the syllables "la-la-la" or count while reading passages in prose. The author concluded that comprehension while reading without articulation may approach normality [260].

6. N. Reed (1916) investigated tongue movements by placing into the subject's mouth a very sensitive rubber balloon connected to a kymograph. He experimented with reading aloud to oneself and in a whisper, mental multiplication, etc. His findings show that in all these cases movements of the tongue represent an individual characteristic rather than a general one [262].

7. R. Clark (1922) recorded movements of the tongue and of the larynx simultaneously by placing the drum on the larynx and a small rubber balloon on the tongue, while the subjects were given some task to think over. Her experiments showed laryngeal and tongue movements to be incidental to thought processes [213].

8. A. Thorson (1925) decided to dispense with pneumatic recording of speech movements, considering it to be very inaccurate since, as she pointed out, it is not only movements of the organs of articulation that may be recorded, but also the small changes in air pressure produced by respiratory or swallowing movements, and so on. Thorson used the Lashley-Sommer apparatus to record movements of the tongue during her experiments. The device

consists of a system of levers which permit the simultaneous recording on a smoked kymograph tape both vertical and horizontal movements of the tongue. The author concluded:

a. tongue movements are not necessary for internal speech;

b. when tongue movements did occur in internal speech, they were found in a form completely different from that characterizing explicit speech (their forms coincided in only 4.4% of all cases);

c. tongue movements were of a different kind also with repeated reproduction of the same verbal material (they were similar in form in only 10% of those cases where such movements were noticed).

Thorson concludes from her experiments that tongue movements depend not so much on internal speech as on the conditions of nervous irradiation and muscle tone. In this respect they are indistinguishable from finger tapping or from the face distortions which people have during tics or emotional stress [276].

9. E. Jacobson (1931) recorded the action potentials of speech musculature (tongue and lips) with the aid of a galvanometer which was very sensitive for those times. All subjects first were trained to relax their muscles voluntarily to exclude, in subsequent experiments, tension in the muscles extraneous to the test, which might augment the potentials recorded from the muscles under investigation [243; 244; 245].

V. M. Borovskii, the first in our country to turn his attention to these experiments, said: "To study the speech musculature, electrodes were inserted into the muscles of the tongue or lower lip. The subjects were instructed to multiply numbers mentally, to imagine themselves to be counting something, to recollect verses, to think of abstract matters such as 'eternity,' etc., to compose a schedule for the next day.... The apparatus was set for low sensitivity, and in response to the first signal the subject is asked to whisper as softly as possible, 'one, two, three.' The photogram shows three vertical lines separated by intervals. Then the apparatus is set for the highest sensitivity, and the subject is asked merely to imagine counting. The resulting photogram is very similar in appearance. The same can be done with the recollection of verses and with the whispering of them, the only difference being that in voltage" [34: 221-223].

Jacobson's experiments thus demonstrate that "in so-called internal speech the muscles of the tongue and lips contract as if words were pronounced in a rapid and abbreviated manner."

Subsequently, Jacobson's experiments found a broad response and confirmation in the work of a number of researchers in our country and abroad (Yu. S. Yusevich, F. B. Bassin and É. S. Bein, L. A. Novikova, K. Faaborg-Andersen, A. Edfeldt, and others). We shall deal with these studies later on in relation to our investigations of inner speech.

2. DISCUSSION OF INNER SPEECH IN SOVIET PSYCHOLOGY

The first investigations of inner speech in Soviet psychology had been predominantly theoretical in character, touching chiefly on the general issues related to the genesis of inner speech and its semantic and syntactic structure.

The most important work in this respect was that of L. S. Vygotskii and P. P. Blonskii who stressed the importance of inner speech as a mechanism of verbal thought and logical-verbal memory. In his book *Thought and Speech*, Vygotskii demonstrated clearly the scientific importance of studying inner speech as the psychological core of the entire problem of relations between thought and speech; he made the first attempt at a theoretical elucidation of the specific characteristics of inner speech as a speech "to oneself" and "for oneself," and he outlined a number of assumptions concerning the genesis, syntax, and semantics of inner speech.

It was clear to Vygotskii that "without proper understanding of the psychological nature of inner speech there is not and cannot be any possibility of explaining the relationship of thought to speech in all of their real complexity" [43: 338]. He was quite critical of the concept which held inner speech to be merely verbal memory (retention of acoustic, optic, motor, and synthetic images of words). He was fully justified also in repudiating the rather simplified behaviorist concept of inner speech as merely a soundless form of external speech ("speech less sound"), believing that the principal, determining factors of inner speech were its semantic features. Vygotskii rejected both the idealist and spiritualist doctrines of the Würzburg school and Bergson's concept of the total independence of thought from word and of the "distortions" which the word introduces in the thought.

According to Vygotskii, in all its principal attributes and aspects—genetic, structural, and functional—inner speech is a very special and unique psychological phenomenon: it is "the living process of the birth of thought in the word" and, as such, reflects an extremely complex interrelationship between thinking and speech, their paradoxical unity.

On the basis of material from researches in child psychology, Vygotskii shows that speech "does not represent a simple mirror reflection of the structure of thought. Hence it cannot fit the thought as a ready-made dress. . . . Thought, converting to speech, is reconstructed and modified. Thought is not expressed but is achieved in the word" [43: 331-332]. The absence of the mechanist identity of thinking and speech is manifested, specifically, in the fact that in the child the semantic aspect of speech proceeds in its development from whole to part, from sentence to word, whereas the external aspect of speech proceeds from part to whole, from word to sentence; that in general the flow and movement of thought does not coincide directly and immediately with the development of speech. "That which is contained in thought simultaneously, is developed in speech successively. Thought might be compared to an overhanging cloud pouring out in a rain of words" [43: 378].

In this connection Vygotskii also notes that grammar develops earlier in children than does logic. "The child masters the subordinate clause and forms of speech such as 'because,' 'since,' 'if,' 'when,' 'on the contrary,' or 'but' long before he masters causative, temporal, conditional relationships, oppositions, and so forth. The child masters the syntax of speech before he masters the syntax of thought" [43: 138].

Vygotskii also points out that the grammatical and psychological subjects and predicates do not coincide. Psychologically, any part of the sentence, singled out by logical stress via intonation, can be a predicate in a complex sentence. It is for this reason that the logical and grammatical predicates do not coincide. However, the thought content of a phrase cannot be understood without singling out the psychological predicate. This is additional testimony to the paradoxical unity of thinking and speech, logic, and grammar.

Turning his attention to the genesis of inner speech, Vygotskii considered it most likely that inner speech originates and develops from the so-called egocentric speech of the preschool child. According to Piaget's description, egocentric speech is a conversation of the child aloud with himself. Egocentric speech is often observed during play and is not directed toward a playmate. In this characteristic of egocentric speech Vygotskii saw a functional and structural similarity to inner speech and on it formulated his hypothesis concerning the evolution of egocentric speech into internal speech, all the elements of which he claimed to find in egocentric speech.

Syntactically, inner speech was characterized by Vygotskii as extremely fitful, fragmentary, and abbreviated in comparison to external speech. Inner speech is characterized by a "simplification of syntax, a minimum of syntactic breaking down, expression of thought in condensed form, a considerably smaller number of words" [43: 359], which, in Vygotskii's opinion, is achieved by virtue of a sharp increase of predicativeness in inner speech through omission of the subject and the parts of the sentence related to it. In support of this thesis of the "absolute and complete predicativeness of inner speech" Vygotskii argued that the predicate of our inner judgment is always present in our thoughts and is always implied by us without being stated. "In inner speech, it is never necessary for us to name that about which we are speaking, i.e., the subject. We always limit ourselves only to what is being said about this subject, i.e., to the predicate. But this is precisely what leads to the dominance of pure predicativeness in inner speech" [43: 366]. "The child talks about that which preoccupies him at the moment, about that which he is now doing, about that which he has before his eyes. He therefore leaves out more and more, abbreviates, condenses the subject and the words related to it. And he reduces his speech, to an ever-increasing extent, to the predicate alone" [43: 367].

On this basis Vygotskii believed, further, that as a result of this peculiar syntax of inner speech, the semantics of inner speech must also undergo fundamental changes: it must become more contextual and idiomatic and include not only the objective meaning of words but all of the intellectual and affective content connected with it; this must lead to the dominance, in inner speech, of the contextual meaning of words over their objective meaning.

Subsequently, Vygotskii outlined a broad and bold plan for the psychological study of inner speech as a mechanism of verbal thinking, which has influenced greatly all the subsequent research on this problem. Much, however, remained obscure and debatable in this scheme.

The first criticisms of Vygotskii's concept of inner speech were made by P. P. Blonskii in his book *Memory and Thought*, where he also made a number of proposals which were to have great influence on the subsequent experimental development within this field.

In considering the relation of thought to speech, Blonskii consistently developed the principle that they were inseparable; he held that, regardless of the arguments brought forward by the adherents of the independence of thought from speech, "in reality no thinking is possible even for a minute without words" [29: 441]. In support of his statement he alludes to Mesmer's unsuccessful attempt (described by Hegel [50: 273], to think without words, an attempt that brought him to the brink of insanity. Blonskii also criticized the views that equated thought with speech (including inner speech); he pointed out that psychologically it was possible to articulate words unconsciously, as in the case of automatic speech.

In opposition to Vygotskii, who shared the view of Köhler and Rühler that thought and speech had different genetic roots, Blonskii stood solidly on the position that they originated from one source. "This common root is work: both speech and thought have developed from work. Primitive speech was really action. Primitive intellectual operations were actions, and it was only gradually that true action became replaced by mental action: actual division, by mental analysis, actual act of addition, by mental addition" [29: 500]. Blonskii was also very cautious in treating the language of gestures, believing that "only articulate verbal speech . . . deserves the name of speech" [29: 446-447].

On the genesis of inner speech, Blonskii held that inadequate study of this problem prevented its solution in a more or less definite manner. Vygotskii's hypothesis on the evolution of inner speech from egocentric speech was not considered reliable by Blonskii because it placed the origin of inner speech in a rather late period of child development—the school age, thus depriving all preschoolers of inner speech; this, in Blonskii's view, is at variance with the facts.

Blonskii considered it more likely that inner speech originates simultaneously with spoken speech from a common source—social intercourse among people, which presupposes not only that words are spoken but also heard; and listening to words, particularly in early childhood, is, according to Blonskii, always accompanied at first by audible and later on by soundless, internal repetition of the speech of the speaker, its "simultaneous reproduction," or "echolalia." "Listening to speech is not simply listening: to a certain extent we, as it were, talk together with the speaker. There is, of course, no complete repetition of his words here, not even complete internal repetition (although at times such complete repetition, even audible, does take place, e.g., repetition of a refrain in chorus). But it is possible that it is precisely here that we have the rudiments of inner speech" [29: 451].

Blonskii used a very simple experiment to demonstrate that it is necessary for the listener to reproduce the speech of the speaker at the moment of listening; namely, he showed that it was impossible (or extremely difficult) to think about something else while one listens attentively to some utterance—a fact which subsequently was made use of as one of the techniques in the experimental study of the processes of inner speech.

Blonskii made no special analysis of the syntactic and semantic aspects of inner speech, but in his overall characterization of "thinking in everyday life" he, like Vygotskii, pointed to the extremely fragmentary nature of inner speech, its underdevelopment and incompleteness, and this to such a degree that if there were some way to record the verbal expression of thoughts in our inner speech, we would get the impression of something like the *Ideenflucht* of manic patients: "An extremely rapid and changeable flow of thoughts, making little sense for an outsider because of its jumps and incompleteness of reasoning and judgments, continually reverting to fragments of phrases or even to individual words, which would surprise the listeners" [29: 480].

Further theoretical analysis of the problem of inner speech was undertaken by B. G. Anan'ev in an article titled "On the theory of inner speech in psychology" [7]. Noting that there are a great many debatable issues in the theory of inner speech, Anan'ev believes that this should not prevent us from establishing a number of very important and indisputable facts and propositions which would serve as a starting point for the planning of further studies of the problem. Among such indisputable facts he places: a) the soundless character of inner speech; b) its contracted, abbreviated nature; c) its secondary nature, i.e., derivation from external speech; d) the systematic and phasic nature of transition from internal to external speech. Hence, the three chief issues in the theory of inner speech as seen by Anan'ev: 1) mechanisms; 2) motivation; 3) phasic character.

Anan'ev holds that Vygotskii's and Blonskii's genetic hypotheses on the origination of inner speech in the act of speaking or listening to speech do not exhaust the essence of the problem, since they do not take into account the entire system of speech activity, which includes not only speaking and listening, but reading and writing also; these too are a source for the formation of inner speech, especially of its higher and more developed forms. "It is precisely because of this that the forms of inner speech, their mechanisms, and the phases of the process are always original, depending on the speech activity from which they arise" [7: 367].

This thesis enabled Anan'ev to overcome Vygotskii's one-sided concept of the "absolute" and "pure" predicativeness of inner speech, and to develop the proposition that the logical-syntactic structure of inner speech may be quite diversified, depending on the cognitive content of thought. Inner speech can be both predicative and substantive. "Inner speech based on a certain concreteness of thought is predicative. When, on the other hand, an object is as yet not recognized and identified in perception, not outlined in thought, inner speech is substantive" [7: 336]. Starting from certain characteristics of external speech, in particular the presence in it of one-component predicative and nominative sentences, Anan'ev and Podol'skii [131] hold that inner speech may be interpreted as a system of "zero syntactic categories" with a zero predicate in the nominative sentence (of the type "Night," "Stars") and with a zero subject in an impersonal predicative sentence (of the type "It is dawning," "It is late"). From this point of view, the reduced quality of inner speech, its syntactic abbreviatedness and fragmentariness, can be explained by the effect of the "zero" syntactic categories mentioned above. Anan'ev also allows for the possibility of a phonemic reduction of inner speech, the dropping of many phonemes, primarily of the vowel type, similar to the abbreviations usually used in the Russian written language (e.g., *L-d* or *Lngr* instead of Leningrad, *d-r* instead of doctor, etc.). This is what explains the sometimes observed "initialness" of inner speech, its functioning in the form of the initial sounds or letters of words.

Some interesting ideas were also advanced by Anan'ev in regard to the regular development and phasic nature of inner speech—its development from the initial poorly-differentiated forms (among which he places the "set for designation" and the process proper of mental designation in a reduced phonemic and syntactic form) to "internal speaking," or "internal monologues" as the final stage of inner-speech development during its conversion to external speech, when it is maximally unfolded and is similar in structure to external speech. He finds excellent examples of such internal dialogs in the classical works of Russian literature (especially in the novels of Tolstoy and Dostoyevsky), which have been subjected to special analysis by I. V. Strakhov [164; 165]. In this connection, Anan'ev proposes a broad "personal" approach to the problem of inner speech, which would encompass not only its intellectual functions but also "the entire personality structure of consciousness," including its moral-ethical aspect.

Anan'ev demonstrated further that the study of inner speech may well be not only of theoretical but also of practical significance, particularly in the teaching of cultured oral and written speech—precision in the expression of thought, development of good speaking style, and so forth. He attaches great importance to the study of inner speech because it may also be helpful in developing practical methods for the restitution of speech in motor and sensory aphasias.

Of great value to a discussion of inner speech also, is the study of "internal singing" and "inner (musical) hearing." The bulk of the material on this issue can be found in B. M. Teplov's book *The Psychology of Musical Aptitudes* [168]. In analyzing auditory (musical) images, Teplov concludes that motor factors (overt or rudimentary vocal-cord or finger movements) play a very important role in the operation of "inner (musical) hearing" and "internal singing," providing a necessary basis for them. However he allows for the possibility that in individual cases auditory images may also arise without the cooperation of the vocal or instrumental motor apparatus. Thus, referring to Stumpf and Abraham, he points out that "one can imagine with complete clarity passages of such virtuosity as would be impossible for one either to sing or to play." It is also possible to image multivoiced (both homophonic and polyphonic) music, while only one voice can be reproduced by "inner singing" [168: 253-254].

Teplov sees a way out of this paradoxical situation (acknowledging, on the one hand, the necessity of the vocal motor apparatus for auditory representations, and denying it in some cases, on the other hand) in classifying auditory representations as "voluntary" or "involuntary," regarding the participation of the vocal motor apparatus obligatory for the former and nonobligatory for the latter. To argue this point, he falls back on N. N. Lange's theory [95], according to which voluntary concentration of attention is only possible when it is maintained and reinforced by appropriate muscular movements, since a "reinforcement of the m..tor component of the recollection complex has to entail the reinforcement of the entire complex as well." Lange did not mean that "representations in general arise in consciousness only through muscular movements"; he only meant that "in this manner ideas become fixed in the process of voluntary attention" [95: 191, 206, 243]. Starting from this principle of motor "reinforcement" and "fixation" of representations, Teplov held that the "motor factors acquire a fundamental significance (becoming, perhaps, even a necessary, required condition) when a musical representation has to be evoked through a voluntary effort" [168: 255]. As for the involuntary auditory images, (in particular, persevering images and primary auditory memory images) they can arise without any participation of the vocal motor apparatus whatever. L. V. Blagonadezhina arrived at similar conclusions, too, as a result of questions put to her subjects. In her experiments, voluntary reproduction of auditory images was usually related to "muscular experience"; in those cases where an auditory image appeared involuntarily ("sounded by itself"), the subjects noticed neither motor movements nor "internal singing" [27].

Further investigation of this problem was carried out by A. N. Leont'ev and his collaborators, Yu. B. Gippenreiter and O. V. Ovchinnikova, who used an original technique to evaluate the "separation threshold" of pitch. With this method, they established that when subjects had had previous training in intoning the sounds of the voice, their "separation thresholds" of pitch for the most part went down, whereas in the absence of such training, i.e., when the subjects practiced the comparison of sounds by ear only (without intoning them), no noticeable lowering of thresholds was observed [95; 98; 99; 116].

These data indicate that development of tonal hearing depends directly on vocal activity, and that in the process of intonation (aloud or silently) there arises a link between the pitch of sound and the movements of the vocal cords and even of the hands, which, as it were, imitate the perceived auditory stimuli and become isomorphous with them, thus copying and modelling them. This is in agreement with the general theory of "motor isomorphism" being developed by Leont'ev, according to which the motor apparatus and the motor mechanisms of the brain, associated with it, necessarily become engaged in all the brain's functional systems which are formed in one's lifetime and whose combined activity ensures the accuracy of our perceptions [98: 146-156]. In the process of perception the overt motor acts are, moreover, replaced by "internal motor acts" in the form of positional-tonic changes connected with the subject's former activities (A. V. Zaporozhets [67: 385]. In this particular case the vocal motor acts appear as the modelling mechanism of auditory perception.

In summing up the discussion of inner speech in the work of Soviet psychologists, it may be concluded that they have not only analyzed critically and generalized the relevant material, but also have advanced a number of novel genetic and psychophysiological hypotheses and proposed experimental means of verifying them. Of great importance in this respect has become the method of verbal interference and verbal activation (i.e., voluntary delay and voluntary reinforcement of articulation), followed by electrophysiological studies of hidden articulation. An array of data have been obtained on the neurodynamics of speech processes with the aid of conditioned-reflex methods, as well as in the clinical studies of speech disturbances in various forms of aphasia. The main results of these studies are given below.

3. VERBAL INTERFERENCE METHODS IN THE STUDY OF INNER SPEECH

The lack of reliable techniques for recording inner-speech processes makes the testing of the physiological and psychological hypotheses proposed to account for observations of the relations of the speech mechanisms to thinking very difficult, compelling researchers to experiment within very narrow limits. The question most accessible to experimental study is that concerning the relation of articulation, and speech kinesthesis associated with it, in the various mental operations, such as arithmetic calculations, reading, writing, listening to speech, etc., to the various graphic and abstract components in these tasks. In some cases, researchers resorted to methods of inhibiting external and internal articulation of words, going back to the old experiments of Binet; in other cases articulation was, on the contrary, reinforced by means of obligatory audible enunciation of experimental material. Experimenters were fully justified in interpreting the changes occurring in the process of task performance as a functional dependence of mental activity on the degree to which speech articulation is expressed in it.

The method of delay and reinforcement of external articulation proved fruitful in the study of speech kinesthesis during the initial stages of mastering mental operations, e.g., in teaching children to read and write (L. K. Nazarova's [112] and L. N. Kadochkin's [76] experiments), as well as in the study of the role of articulation in patients with various types of aphasia (A. R. Luria [101; 103]; S. M. Blinkov [28]; and others). In these conditions it was found that mechanical retardation of articulation (e.g., by clamping the tongue and lips between the teeth or by opening the mouth as wide as possible while the tongue and vocal cords remained in a maximally passive position) hampers considerably mental operations of verbal type, first of all because it hinders the perception, understanding, and remembering of words and their logicogrammatical connections in word combinations and phrases; these difficulties disappear when articulation is reinforced by enunciating verbal material aloud.

In laboratory experiments of this kind, carried out on normal adults (A. N. Sokolov [151; 152]) it was found, however, that as mental operations become automatized, retardation of articulation ceases to have any negative effect on their implementation; occasionally it can even appear as a positive factor that accelerates mental operations. At the same time, reinforcement of articulation by an audible enunciation of words at this stage becomes a negative factor which retards mental operations. In children, mechanical retardation of articulation exerts negative influence for a longer time than it does in adults. The most likely explanation of these facts is that cessation, in the experiments, of external articulation did not signify cessation of articulation in general. Articulation became concealed, internal, implemented through imperceptible movements of the speech apparatus, and no mechanical delay is capable of inhibiting them.

Starting from Blonskii's assumption that it is impossible to have two internal speeches going on simultaneously—one, for instance, for listening to somebody else's utterance, and another for the enunciation of extraneous words—in a number of studies (A. N. Sokolov [148]; N. K. Indik [72]; and others) a more complicated variant of the method of speech interference was used, consisting in the performance of various mental tasks with simultaneous continual enunciation aloud (without pauses) of word series (e.g., ordinal count to ten, enunciation of verses learned by heart, etc.) well learned by heart, or of individual syllables ("ba-ba" or "la-la").

The continuity of enunciation of these words or syllables was controlled by means of laryngograms.

Speech interferences of this type obviously occupy not only the peripheral apparatus of the organs of articulation (lips, tongue, larynx) but also their representation in the cerebral cortex, loading the motor speech divisions of the brain with extraneous impulses, irrelevant to the performance of the tasks assigned, setting up inside them negative induction. Also, in carrying out these experiments, it was taken into account that the enunciation aloud of extraneous word series or syllables, while demanding a certain auditory control over the correctness of their pronunciation, must to some degree or other generate negative induction in the auditory cortex as well.*

The results of the experiments showed that such a load imposed on the motor speech and auditory speech analyzers† in the form of extraneous verbal stimuli produces, at first, a state resembling sensory aphasia (in that stage when words are yet heard as words, but the meaning of a phrase as a whole is not understood), so that performance of any kind of mental operations becomes impossible at that moment. This state quickly fades away, however, and is replaced by instantaneous amnesia: an extremely rapid forgetting of a text heard or read, resulting in a considerable reduction of the volume and accuracy of perception and memory, and speed of reading and problem solution. Later on, as the enunciation of extraneous verbal material becomes more automatized, internal (concealed) articulation of words is gradually reinstated, and the subjects, despite the preoccupation of the speech apparatus with the continual enunciation of word series or syllables learned by heart, grasp and retain the meaning of the words perceived and manipulate them correctly by means of concealed articulation of certain generalizing words. Moreover, along with the rudimentary articulation of the key words, all subjects noted during these experiments the appearance of vivid visual images which are usually absent under normal conditions and which they use here as a means for comprehending and retaining the meaning.

---

* The method of mechanical inhibition of the motor speech analyzer has recently been developed further and found application in neuropsychology (E. Weigl [38]) and the interference method, in engineering psychology (F. D. Gorbov [581]).

† The "analyzer" concept which we use here designates, according to Pavlov [117: 101-102], an anatomic-physiological system consisting of a receptor (in this case, a motor speech or speech auditory receptor, outgoing afferent pathways, and the corresponding higher and lower segments of the brain, which constitute the "cerebral projection" of the receptor, or the "cerebral terminal" of the analyzer.

The principal theoretical significance of these experiments is that they graphically demonstrate the possibility of implementing stereotyped analytico-synthetic operations under conditions of maximum suppression of speech movements and, hence, without any unfolded silent enunciation of words. This poses a number of important, acute theoretical and experimental questions.

From the principle of unity and interrelation of thought and speech, it has to be assumed that we are dealing with rather abbreviated (reduced) speech processes, under conditions of maximal reduction of phonetic and syntactic word structures or word combinations, and with simultaneous reinforcement of the graphic-image components of thought. The existence of such fused, graphic-speech complexes seems to make their instantaneous retention, selection, linking together, and mutual comparison possible and, on this basis, the construction of new thoughts in accordance with the given premises, former experience, and the tasks arising at present possible as well. As for the process proper of the reduced enunciation of words to oneself, in these experiments it might have been implemented during micropauses which inevitably arise whenever some extraneous verbal material is enunciated.

Further, what attracts attention in these experiments is that negative induction is equally strong during the operation of both motor speech and auditory speech interferences (i.e., both during imperative enunciation of extraneous words and during imperative listening to them), as well as the fact of the diminishing of negative induction with a diminishing of auditory control over the enunciation of extraneous words, which attests convincingly to the presence of constant interaction between the motor speech and auditory analyzers. Hence the likelihood of the assumption that inhibition of the motor speech component may not be reflected in the developed forms of thought because in this case, along with the rudimentary articulation, other speech components, too, may be functioning—auditory and visual ones. This entitles one to speak of all the speech kinesthesias as being internally "sounded," i.e., being associated with auditory-speech stimuli, while the auditory and visual perception of words is linked with speech kinesthesis. From the latter it also follows, evidently, that the usual characterization of inner speech as "soundless" is justified only from the point of view of an outsider; for the thinker himself, however, inner speech remains linked to auditory speech stimuli even in the case of maximal inhibition of speech movements.

Finally, it is also permissible to speculate about an effect of trace speech stimuli from all the speech components, since verbal stimuli, as any other kind of stimuli in general, possess more or less prolonged trace effects, aftereffects, which may be actualized even without ongoing verbal stimuli, just under the influence of object stimuli or graphic images associated with them.

The experimental data obtained by B. F. Baev with the aid of the interference methods described distinctly indicate that the participation of

internal speech (internal enunciation) is far from being equal in solving problems of different types: graphic problems are solved with minimal participation of internal enunciation, while problems involving abstract content, having
no immediate relation to graphic objectivity, can be resolved with the aid of
inner speech alone. In this connection, the author also notes the dependence
of the structural-grammatical features of inner speech on the degree of graphic
content and "abstractness" of the mental operations being carried out: "With
the presence in thinking of a graphic support there is observed a tendency
toward contraction of inner speech; in the absence of such support, a tendency toward expansion, since in this case the work of thought becomes reduced to a manipulation of only the verbal content, so that the scope of
utilization of verbal means becomes much expanded" [20: 50].

The situation is identical to the action of vocal interferences, when one
has to intone extraneous sounds of a certain pitch while evaluating the pitch
of other sounds. As shown by O. V. Ovchinnikova's experiments [115], this
technique has produced great difficulties only with those subjects who usually
make use of intonation in comparing the pitch of sounds; it had no effect
whatever on pitch discrimination in subjects who possessed either a very bad
or a very good sense of pitch. The latter result seems to be due to the fact
that subjects with very bad pitch discrimination never resorted to singing the
tones, with the result that their evaluation of sounds in terms of pitch was
bad in all cases; in subjects with good pitch discrimination, however, the vocal
acts were automated to such a great extent, even prior to experiment, that
kinesthetic signals could operate in a contracted form, so that vocal interferences were unable to exert any noticeable inhibitory effect on the process of
pitch analysis.

Recently, N. I. Zhinkin [65; 66] has made an attempt to interpret the
speech and nonspeech interference method and the results obtained from it, in
the light of certain problems of information theory. As is known, one of the
models upon which information theory is built is that of communications, i.e.,
the transmission of information over channels, taking into account their
information-carrying capacities and the potentialities of the mechanisms for
conversion and reception of information. In this context, the concept of
"interferences" acquires great significance in information theory; they may
appear in the transmission channel and their harmful effect must be taken
into consideration so that appropriate measures may be taken to ensure correct transmission of information.

According to this model, speech too can be regarded as a combination
of signals (sounds and letters), by means of which information is transmitted
from one person to another. Moreover, as in all lines of communication,
external and internal interferences of various types are possible. By external
interferences in the transmission of speech we have in mind those which arise
in the environs of the acoustic signal and which may impede its reception (for

instance, noise in a room). By internal interferences in speech channels may be understood those which occur in man's organism proper, beginning with the moment the acoustic signal arrives at the auditory receptor and ending with the moment of "delivery" [presentation] of speech signals by the motor speech analyzer. If in terms of their algorithm (a certain sequence of combinations of elements) the interferences approximate the speech algorithms, their effect will be maximal; if the algorithms are dissimilar, their effect will be minimal or will be not noticed at all. Starting from this, Zhinkin used the techniques of nonspeech rhythmic interference for the study of the mechanisms of inner speech.

Investigated was the question of the role of enunciation, and of speech kinesthesis related to it, in inner speech. If in the process of inner speech enunciation does take place, it becomes evident that the motor speech analyzer has to set up an algorithm of speech movements, which corresponds to the elements of the words being enunciated; this algorithm must be, moreover, multirhythmic, since Russian words do not have fixed accents. By introducing interferences which disturb this algorithm, we can form judgment as to whether speech movements do indeed participate in the process of inner speech.

The following techniques were used in the researches. While solving mental problems of various kinds, the subject was to tap his hand in a certain rhythm. It was thought that the steady tapping rhythm would upset the intermittent rhythm of speech movements during the internal enunciation of words, i.e., the tapping would become an interference. The rhythms were simple, and the accuracy with which they were executed was recorded, *via* pneumatic transmission, on a kymograph. The results coincide, to a considerable degree, with the experiments described above: for certain problems and for certain subjects, there was strong interference, while with other problems and other subjects there was a lesser amount of interference; sometimes it was almost absent and, in all cases, the effect of interference gradually weakened.

The following result was the most interesting one. The experimenter succeeded in finding such a problem whose solution becomes very difficult for all the subjects during the tapping of a rhythm. This was the very easy operation of counting sequentially to a particular square within a line of checkered writing paper (25 or 28 squares). The author's explanation for this is that, in counting, a word cannot be replaced by anything: it has to be enunciated to oneself completely, whereas in other cases (for instance, in reading a text or listening to extraneous speech) words can be replaced by graphic representations or diagrams, or whole groups of words can be replaced by one short word, generalizing the meaning of the entire phrase. Thus, the diversity of all the cases described above for the effect of rhythmic interference may be explained by the fact that, while solving problems, the subject begins to replace words by nonrhythmic structures, avoiding thereby the effect of rhythmic interference.

Subsequently the author, breaking down the mechanism of speech into two basic components—word composition from sounds (and, correspondingly, of speech movements) and message composition from words—shows that return kinesthetic connections are necessary for the formation of the first component, whereas in the second component (message composition from words) the feedback from the speech organs becomes weakened to a considerable degree because of the possibility of replacing the complete enunciation of words by other (graphic) signals. However, toward the end of the process of message composition from words ("at the output of the speech effector") the interference begins to act with its former strength. This means that complete words in which the utterance is made, have been prepared. Here, the author distinguishes between "complete" and "incomplete" words, the latter meaning any equivalents substituting for words in the process of inner speech.

4. DETECTING CONCEALED SPEECH REACTIONS BY CONDITIONED-REFLEX METHODS

The findings available on this problem have for the most part been obtained from experimental investigations of "the interaction between the first and second signal systems" (in the laboratories of A. G. Ivanov-Smolenskii and N. I. Krasnogorskii) and from those devoted to the interrelation of verbal stimuli (in the laboratories of Krasnogorskii, G. Kh. Kekcheev, and others). Although inner speech was not directly recorded in these investigations, the fact itself of the formation of conditioned reflexes to the words which are heard, seen, or pronounced by the subject either aloud or to himself undoubtedly attests to the functioning of "internal speech chains" (neural verbal connections) in all the experiments.

The basic facts established are:

1. Conditioned reflexes elaborated to concrete (nonverbal) stimuli subsequently take place when these stimuli are merely named; moreover, the verbal stimuli replacing them in such cases evoke a conditioned reflex at once, without preliminary reinforcement by an unconditional stimulus.

For example, O. P. Kapustnik [79] elaborated a conditioned motor reflex to the sound of a bell in children. When the experimenter then uttered the word "bell," he obtained the same reaction. The same response was found when the subject was shown a card on which the word "bell" was written. The ability of verbal stimuli to substitute for graphic ones was also observed in the elaboration of inhibitory conditioned reflexes (N. N. Traugott [172] and in the elaboration of conditioned reflexes to a sequential complex of stimuli. In É. P. Smolenskaya's experiments [147], the positive signal complex was the sequential flashing of red, white, and yellow light; and the negative (inhibitory) signal was the reverse sequence. After these conditioned responses were elaborated, the same effect was obtained by pronouncing the verbal designations of these stimuli in the appropriate order.

Similar results were also obtained during the elaboration of autonomic conditioned reflexes. L. I. Kotlyarevskii [85] combined the sound of the bell with Ashner's ocular-cardiac reflex and obtained a decrease in heart-beat rate as a conditioned reflex to the bell. In another experiment, Kotlyarevskii [84] elaborated a conditioned pupillary reflex (by combining the sound of the word "bell" with light), whereupon he tested the effect of the word "bell," pronounced by the subject himself aloud, in a whisper, or to himself. In all cases the word "bell" evoked the same pupillary reflex as did the sound of the bell.

The authors of these works explain similar immediate replacement of nonverbal stimuli, within conditioned reflexes, by their verbal designations by the fact that verbal stimuli usually become firmly linked with concrete stimuli in early ontogenesis. If, therefore, a person forms a conditioned reflex of some kind to first signal stimuli (e.g., sound, light, etc.), subsequently the associated verbal stimuli spread selectively over the neural pathways previously (in ontogenesis) closed and thus at once evoke the corresponding reflex. Ivanov-Smolenskii [69; 70] called this phenomenon "selective irradiation" as distinct from the "diffused, or broad, irradiation," arising in the early stages of the development of conditioned reflexes.

2. During the elaboration of conditioned reflexes to complex stimuli of the first signal system, whose components are of varying intensity, usually it is only the strong components that are verbalized (transferred to the second signal system); the weak components are not always noticed in such cases and therefore are not verbalized.

This masking of weak first signal stimuli by strong ones is demonstrated well by one of Kotlyarevskii's experiments [83]. In children 8 to 12 years of age, a conditioned motor reflex (squeezing a rubber balloon) was elaborated in response to a brief illumination of a green square and a simultaneous slight increase in the illumination of the experimental room. The children were found to respond with a motor reaction to each of these stimuli, but they noticed, as a rule, the connection of their response only with the stimulus (illumination of the green square). When a weak stimulus was tested (i.e., slight increase in illumination of the room), they squeezed the rubber balloon without being able to explain the reason for their actions. They could not pick out the weak stimulus clearly enough, although a motor response to it was present. Subsequently, similar results were also obtained in other studies [181; 166]. It is assumed that such "unnoticeability" of weak components of an established conditioned link is produced by negative induction from the strong component. Negative induction may arise both within the bounds of the first signal system and along the excitation transmission paths from the first signal system to the second.

3. Conditioned reflexes elaborated in response to certain verbal stimuli continue to function when these are replaced by other verbal stimuli if the latter have some logical or semantic connection with the former.

This is exemplified by the experiments of A. Ya. Fedorov, described by Krasnogorskii [88: 307; 89: 467]. In a child 12 years of age repetition was used to establish a firm association between six words: "pigeon," "turkey," "hawk," "owl," "chicken," and "swallow." One of these words ("pigeon") was then reinforced several times with a food stimulus (cranberry with sugar). All the words of this complex were found to have turned into conditional stimuli, each one evoking intense secretory (salivary) conditioned reflexes. However, all other words designating, for instance, animals, trees, and fruits did not evoke this response. Nor was the response evoked by the names of other birds not belonging to the original complex, but the general name "bird" produced an intense response without any preliminary reinforcement. Subsequently, V. D. Volkova [40] confirmed these observations by new, analogous experiments and found that the magnitude of the conditioned reflex decreased as the initial verbal stimuli became more and more remote.

Another example of the influence of semantic associations of words on conditioned reflexes is furnished by experiments where words, to which conditioned reflexes were elaborated, were replaced by their synonyms and homonyms. The experiments of L. A. Shvarts [190; 191; 192] are quite illustrative. A conditioned photochemical reduction of visual sensitivity was formed by combining a verbal stimulus (e.g., the word *doktor* which is commonly used synonymously with the word *vrach*) with illumination of the eye, and then the conditioned reflex to the synonym (in this case the word *vrach*) was tested. The synonym was found to evoke at once, without any preliminary reinforcement, approximately the same conditioned-reflex reduction of visual sensitivity as the original word. At the same time, words similar in sound but different in meaning (e.g., the word *diktor* used instead of the word *doktor*) barely produced any reflex; if a response did take place, it was quickly inhibited in subsequent trials. Similar results were also obtained by the author with vascular conditioned reflexes with the aid of plethysmography.

Also of great interest in this respect are experiments involving conditioning to verbal complexes (phrases and sentences). In investigating this problem, N. R. Shastin [189] found that in 11- to 12-year-old children a much more intensive response is evoked by the subject of a sentence than by the predicate and other parts of sentence. A change in the word order of a sentence produced no noticeable difference in the intensity of the conditioned reflex. Later on, however, in M. V. Matyukhina's experiments using the photochemical method [105], adult subjects were found to respond with a sharp inhibition of the conditioned reflex to a change in the word order, which seems to be connected with the more subtle semantic differentiation of phrase structure by the adults. Also, it was found that adult subjects responded equally well to the subject and the predicate, and in some cases even to the secondary parts of sentences.

5. CONDITIONED REFLEXES TO NUMBERS

We are singling out this variety of semantic conditioned reflexes as a separate group only because their effect has a particularly marked connection to inner speech. In V. Ya. Kryazhev's [93] experiments, a large group of 7- to 8-year-olds was at first conditioned (while pressing a key with the hand or a pedal with the foot) to the word "five," while the word "three" served as the differential (unreinforced) stimulus. After the conditioned reflexes to these words had been established (in the first case, positive, in the second, negative, or inhibitory), the number 5 was presented, followed by 3; they evoked the same conditioned responses as the corresponding words did at once, without additional reinforcement. Subsequently, during mental execution of arithmetical tasks, if the end result was "five" $(3 + 2; 10 \div 2; 100 \div 20)$, a positive conditioned reflex was evoked, and if the end result was the number "three" $(5 - 2; 9 \div 3; 3 \times 1)$, a negative (inhibitory) reflex was evoked.

These data were subsequently confirmed in Krasnogorskii's laboratory by V. D. Volkova's experiments, in which an 11-year-old child was conditioned to respond with a salivary reflex to the word "ten" and differentiation to the word "eight" ("ten" was reinforced with a food stimulus, and "eight" was not). In control experiments, the child was given the task of "adding five and five." Conditioned-reflex salivation took place during the solution of this problem. In solving the second problem, "subtract two from ten," there was no salivation. The more complex the arithmetical operation, the longer was the latent period of the conditioned reflex: in operations involving simple numbers, the latent period was 2 sec; with two-digit numbers, from 6 to 11 sec. Generalizing the results of these experiments, Krasnogorskii concludes: "thus, due to the fact that earlier the word (ten) was associated with the food reflex (first signal system), the appearance of this word in the internal speech chain (second signal system) produced conditioned salivation, which objectively proved the intimate interaction of the first and second signal systems" [90].

Experiments of this kind are few, and it is difficult to draw conclusions concerning the dynamics of functioning of "internal speech chains" from them. It seems that in the future it may be necessary to combine conditioned-reflex methods with other methods permitting a simultaneous study of the different aspects of the speech process.

6. CLINICAL OBSERVATIONS

Of great interest in the study of the speech mechanisms of thought also, are the results of clinical observations on speech and thought disturbances accompanying the various forms of aphasia. In the most comprehensive form these problems are treated in the monographs of A. R. Luria [101; 103] and in a series of separate studies of other authors (M. S. Lebedinskii [96], É. S. Bein [23; 24], S. M. Blinkov [28], O. P. Kaufman [81], B. G. Anan'ev [8], and others). We shall discuss here only one aspect of this problem—inner speech disturbances in motor and sensory aphasia.

It was noted in the early investigations of Soviet neuropsychologists and psychopathologists that both external and internal speech are disturbed in all more or less pronounced forms of aphasia. The basic objective index of disturbances of internal speech in aphasia is that the patients perform various thought operations considerably better aloud than to themselves. Aphasics better understand and remember material that is read aloud than that read to themselves, and they are compelled to translate all more or less complex reasoning into the spoken word. Hence the inference that "There is no aphasia without disturbances of inner speech" (Lebedinskii [96]). Disturbances of inner speech become less pronounced in marginal forms of aphasia (which seem to include the so-called conducting aphasia); in these cases patients can read to themselves, albeit slowly, solve arithmetical problems mentally, and perform similar thought operations.

Subsequently, it was found that the most severe inner-speech disturbances occur in motor, and not in sensory, aphasia, as had been assumed in earlier studies of aphasia. With the aid of rather simple yet effective techniques it has been established that motor aphasics are unable to understand, because of functional disturbances in the fine verbal kinesthesis characteristic of inner speech, grammatically complex phrases and sentences, to perform mentally more or less complex counting operations, to solve arithmetical problems, etc., if their external articulation is disconnected, for example, by clamping the tongue between the teeth. The same is true of the process of writing: if the motor aphasic has his tongue clamped, his writing deteriorates instantly.

In view of the great importance implicit in these facts, I shall quote several instances of similar observations from a study by Luria [103: 279-292].

Patient L., 30, a mechanic with a seventh-grade education, had suffered an injury to the premotor areas of the cerebral cortex, resulting in right-sided hemiplegia and motor aphasia, while the temporal (auditory) cortex remained relatively intact. In experiments aimed at testing the patient's understanding of speech, it was found that in those cases when the verbal structure of a phrase was relatively simple, the patient experienced no appreciable difficulty in understanding it, even when external articulation had been excluded (by clamping his tongue between his teeth). Thus, with the external articulation cut off, the patient is presented with a simple descriptive sentence: "Today, a dense fog rolled in, and driving was very difficult." After a 15-sec delay, during which time the tongue remained clamped, the patient readily reproduced the sentence and stated: "I understood right away; I pictured to myself how hard it was to drive in the fog."

Under the same conditions, considerably more time was required for him to understand a more complex sentence. For instance, he was instructed to perform a task of this type: "Place the comb to the left of the pencil." With his tongue free, he enunciates this instruction: "That means, place his ... to the left ... ," and solves the task in 7 sec. This process slows down considerably when normal speech kinesthesis is obstructed; the patient begins to probe the objects, making trial attempts at arranging them, and spends 1 min and 20 sec (i.e., 12 times longer than before) on the problem, saying: "I figured it by my hand, so this is how it came out."

Still more illustrative are experiments where the patient was given sentences containing grammatical inversions: when external articulation was impeded, these sentences remained beyond the patient's grasp. For instance, the patient was presented with the sentence: "The girl is bigger than the boy," and asked which of the two was smaller. With his tongue clamped, the patient spent 1.5 min in tracing the individual words with his finger, in the end refusing to answer the question, saying: "I read it and it is as if I understand it, but I cannot figure it out." With his tongue free, he solves the same problem in 10 sec, repeating: "The girl is bigger ... the girl is bigger ... That means the boy is smaller," adding: "I can visualize it, yet nothing comes out of it... I just don't get it... But if I repeat it aloud, I understand. Then I can figure it out right away... I can't understand what it is that helps... When my tongue is clamped, it seems as if the words are there, yet it's impossible to connect them."

Similar results were obtained with this patient also in experiments involving counting operations. Whereas under normal conditions he was able, albeit slow, to perform correctly in writing operations of addition and subtraction, multiplication and division of numbers up to ten, when external articulation was blocked, these operations became impossible for him. The results of these experiments were summed up by Luria as follows:

Adding and Subtracting Numbers to Ten Mentally

Experimental conditions	Correct solutions, %	Average time in seconds
Tongue free	100	26
Tongue clamped, counting on fingers	100	15
Tongue clamped, counting on fingers not permitted	0	30
With eyes closed	100	6.5
With left hand clenched into a fist	100	8.4

As may be seen, a disintegration of the patient's counting ability is observed only when speech kinesthesis (and acts substituting for it) is weakened; it does not occur when the execution of a task is accompanied by other auxiliary muscular efforts (closing the eyes, clenching the fist, etc.).

Thus, these clinical observations and experiments indicate the important role played by speech-kinesthetic impulses in the performance of verbal (and in many cases, visual-graphic) tasks by motor aphasics, and the necessity for speech kinesthesis to be immensely intensified if thought operations are to be performed by motor aphasics. However, the performance of elementary verbal thought operations (for example, retention and comprehension of individual words and phrases, addition and subtraction of numbers up to ten, and other automatic actions of this kind) are within the capabilities of motor aphasics. The insufficiency of kinesthetic afferent impulses used in the speech act seems to account for the origin of conducting aphasia in which the greatest injury is to the ability to repeat aloud individual speech sounds and words, while the ability for spontaneous phraseological speech and silent reading remains relatively unimpaired.

Taking into account the motor aphasics' need for intensification of motor speech impulses in order to perform mental operations, their rehabilitation is based on operations accomplished in a loud voice with subsequent shift to internal performance, to oneself. The system of external speech operations thus is internalized into an internal speech order which itself becomes a basis for subsequent detailed oral and written statements; this is what one always encounters in a normal functioning of inner speech. In addition, another peculiarity of the motor aphasics' speech has to be taken in consideration when their speech is to be restored, namely, the predominance of substantives and related words and the extreme paucity of verb forms ("telegraphic style"). Special attention must therefore be given to the restoration of the predicative aspect of inner speech [81].

In sensory aphasia, as far as can be judged from aphasics' oral speech, reading, and writing, inner speech is less impaired than in motor aphasia. Sensory aphasics retain the capacity for abstract operations and for an understanding of logicogrammatical relationships, but because of their disturbed phonemic hearing (differentiation and recognition of phonemes by ear), they often lose the ability to recognize the objective meaning of words, which is the main reason for their failure to understand what they hear. As a result, the speech of sensory aphasics differs from that of motor aphasics by being predominantly predicative, idiomatic, and deficient in substantive forms (subjects). While retaining the ability to perform abstract operations, the thought process of the sensory aphasic is therefore often interrupted, is not carried to the end, and may be absent altogether because of a disturbance in direct associations between the word heard and the object it refers to.

At the same time, the inaccurate differentiation between speech sounds leads to manifestation of a compensatory set for meaning; the patient attempts to catch the phonation with the aid of any semantic context he can think of at the moment, which is what produces the verbal paraphrasia (substituting words according to sound or meaning) so characteristic of these patients. Due to the disturbed phonemic hearing, sensory aphasics also find it difficult to write to dictation, even though they can copy a written text. Because their articulatory mechanism and the understanding of logicogrammatical relationships remain relatively intact, the work toward the rehabilitation of speech is greatly facilitated (Bein [24]).

The above observations on the antithetical nature of speech disorders in motor and sensory aphasia may be regarded as evidence of the fact that both of the brain mechanisms of speech—motor and auditory—are necessary for the normal development of thought, since the former ensures that logicogrammatical relationships will be established in speech, while the latter ensures the acoustical analysis of the speech perceived. On the other hand, these findings lend probability to the assumption that the motor mechanism is predominant while words are pronounced, whereas the auditory mechanism, supported by the speech motor system whenever acoustic analysis becomes difficult, predominates in the auditory perception of speech.

7. INTERRELATION OF INTERNAL AND EXTERNAL SPEECH AND THEIR INTERMEDIATE FORMS

The studies of inner speech discussed above leave no room for doubt as to its immediate genetic relationship with external—oral and written—speech. Inner speech takes its origin from external speech; it represents its psychological transformation, where it is not so much its "soundlessness" that is of the greatest significance as its more basic psychological characteristics—primarily, its *ad hoc* character, generality, and hence verbal fragmentariness. Let us also note that under certain conditions all of these specific features of inner speech (e.g., a common situation) appear in external, colloquial speech, as demonstrated by Vygotskii in numerous examples from the literature. This means that inner speech cannot be separated from external and regarded as an independent phenomenon.

It is also quite evident, however, that external speech is functionally dependent on inner speech. A sufficient reason for this inference is the fact that whenever we delay communicating our thoughts (concrete or verbal associations), we first fix them in our mind with the aid of inner speech, formulating a mental plan or a synopsis of some sort for our future statement. This takes on an even more definite shape in writing when each contemplated phrase or even word to be written is preceded by its mental enunciation, followed by selection of those most suitable. But, even if thoughts are communicated immediately as they occur, before they become expressed through external speech they still are preceded by a discharge of motor speech impulses; as will be shown later, they are always antecedent to the utterance of words, be it even a matter of fractions of a second.

The foregoing permits us to conclude that, although inner speech cannot, as such, serve as a means of direct communication among people and is chiefly a vehicle for thought (in this sense Vygotskii was fully justified in calling it speech "to oneself" and "for oneself"), it nevertheless carries out very important preparatory functions for human communication. Owing to inner speech, there arises a "set for speech" (Anan'ev [7]) or a "set for communication" (Baev [21]) which activates the appropriate verbal stereotypes, so that words and phrases are selected for subsequent oral and written statements.

A large amount of relevant material may be obtained not only through a study of the literary output of writers and poets—the object of numerous special investigations (A. L. Pogodin [130]; D. N. Ovsyaniko-Kulikovskii [114]; A. G. Gornfel'd [59]; and others)—but also through observations on the development of oral and written speech of schoolchildren. Although in the latter case the conflict between the "internal scheme" and its verbal realization, is frequently accompanied by the specific literary "throes of creation," still, the divergence between external speech and inner speech is very much in evidence here too.

Of particular importance is the study of errors in oral speech committed by junior schoolchildren, which brings out clearly the difficulties involved in the transition from the internal scheme to its external manifestation in speech. D. G. Pomerantseva [134] has made a detailed description and classification of such errors.

She concludes from her observations that, as a rule, the speech of young schoolchildren "does not flow freely, does not shape itself into well-turned sentences." On the contrary, what we hear them say are often fragments of various sentences, "trial-and-error incomplete phrases" of some sort. In the speech of young schoolchildren there are often errors of anticipation, when the pupil utters some part of his statement before he should (for example, a girl of the fourth grade says, "*gravnyi gorod*" instead of "*glavnyi gorod*," anticipating the second word in the first) and errors of speech inertia, when the stimulus from the first word is as it were superposed on the succeeding one (for example, having said the word "*ust'e*," the girl then pronounces the word "*ruslo*" as "*rust'e*").

There are also errors involving a collision of thoughts, when, for instance, in answer to the teacher's stern question, "Ty pochemu tetrad' ne sdala?" [Why haven't you turned in your notebook?] the girl replies, "U menya sdalas'" [I turned myself in] instead of "*konchilas'.*" The expressions "*sdala*" and "*konchilas'*" turned into the absurd "*sdalas'*" in this case. Of a similar nature are errors involving a shift in the set for speech, occurring when some modification of design takes place in the speaker's internal scheme of speech, "disruption of the previous verbal set," externally manifested in false agreement. For example, in the course of story telling there may occur a transition from a singular subject to plural, and so on. These errors in oral speech all attest the extremely complex functioning of verbal thought mechanisms during transition from inner speech, where thought appears in a very abbreviated and complex form, to external speech intended to make the thought understandable to the listener or reader (i.e., it has to be transformed into a logically and grammatically presented series of judgments or sentences).

Some data concerning such a transformation (decoding) of inner speech into external speech can be obtained from studies devoted to the development of written speech in students. Although many details of the decoding, in writing, of inner speech are far from being fully revealed in this case, the main tendencies in the development of inner speech during its transition to written speech can be discerned quite clearly. Of great interest in this respect is Zhinkin's analysis of the compositions of third- to seventh-graders. The compositions were written on the basis of pictures which enabled the experimenter to trace the transition from an image (perception of picture) to its verbal description [63].

Analyzing these compositions, Zhinkin distinguishes four basic elements common to all speech, including internal, which enter into the process of written exposition and with which the process of description begins. These elements are: 1) selection of words in accordance with the subject of discourse; 2) selection of phrases and sentences in accordance with the distribution of object attributes in a group of sentences; 3) singling out of predicates by fixing the order and internal intonation of words during writing; 4) connection of sentences according to meaning.

Of particular interest are the author's conclusions concerning the relationship of subject and predicate, depending on whether they are considered within the limits of a separate sentence (judgment) or within the context of several sentences, i.e., in an interconnected system of judgments. In an individual sentence the main constituent is the predicate, i.e., whatever new is being stated about the subject of statement; in a context, however, the main thing is the subject of statement which at first appears as an unknown and whose attributes are gradually revealed through the succeeding series of judgments.

The psychological aspect of this problem consists in the fact that, while sentences are being written down, the subject of statement must at all times be inwardly retained by the writer. Only under this condition can a word series be synthesized into a definite system. This involves anticipation of the imminent writing of the text both as regards proper agreement and government of words and the logical sequence of content. The concrete form in which the anticipation of the forthcoming text is manifested in inner speech— this, of course, cannot be established by analyzing the compositions, but the fact itself of the singling out of individual object attributes, some as main and others as subordinate or coordinate—can be objectively ascertained by contextual analysis of the intonational articulation of a text.

Since the writer enunciates the text before writing it down (this will be confirmed by electromyographic recording of motor speech impulses), the intonational articulation of a text in inner speech becomes an important factor in determining the syntactic structure and the entire style of the text: separating, by means of internal intonation, individual words or groups of words as logical predicates, the writer, by the same token, is already determining to a considerable degree the arrangement of words and their syntactic connection in the sentence. Internal intonation of words during writing is significant for another reason, namely, because it makes still more evident the interrelationship between the auditory and motor analyzers, not only during external but also during internal enunciation of words, for internal intonation necessarily presupposes the presence of internal listening or auditory representation of intonation as a means of control over it. It follows that verbal hearing is necessary as a major condition for the articulation of a sentence in semantic parts and for the determination of the syntactic structure of the sentence and of the text as a whole.

We return once more to the problem of the relationship between the motor and auditory components of inner speech and, on the basis of the foregoing, emphasize again their constant interaction during the writing process, the motor speech component being predominant—it enables one to carry out voluntary (intentional) analysis not only of the sound composition of words but of the semantic structure of phrases and the text as a whole. This is beyond a shadow of doubt, at least so far as the period of instruction in written speech is concerned.

As has been demonstrated by L. K. Nazarova's experiments [112], in this case any interference with the enunciation of words (e.g., by clamping the tongue between the teeth) makes the process of writing extremely difficult, causing numerous gross errors due to the absence of motor speech control. According to L. N. Kadochkin's [76] experiments, the enunciation of words is of particular importance during the formation of writing habits in spelling Russian words which are not governed by the rules of orthography (specifically, in spelling words containing unverifiable unstressed vowels), and in those cases where the difference between the orthoepic and orthographic norms can be ascertained by enunciating words syllable-by-syllable. As the written-speech habits develop, the need for enunciating syllables disappears, reappearing only whenever difficulties of an orthographic nature arise. As for mental fixation of the order of words and phrases, their reduced (abbreviated) enunciation in inner speech is quite adequate.

A similar phenomenon is also observed during formation of all other intellectual habits and skills where automatization of thought operations is accompanied by speech reduction, while verbal control over their implementation is exercised by intensified and unfolded speech activity. This transition from external to internal speech is a necessary link in the "interiorization" of mental acts (J. Piaget, A. N. Leont'ev, P. Ya. Gal'perin), i.e., gradual replacement of the actual manipulation of objects with their mental manipulation, accompanied at first by external and then only by internal speech. According to Gal'perin, a mental act is nothing but a "recollection of an external act," an "automatized flow of notions about action" [44]. From this standpoint, an act becomes mental when all the external operations which earlier formed its genetic basis are excluded, when the act "becomes a silent act, an act of verbal thought" [47].

Owing to the great theoretical and practical importance of this problem, we shall consider it in greater detail in the next chapter, where we shall also present our experimental findings.

Chapter III

Generalization and Reduction in Speech during the Emergence of Mental Acts

1. GENERALIZED ASSOCIATIONS AND ABBREVIATED INFERENCES

The basic fact related to the problem of speech reduction during the formation of mental acts is that, as intellectual habits (reading, writing, mathematical problem solving, etc.) are developed, verbal operations (judgments) gradually become abbreviated, or reduced, in the manner of enthymemes in logic, (i.e., abbreviated syllogisms in which some of the elements are omitted—a major or a minor premise or even the conclusion therefrom). It is usually assumed that the omitted premise or inference is in this case being kept in one's mind or implied as an obvious proposition (V. F. Asmus [17: 228]; D. P. Gorskii [66: 117]. As pointed out by P. A. Shevarev [195: 43-44], however, the term "being implied" is very vague and does not answer the question: Does one think the omitted elements or does one not? In other words, are there cases where one not only does not state the intermediate links of a judgment but does not reproduce them mentally either? Asmus seems to admit the existence of such cases. He relegates the need for complete syllogisms to the mathematical sciences only, believing that "in other sciences and in artistic and particularly everyday thinking it is not always, far from it, necessary to reproduce in thought and to express in speech all the links of a proof, all the parts of an inference" [17: 227].

Shevarev's psychological studies of this problem led him to the conclusion that, in principle, such mental acts are quite feasible without one's being conscious of the underlying rules. Many mathematical, spelling, and other study habits operate in such an automatized form, for instance, in schoolchildren. At first they are carried out by students on the basis of certain rules as major premises for deductions; subsequently, however, as the operating with like rules expands in volume, there arise generalized, or "variable," associations, where the first member (conditions or the unknown of a problem) at once evokes the second member of the association (appropriate actions) without restating the corresponding rules. Moreover, as an association of this kind becomes firmer, the underlying ground propositions may entirely be forgotten; yet the necessary operations will be carried out correctly [195: 71, 140, 289].

Such abbreviated inferences, carried out without verbal reproduction of the underlying rules, must of course result in a maximal abbreviation of verbal operations not only in external but also in internal speech, thereby accelerating the performance of all mental acts. Shevarev has calculated, for example, that even such an elementary mental operation as the process of multiplying simple binominals would have to contain no less than 100 to 150 inferences if every act were to be substantiated in detail. Actually, however, people with developed algebraic habits bypass all these inferences, so that the process of binominal multiplication is reduced to simply multiplying the numerical indices of the coefficients, writing out the letters, and adding their indices [194: 171].

If this is true, we have to assume that in the thought process the reduction of speech must take place not merely by virtue of a "devoicing" of external speech and its conversion to "speech minus sound" but by virtue of a more radical rearrangement of the entire verbal structure of mental operations, so that unfolded reasoning is absent in internal speech as well, the latter turning into a very abbreviated and generalized code—a language of "semantic complexes" (reduced verbal statements sometimes combined with graphic images).

The presence of semantic speech complexes of this type is easily detected in many psychological studies of thought, especially when the subject is asked to solve some problem aloud, verbalizing all of his thoughts at the moment of their emergence (*in statu nascendi*). The protocol of the solution thus fixed will be the principal document for subsequent analysis of the solving process. In addition, should the report be incomplete, the subject may be asked to substantiate his solution *post facto*, ascertaining in this manner by what hidden (implied) propositions he had been guided.

The method of thinking aloud cannot, of course, guarantee that all the hidden verbal processes will be translated into external (oral) speech, but, still, this method brings out well enough all the basic logicosemantical peculiarities of inner speech, especially if the results obtained in this manner are correlated with the logically unfolded algorithm of the solution. In this connection let us note the following:

1. The main purpose behind the correlation of the logically-assumed and the actual course of problem solving is not, by any means, to juxtapose the logic and the psychology of thinking but to investigate their interrelation and interaction, since in reality all correct thinking is logical and all rules of logic are, after all, nothing but a more or less precise verbal generalization of the basic principles of the brain's cognitive activity. The logic and psychology of thinking cannot therefore be divorced from each other. The interrelation of

the logic and psychology of thought is brought out with particular clarity by an operational approach. In essence, psychology studies the genesis and mechanisms of thinking, starting with the logical norms, or algorithms, of thought operations. On the other hand, psychological studies of thought operations (particularly in relation to scientific thought or creative thought in general) widen the bounds of logical norms, and are thus capable of serving the progress of logic itself.

2. The concept of "thought operation" must be applied to all thought acts, both verbal and nonverbal; the latter may be regarded as a reflection of concealed, outwardly nonverbalized thought operations. In other words, both a judgment stated directly and other thought acts (e.g., arithmetical calculations, drawing of diagrams, etc.) may appear as thought operations.

3. Finally, in comparing the logically-assumed and the factual course of problem solving one must take into account the possibility of solving the same problem in a number of ways and on the basis of different starting principles. Accordingly, variations of the logically-assumed course of problem solving must be anticipated.

We shall illustrate the use of this method by citing two examples of which we have made special study: the solution of physics problems and translation of foreign-language texts. In the former case we had to deal with a transformation of the solution algorithm on the basis of mathematical formalization of thought operations; in the latter, with a transformation ("recoding") of a foreign text in accordance with the lexical and grammatical norms of the Russian language. Let us consider both cases in greater detail, for they reveal in a graphic way some of the structural and functional characteristics of interiorized speech.

2. REDUCTION OF THE LOGICAL ALGORITHM IN THE SOLUTION OF PHYSICS PROBLEMS WITH FORMALIZATION OF MENTAL ACTIVITIES

The graphic variant of the method for comparing the logically-assumed and actual course of solution of a problem was used in the first case [158]. In a rectangular coordinate system the logically-assumed and developed sequence of solution (judgments and operations) was plotted on the abscissa and the actual sequence (judgments and operations) on the ordinate. Whenever in the course of solution there appeared logically redundant judgments and operations, we plotted them on the zero ordinate without moving along the abscissa, while the appearance of erroneous judgments and operations was marked off to the left of the zero point of the abscissa. The resulting curve expressed the relationship of two series of solutions, the logically-assumed and the actual.

Theoretically, different cases of such a relationship are possible. When both courses of solution coincide, we obtain a straight line dissecting the coordinate field at a 45° angle (Fig. 1a). The picture changes drastically when the courses of solution diverge. The curves obtained in this case illustrate the dynamics of thinking so graphically as to indicate, in each individual case, all points where the actual and the logically-assumed and unfolded courses either coincide or diverge, as well as all instances of redundant and erroneous judgments and operations, and the omission of logically-necessary judgments and operations (Fig. 1b).

We shall now turn to some specific examples illustrating a comparison between the logically-assumed and actual course of problem solving by secondary-school students. The problems relate to one of the first sections from a school textbook in physics (topic—"Specific Weight"). Their logical sense consisted in determining the physical relationships between weight volume, and specific weight of physical bodies, and in manipulating these relationships. It was on the basis of these physical relationships that the logically-assumed sequence of solving the problem was built; this solution may be regarded as a simplified or schematized algorithm of solution. Below are adduced the texts of these problems and the logically-assumed and actual sequences of their solution by the students.

Problem 1. A glass is on one pan of a balance; weights totalling 450 g on the other. Equilibrium is achieved by pouring mercury into the glass. The volume of mercury used is 32 cm³. Specific weight of mercury is 13.6. Determine the weight of the glass.

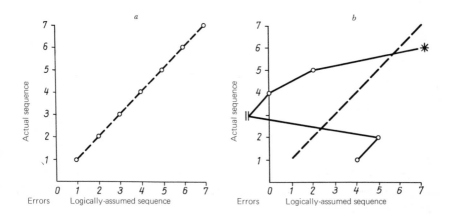

Fig. 1. Coincidence (a) and divergence (b) of logically-assumed and actual sequences in problem solving. Dotted line designates the logical course; solid line, the actual course of solution. Breaks (dead ends) in the sequence are designated by double vertical strokes, correct final answer, by an asterisk.

Logically-assumed sequence of solution	Actual sequence of solution
1. One pan of the scale contains a glass, another weights totalling 450 g.	Student L. B. (8-th grade). The weight of mercury is to be determined. 13.6 g/cm^3 × 32 cm^3 = 435.2 g. We shall determine now the weight of the glass: 450 g – 435.2 g = 14.8 g.
2. The glass with mercury is balanced by the weights.	
3. Hence the glass with mercury weighs 450 g.	Student B. S. (6-th grade). Specific weight of mercury is 13.6. The volume of mercury is 32 cm^3. We have to divide (??) 32 cm^3 by specific weight. We learn how many times it's contained there. This will be the weight of mercury (??) . . . Specific weight of mercury is 13.6. Let us divide 32 cm^3 by 13.6 and we get 2.4 g . . . (prolonged pause).
4. Hence the empty glass weighs 450 g minus the weight of mercury.	
5. Therefore, the weight of mercury is to be found.	
6. The weight of mercury is not known but its volume is known.	
7. In this case, the weight of mercury can be found from the volume and specific weight.	Experimenter: What are you thinking about? What are you going to do next?
8. To do this, specific weight has to be multiplied by the volume.	Student: When I got 2.4 g, I would divide 450 g by 2.4 g to find out how many times mercury is contained in 450 (??). Then I stopped and didn't know what to do. I understood that it was wrong when I got 2.4.
9. The volume of mercury is 32 cm^3.	
10. Specific weight of mercury is 13.6.	Exp.: Still, how is the problem to be solved?
11. Hence, mercury weighs 13.6 × 32 cm^3 = 435.2 g.	Student: . . . We have to find the weight of the mercury.
12. Hence, the glass weighs 450 g – 435.2 g = 14.8 g.	Exp.: But why?
	Student: Now I know: 450 g is the weight of mercury together with the glass. Therefore, the weight of mercury has to be subtracted from 450. I didn't think of it right away. My trend of thought was different before. Now I understand. First we have to find the specific weight of mercury, then the weight of mercury. To do this, we have to multiply the specific weight by volume. We find the net weight of mercury: 13.6 × 32 cm^3 = 435.2 g; 450 g – 435.2 g = 14.8 g. This is the weight of the glass.

Problem 2. Two weights, one of iron and another of lead, of equal weight are made. Which weight is larger in volume? (Specific weight of iron is 7.8; that of lead, 11.3).

Logically-assumed sequence	Actual sequence of solution
1. Given are two weights of equal weight.	Student Kh. S. (8-th grade). The iron will have a greater volume because the specific weight of lead is greater. . . Since the
2. One weight is of iron, another of lead.	
3. Their weight being equal their volume	

is greater the smaller their specific weight.

4. Specific weight of iron is 7.8.
5. Specific weight of lead is 11.3.
6. Therefore, the specific weight of iron is smaller than that of lead.
7. Hence, the volume of the iron weight is larger.

specific weight is smaller the volume will be greater.

Student Z. B. (6-th grade). Specific weight of lead is 11.3. That of iron is 7.8. We will determine now the volume of one weight, then of another and the difference between them (??).

Exp.: But couldn't this be done in a simpler way?

Student: ... Lead is heavier than iron, and if their weight is equal the iron weight is larger in volume. If we take 10 kg of lead its volume will be smaller because lead is heavier than iron. But the volume of iron will be greater.

Problem 3. What is the volume of a copper 500-g-weight? (Specific weight of copper is 8.9.)

Logically-assumed sequence

Actual sequence of solution

1. The copper weight weighs 500 g.
2. To determine the volume of a body from its weight one has to know its specific weight.
3. Specific weight of copper is 8.9.
*4. Therefore, 1 cm^3 of copper weighs 8.9 g.
*5. Therefore, a copper weight of 500 g contains as many cm^3 as 500 units contain 8.9 units.
*6. To find it, 500 must be divided by 8.9 (in other words, weight divided by specific weight).
*7. The quotient obtained will indicate the volume of the weight in cm^3.
*8. The volume of the weight is: $500 \div 8.9 = 56.2$ cm^3.

Student N. K. (8-th grade). Specific weight of copper is 8.9. $500 \div 8.9 = 56.2$ cm^3.

Student Ya. K. (6-th grade). Specific weight of copper is 8.9. To determine the volume, the specific weight must be divided by weight: $8.9 \div 500$ (??) ... No, the volume of the weight cannot be less than one. The weight must be divided by the specific weight: $500 \div 8.9 = 56.2$ cm^3.

Exp.: Tell me, what's specific weight?

Student: ... Now I know. Since the weight has a total of 500 g, and specific weight is the weight of 1cm^3 or 8.9. And we have to find the volume of the entire substance: 500 must be divided by 8.9 and we get the volume.

Note: When this problem is solved algebraically by the "volume rule," the number of logically necessary judgments is reduced to five since the steps marked by an asterisk are replaced with the formula

$$V = \frac{P}{d}$$

Graphic comparison of the logically-assumed and actual sequences of solution revealed readily the very diverging degrees to which reasoning is unfolded, depending on the complexity of the problems being solved and on the degree to which problem-solving habits are developed. In some cases the problems were being solved very rapidly and with a minimum (occasionally just two or three) of judgments expressed (Fig. 2). In other cases, the

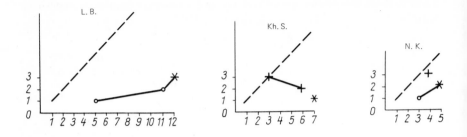

Fig. 2. Graphs depicting problem solving in physics by eighth-graders, with a minimum of judgments expressed. On the left, Problem No. 1; in the middle, Problem No. 2; on the right, Problem No. 3; on top, the initials of students. Crosses designate judgments expressed to substantiate solutions. The rest of notation as in Fig. 1.

problems were being solved, on the contrary, with a lot of redundant and erroneous judgments, with the result that the graphs assumed a very complex zig-zag configuration with large deviations from the logically-assumed course of solution (Fig. 3).

Analysis of the graphs also indicates that, in the case of a correct abbreviated solution, the things most frequently omitted from the students' formulations are, first, the initial data (since they are stated directly in the text of the problem) and, second, the substantiating judgments of a general nature (major premises for a deduction) which are not always reinstated even when the solution is being substantiated later on. What is formulated at the moment of solution is, first of all, operative and formalized judgments related

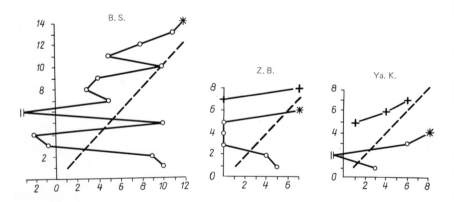

Fig. 3. Graphs depicting problem solving in physics by sixth-graders with logically-redundant and erroneous judgments. Notation as in Figs. 1 and 2.

TABLE 1. Judgments in Actual and Logically-Assumed Sequences of Problem Solving by Sixth- and Eighth-Graders (the number of judgments in the logically-assumed sequence is taken as 100%)

No. of problem	Sixth grade		Eighth grade	
	Total number	Number correct	Total number	Number correct
1	93	55	50	46
2	69	60	50	48
3	71	48	50	45
Arithmetic mean	77.7	54.3	50	46.3

to mathematical operations.* Such are, for instance, all solutions according to ready-made formulae for volume $V = P/d$, weight $(P = Vd)$, and specific weight $d = P/V$.   The largest number of formalized solutions of this type are encountered in eighth-graders; to a lesser extent they are found in sixth-graders (see Table 1).

As for solutions involving logically redundant premises and judgments, they were usually provoked by the necessity to concretize general propositions which have not been sufficiently mastered by students (in this case these were the rules for the volume, weight, and specific weight of physical bodies). Psychologically, therefore, solutions involving logically redundant premises (usually they are encountered when transition to formalized operations is too rapid) are to be regarded not as a deviation from logic but, rather, as search for correct solution by seeking support in concrete images and examples.

Thus it may be stated that, as habits in solving physics problems are developed, verbal statements become abbreviated by virtue of omission of sufficiently mastered general propositions and use of formalized operations, i.e., thought operations involving any system of conventional signs in the form of letters, numbers, or concrete pictures. Since in the process of problem solving the latter are not verbally decoded, being used as substitutes for a series of logically formulated judgments and deductions, we may class them under hidden verbal complexes.

---

* The concepts "substantiating" and "operative" elements have been worked out in detail in N. K. Indik's dissertation titled "Thought processes during formation of a new operation" and based on material involving construction of chemical equations [72].

3. VERBAL GENERALIZATIONS AND VERBAL SEMANTIC COMPLEXES IN TRANSLATION FROM FOREIGN LANGUAGES

Another operation with such verbal semantic complexes is the singling out of semantic points of reference, or key words, in reading or listening to somebody else's talk. Investigation of such points of reference in the process of remembering and reproduction of texts has led A. A. Smirnov to the conclusion that they involve a "recoding" of text and that in their psychological mechanism they are by no means mere members of an association; on the contrary, they represent a generalization of an entire complex of words and phrases. "A semantic point of reference is a point of understanding." At the same time it is a point of "decoding," reproduction of what has been learned or read by means of a code set up in the process of reading or learning by heart [145: 231-232]. As defined by P. I. Zinchenko, semantic points of reference are a means for "mnemonic orientation in material" [68: 412, 420].

In our experiments [149] the operation of semantic points of reference was particularly well manifested in the course of translation from foreign languages into Russian. English texts of varying complexity, with respect to both word content and grammatical forms, were selected: least difficult (very short stories from an ABC book); more difficult (excerpts from stories by Conrad, Stevenson, and London); and finally, scientific texts (excerpts from an English textbook on logic). The subjects were people with varying degrees of knowledge of English, as well as those who knew no English at all but were a little familiar with German.

The subjects were given an English text, a dictionary, and a grammar manual (the subjects preferred to address themselves to the experimenter whenever grammatical information was needed) and asked to read the text and give an account of its contents. The subjects were also told that in translations from a foreign language accuracy does not always mean literalness and that therefore no literal translation was required of them. In addition, just as in the preceding physics problem solving experiments, the subjects were instructed to think aloud when working with the text, i.e., to express their thoughts no matter how redundant, extraneous, or absurd they might seem to them. The majority of subjects were eager to comply with this request, particularly in the initial tests. We were thus in a position to gain an insight into the very process of translating and understanding texts.

Whenever any particular instances of the understanding process had to be clarified, we would keep the subjects at them by various techniques: the subjects sometimes were not allowed to use the dictionary or the grammar, or they were given very fragmentary texts where certain semantically very important words or phrases had been left out. In other cases the subjects were asked to read a text cursorily and give an account of what had been grasped in this manner; at other times, however, the subjects were, on the contrary, prevented from preliminary familiarization with the text.

We shall now present the principal data obtained in these experiments on the role and grammatical structure of the semantic points of reference in understanding the texts read.

The first of the texts presented to the subjects was titled "The Monkey and the Looking-Glass," but in order to make understanding more difficult we presented it without its title, as we did with all the other texts.

The Monkey and the Looking-Glass

Jack and Jim are two young monkeys. One morning people come and take Jack away. The other monkey has no friend to play with.

There is a looking-glass on the table. Jim comes to the table and looks in the looking-glass.

"Here you are at last," he cried. He rubs his head and looks again. The monkey in the looking-glass rubs his head too. He waves his hand, and the other monkey waves his hand. He makes a face, and the other monkey makes a face too.

"Oh, ho," cries Jim, "you make faces at me!" Then he strikes with his hand, howls with pain, and runs away.

The subjects who knew no English but were familiar with German, translated the text by looking up in the dictionary the meanings of all the words as they occurred and reading them "as if in German." Here is an example of such a translation, vividly reminding one of the decoding of ancient inscriptions in an unknown language.

Subject A., reading the first phrase "Jack and Jim are two young monkeys," exclaims, "I haven't understood anything!" This is followed by a pause, and the subject says: "Obviously, this is how it is: Yak and Yim are names, the story obviously is about people." The subject next determines the meaning of the rest of the words from the dictionary. The word "are" is a matter of some difficulty since it is not in the dictionary. The subject makes therefore a guess: "Perhaps this is an untranslatable term of some kind" and continues to determine the meaning of the remaining words: two, young, monkey. "Ah so! And I thought they were people. This means Yak and Yim are two young monkeys. Were there here a link-predicate, then this would be so." In a second the subject adds, "Perhaps 'are' is a copula?" The experimenter confirms this assumption, and the meaning of the phrase becomes clear.

Analysis of how the subject came to understand this phrase establishes the following individual steps:

1. The singling out of understandable words (Jack and Jim) which the subject pronounced as Yak and Yim;

2. The first guess as to the general meaning, arising on this basis, which creates in the subject a general orientation toward the subsequent content of text ("Yak and Yim are names: obviously, the story is about people");

3. Determination of the meaning of unfamiliar words from the dictionary;

4. Sudden grasp of the meaning on seeing the word "monkey" ("Ah so! This means, Yak and Yim are two young monkeys");

5. Discarding the previous concept—a guess as to the meaning ("story about people"); appearance of a new concept, for the time being, just a hypothesis ("Were there here a link-predicate, then this would be so");

6. Grammatical guess as to the link-verb, arising on the basis of the guess concerning meaning ("Perhaps 'are' is a copula?").

Thus, the process of understanding proceeded here from the recognition and determination of the meaning of individual words via a guess (hypothesis), at first semantic and then grammatical, as to the general meaning of the phrase. In the beginning, moreover, when all that had been known was the first two words, there arose just a vague notion, and even that was erroneous. The following determination of the meaning of words resulted in a clarification of the meaning of the phrase, to be sure so far in the form of a hypothesis only, since the subject was not familiar with English grammar.

Let us note that not all the words were of equal significance for an understanding of the meaning of the phrase. The most significant were "Jack," "Jim," and "monkey." The hypotheses on meaning were linked to these words; they set up the orientation toward the subsequent content. True, the first two words had created a false orientation; the true carrier of the meaning of the phrase turned out to be the word "monkey" which brought together the disconnected word meanings into a unified idea, created a context, and thus brought about understanding of the general meaning of the phrase. It was precisely the discovery of the meaning of this word that produced the "aha-experience (a typical psychological attribute of any "sudden" and "instantaneous" understanding) and the correct guess as to the grammatical structure of the phrase.

Our subjects called words of this type "main," or "key," or generalizing, words, and in looking for meaning they usually oriented themselves by them; and this is what these words were for them: reference points, landmarks in the process of understanding. Starting with the function of these words as reference points, they may also be called semantic landmarks or, more precisely, operators, with the aid of which the text is broken down into separate semantic groups and generalizations are made. We shall satisfy ourselves later on, that the understanding process, particularly in the instances of "sudden insight," inevitably contained the discovery and fixation of these semantic landmarks.

Understanding of the second sentence, "One morning people come and take Jack away," took almost the same course in the same subject. The latter begins again by determining the words unknown to him, and with the very first words there again arises in him a vague, undifferentiated notion concerning the meaning of the phrase. The subject says: "Some kind of a meaning looms before me: something about people and monkeys. Evidently, Jack is here the main character—here is his name." This is a very vague notion, and the subject is not satisfied. The dissatisfaction gives rise to questions like

"Why are there people here? What are they doing?" which are followed by hypotheses: "Perhaps this is a zoo?", "Perhaps this is a circus?", etc.

At last the subject determines from the dictionary the meanings of all the words, but this is not itself final understanding. The words are disconnected, and the subject for quite a while fails to establish a direct link between them. The multimeaning word "take" presents particular difficulties: the subject is at a loss as to what meaning is to be selected for it. New hypotheses arise. At first the subject selects for "take" the Russian word meaning "to take," starting from the hypothesis: "Perhaps the monkeys are going to take food," and on this basis tries to interconnect all the words of text. "One morning ... people ... come ... and to take...." The subject is puzzled: "Something doesn't fit. I'll look up 'take' once more." The subject now selects the Russian word with the meaning of "take away." The difference is small, yet it channels the subject's thought in an entirely new direction: "To take away; then: "One morning people came and took Jack." A pause, followed in a next second by the exclamation: "Could it be that they took him and led him away?! Yes, they led him—away."

The understanding came here together with the meaning of "take" as signifying "to take away," it formed a link-up of words without which they hung in the air; it converted the original vague, indefinite notion ("something about people and monkeys") to a clear thought ("people took Jack and led him away"). The verb "take" appeared here as the connecting or unifying word, but unifying in a different sense from that of the word "monkey" in the first phrase. The word "monkey" was there the direct carrier of meaning, a semantic reference point prior to the appearance of the syntactic connection of words; here the meaning of the phrase was grasped only after all the words had been syntactically interlinked.

The next phrase, "The other monkey has no friend to play with," brings out new peculiarities of the process of understanding. As the subject determines the meaning of words, he combines them into separate semantic groups. Three semantic groups arise in this way: "other monkey," "has no friend," and "to play with," which the subject sequentially links up.

Characteristically, however, this breakdown of the sentence into discrete groups and their subsequent link-up did not yet bring the subject to direct understanding. Having divided the phrase into these three groups, the subject asks himself, "What happened, then?", and rereads the text: "The other monkey has no friend to play with ... To play with whom? Ah, I got it. In Russian it's this way: the other monkey had no one to play with, he had no playmate for games."

Referring to the understanding of this phrase the subject pointed out that the words making up the second group became fixed in his consciousness ("has no friend") and this central group became a link connecting all the rest of the words. Here, then, not one word, as was the case with the first two sentences, but a whole group of words played the role of the reference point.

Because this phrase contains certain peculiarities of English grammatical structure (the negation "no" following a verb and the position of the preposition "with" at the end of phrase), its literal translation offered no syntactic link between words. In the beginning (with literal translation) therefore, there was just the general meaning of the phrase, expressed in "has no friend"; next, on the basis of the grasped meaning, there took place a general grammatical reconstruction of the literal translation. Because of this, the understanding involved occurred here in at least four stages: 1) literal understanding by determining the meaning of all the words; 2) singling out the main semantic group; 3) understanding, on this basis, of the general meaning; and 4) rearrangement of an English phrase into a Russian one.

The new phrase, "There is a looking-glass on the table," was understood by grasping the main semantic landmarks of this phrase, the words "looking-glass" and "table." These words, being the main elements in the situation, determined the syntactic interconnection of all the rest of the words, "There is a looking-glass on the table."

The meaning of the next phrase, "Jim comes to the table and looks in the looking-glass," was grasped almost at once, since these words had for the most part been encountered in the preceding sentences, and the connection between words was clear from the situation: "Jim came . . . comes to the table and looks in the looking-glass . . ." The next phrase, however, gave rise to difficulties. These were due to a combination of short and, according to the subject, insignificant words. The expression "at last" presented particular difficulties. The subject broke it down into two independent words, "at" in the sense of "in," "on," "by," "next to," and "last" in the sense of being at the end, most recent. This results in complete puzzlement, the subject asking, "What is this, then? It doesn't make sense." He tries to hypothesize, but hypotheses fail too. After a while I prompt him with the meaning of this expression. One might think that the phrase should become clear now, yet the subject replies, as puzzled as before: "No, the Russian phrase for 'at last' doesn't help either"; then, rereading it, he exclaims: "Ah! This is evidently what he thought about his playmate: he took his reflection in the mirror for his playmate. This is why there is a mirror here. I got it, I got it!" In reply to the question how he hit on the idea, the subject answered: "I went back to the beginning of the story, pictured to myself the monkey and the mirror and then I understood why this 'at last' was there."

Having dismembered the phrase into individual words and found their meaning, the subject was still far from understanding anything. In itself, the phrase "Here you are at last," out of the context of the story, outside a concrete situation, conveyed nothing; it was understood only in the light of the entire context. And indeed, the understanding came only after this phrase had been related to the context as a whole; the phrase came alive, so that the subject exclaimed: "This is evidently what he thought about his playmate: he took his reflection in the mirror for his playmate."

That the phrase "Here you are at last" had not been understood for such a long time is chiefly due to its idiomatic nature and to forgetting of the context. The forgetting of the context was frequently encountered in our experiments; it was related to search for the meaning of individual words and always resulted in a failure to grasp the meaning. Here is another example.

Subject D. reads the phrase "He waves his hand, and the monkey waves his hand." The slow search for the meaning of all the words in the dictionary and their subsequent syntactic unification resulted in his forgetting of the story's situation. The subject says: "All the words are clear, but there is no connection. The monkey was waving his hand... Why should he do that?.. Aha, this is in the mirror. I completely forgot that it's a mirror we are talking about. Then it's clear: he waved and so did his reflection in the mirror."

The subsequent phrases of this story were translated by the subjects without any difficulty, though not always accurately as far as grammar goes. The monkey's behavior in front of the mirror, his outcries, were easily understood because the subjects had been attuned to the situation "monkey and the looking-glass." This situation ordinarily arose at the moment when the word "looking-glass" appeared for the first time in the story. Subject K., referring to this moment, says: "After this everything is clear: the monkey's play with a mirror, the usual monkey behavior." Subject G. stated: "It was difficult so long as I didn't know the plot. It seemed to me at first that we dealt with the relationships between Jim and Jack. When the mirror appeared, everything changed; the former orientation disappeared, and I started looking for meaning on a different plane, on the plane of the fable "The Monkey and the Looking-Glass."

The orientation, or set, thus generated greatly facilitated all the subsequent work with the dictionary. The same subject G. pointed out repeatedly that at first the dictionary was more of a hindrance than help: it gave a lot of meanings for each word, thus disorienting the subject. "But now that I have acquired an orientation, a hint at the meaning, the dictionary no longer hinders understanding: I now look for words of a certain content and a definite grammatical form."

There is no need to adduce the records relating to the other subjects of this group. In analyzing the records, we find, with all the necessary consistency, the same factors in understanding, where of central importance is the detection and fixation of the principal semantic points of the story: the words "monkey," "looking-glass," "make a face," "strike," and some of the others.

For the next two groups of subjects, fairly familiar with the English language, the understanding of this text presented no difficulties and was based in all cases on the singling out and fixation, while reading, the same main, or generalizing, words as in the first group of subjects, with the only difference that those who knew English well did so without translating into Russian. Even for them, however, these words remained the key words, since they at once revealed the plot of the story in its entirety ("The usual monkey behavior in front of a mirror"). Subject V., a teacher of English, said after reading this text: "There arose at once an association with English books for children. It was this association that set the direction for further understanding. Everything was clear, much could be anticipated. Images cropped up, and illustrations from children's books came to mind. While reading, I could at the same time evaluate the text: it is dynamic, affective, humorous."

We are dealing in this case with immediate understanding of text, without translation and grammatical analysis, involving moreover concurrent run of two trends of thought, related, first, to the content of the story and, second, to its evaluation by the reader ("the text is dynamic, affective, humorous"). Grasping of the semantic reference points of the text was here almost instantaneous, to the extent that the most rapid reading can be instantaneous, and the general meaning of the text was determined from these semantic reference points.

It should be noted, however, that without an adequate knowledge of the grammar of a language, such fluent understanding of material read from individual key words becomes very difficult—even impossible if the text contains sentences which are grammatically complex. An excerpt from Conrad's story "The End of the Tether" was such a text in our experiments; it described a fire on a ship on the high seas.

The End of the Tether

> The old man told us to take all the valuable things we could save from the ship with us into the boats. We did so. Then all the boats were put to sea and I received orders to get down into one and keep them all ready, close by the ship. I had two sailors with me. The three of us tied the boats together and did what we could so as to be not too far from and not too near the ship.
>
> By now there was a large circle on the sea, lighted by the fire of the burning ship. It was very dangerous to keep the boats near the ship. The masts might fall at any moment and nobody could tell in what direction they would fall. I could not see anybody on board; I did not understand why they still remained on the ship. What were they doing there? At last I shouted, "On deck, there?" A sailor looked out. "We are ready for you here," I said.

For subjects with poor or no command of English this passage proved impossible to understand due to the complexity of grammatical structure, while guessing the meaning from individual words created a very vague impression as to the topic. Thus in translating the first sentence, subject A., having determined the meanings of all the words from the dictionary and having next singled out some of them as reference points ("ship," "valuable things," "boat," "save"), was still unable to unite them into a single sentence (it remained obscure whether they had to save themselves or the ship). Even one of the principal sentences of the passage—"By now there was a large circle on the sea, lighted by the fire of the burning ship"—which explains the whole topic of the story (a ship on fire) was often misunderstood. One of the subjects from this group understood it in this way: Before us is endless sea illuminated by a ship's lights; another subject translated it as follows: "There now was a large circle on the sea (probably made by the boats) and light from the fire of burned ships."

Even the subjects with a good knowledge of English had some difficulties with this text. These difficulties were, however, not of a linguistic but of a psychological nature, due to the fragmentary nature of the text and a search for a starting point for its analysis and understanding, difficulties usually characterized as "getting the feel of the text" or as "developing a semantic set."

Reading the first paragraph, subject R. says: "The beginning is surprising. Who is this old man? Is he just talking or giving orders? It is clear from the first two lines that this is a shipwreck, and this gave rise to a guess—could it be Robinson [Crusoe]? But next two more sailors appeared, and it became clear that this was no Robinson. When the lighted circle appeared on the sea, the thought flashed—where does the circle come from? The subsequent words "burning ship" made everything clear. Everything that followed was clear to me."

The words "burning ship" thus became the carriers of the meaning of the entire text, clarifying correspondingly the meaning of other words as well (old man is the "captain of the ship" and not just any "old man"; tell means "give orders" and not just "speak," etc.).

In the next test series the subjects were given an abstract text to translate, a passage from an English textbook on logic, in which judgment was defined as a mental act of cognizing the real world:

Judgment

Judgment is the mental act of perceiving and assorting a relation between two distinguishable things. There are two distinct operations in the act of judgment:

1. the operation by which two things are distinguished and related to each other;
2. the mental assertion that this relation thus recognized is a fact in the real world.

As the judgments we make relate to all sorts of matters—things which exist in the sensible world, things that exist only in imagination, things perceived by sense, and things thought only—so the two things which in judging are distinguished and related can be of the most various descriptions, a shade of color in rose, the rose itself in the garden, the little flower plucked from the crannied wall, the universe of which that flower is a part, some action of an actual human being, some deed of a character in fiction, mathematical entities, the symbols of pure logic A, B, . . . D, etc.

Irrespective of their mastery of English, all subjects fell into two groups—
those who had and those who had not studied logic. Even when their
command of English was poor, the former eventually came to understand the
passage, whereas the latter, their good knowledge of English notwithstanding,
understood the text only in vague, indefinite terms, since it was very difficult
to single out any words as reference points without knowing logic. For
example, subject V. who knows English well but who has never studied logic,
says: "I am unable to read this text at one go. I have to go back to the
foregoing, to think it over in order to understand the author's idea. Moreover,
I have to evaluate each concept separately: what does the word 'judgment'
mean here—a conclusion, reasoning, opinion or interpretation? One has
therefore to maintain a critical attitude toward oneself all the time, asking
oneself: Do I understand the author's idea correctly?"

Another female subject from this group stated that she was unable to
understand anything without a painstaking analysis of the author's definitions:
"The main thing for me was to analyze the content and I am not at all sure
whether I understand this text correctly. It would therefore be useful to have
an accurate translation of the author's terminology."

Subjects who knew less English but who had studied logic, translated
this text with comparative ease. Reading the passage, subject T. pointed out
that he was perceiving it just as any other scientific text in Russian:
"Generally speaking, these are international phrases, and to understand them
means just to decipher them regardless of whether this is English or not." He
also noted that in reading this text he not only did not translate many of the
words but even did not read them separately: "Such words as 'logical,'
'mental judgment' are for me not English, French, or German—they are simply
terms, scientific expressions, so that when one reads words like these, it is as
if the Latin type were unnoticed: they are read, as it were, outside the type."

We are dealing here already with elements of immediate understanding,
based on a knowledge of terms and their perception (in this case visual) as a
whole, as verbal semantic complexes whose meaning was well known to the
subjects and required no additional deciphering. The subjects used to say in
such cases that words were perceived by them as "algebraic signs or
formulae." Moreover, just as with physical formulae, the meaning of logical
terms could be expressed by the subjects in an expanded form; but this was
an entirely different task not required for understanding at the moment of
reading: the meaning of the text was clear to them without a deciphering of
this kind, from the key words only. Fixation of such key words preceded the
understanding of the text, making up its principal, central element with which
the phenomenon of the "instantaneousness" of understanding itself was
connected (*die Einsicht*, insight).

Analyzing our material, we find in it words extremely diversified as to
their grammatical forms: nouns (monkey, looking-glass, judgment), occasion-

ally verbs (take, save, etc.), sometimes adverbs (ready), sometimes pronouns (he), link-words (this), and sometimes a whole group of words (too far from). On the face of it there seemed no regular relationship between the key words and the grammatical forms in which they were expressed. The impression was that each word could be the carrier of the general meaning depending on the situation. We observed more than once, moreover, that not only a word but at times even a punctuation mark denoting intonation of speech, e.g., a dash, colon, exclamation point, question mark, quotation marks, etc.–would serve as the connecting, unifying element. Finally, the intonation with which the text was read was itself the connecting element: wrong intonation resulted either in a lack of understanding or in incorrect understanding.

Further analysis showed, however, that a relationship does exist between the key words and the character of their grammatical categories and that this relationship is determined by the level of knowledge and understanding on the part of the subject. For beginners as well as those well acquainted with the English language, nouns followed by verbs served as direct carriers of general meaning in the reading of difficult texts. The primary general notion arose on the basis of semantic landmarks of this type. The remainder of the words were not direct carriers of meaning, and many of them, particularly auxiliary (dependent) words, were frequently consciously ignored by the subjects.

Subsequently, as the syntactic connection of words was better understood and the meaning took on a more definite shape, it was seen that any grammatical form of a word could become the carrier of the more precise meaning. Hence, they became the carriers of general meaning indirectly, via the syntactic connection of words, and this corresponded to a higher level of understanding.

Thus, from the material presented it may be concluded that in the initial stages of textual understanding, nouns and verbs, i.e., words designating objects and actions, play the role of semantic reference points. Subsequently, however, as the meaning becomes better defined, punctuation marks and shades of intonation can perform this function along with other grammatical forms of words and word combinations.

The possibility of understanding a text directly (fluently) was based psychologically on the fact that in this case all the aspects of word meaning–lexical, syntactic, and contextual–in the reader's consciousness became integrated into a common meaning (sense). These generalized semantic verbal associations in some cases (especially in the first two passages) evoked various graphic images which, too, became carriers of the general meaning, its graphic symbols. It would be wrong to assert on this basis that "discursive" processes (analysis, comparison, inference) took no place whatever here. The experiment showed, on the contrary, that these processes did occur, but in an extremely reduced (abbreviated) form, in the form of operations on the key words of text which entered into the reader's internal speech structure.

Keeping in mind the above-mentioned structural and functional characteristics of verbal semantic complexes (their generalized and abbreviated nature, after the type of enthymemes in logic, as well as the possibility of replacing them with graphic-image symbols), we can now pass on to a more detailed study of their operation in the processes of inner speech. As we shall see, semantic reference points of this type will play the role of the principal structural element of inner speech as well as that of a particularizing and integrating mechanism whereby information is processed logically in the process of thinking.

Part Two

Effect of Articulatory Interference on Mental Activity

Chapter IV

Impairment of the Auditory Perception and Under-standing of Speech by Articulatory Interference

1. EXPERIMENTAL APPROACH TO STUDY OF THE FUNCTIONS OF INNER SPEECH

That an understanding of someone else's speech is impossible without it being inwardly reproduced has repeatedly been expressed in psychology and linguistics.

This view seems to be rooted in the classical doctrine on aphasia. Psychiatrists of the last century (P. Broca, J. Charcot, C. Wernicke, and others) who had studied inner speech in connection with aphasic phenomena believed that while listening to speech man reproduces in his mind the auditory, visual, and motor images of words and thus comes to understand speech. Accordingly, failure to understand speech, usually observed in sensory aphasia, was explained by them as due to the inability to reproduce these images. The only debatable question was in which memory images—auditory, visual, or motor—words were reproduced. Stricker, as we have seen, asserted that representations of words were always motor representations; V. Egger believed them to be auditory.

The need to repeat speech in order to understand it has also been noted by lingusts. A. A. Potebnya pointed out that a thought about sound would "inevitably entail a realization (utterance of the sound) since silence is the art of not allowing an image to be translated into a movement of the organs with which it is connected—an *art* which modern man acquires rather late in life and which is completely unnoticed in children. The listener will repeat the sound uttered by another person, his own creation will appear before him in a palpable form and evoke in turn a sound which had been in his mind but whose purpose now is to explain, an image of the object. In this manner a rearrangement of imagery will take place, required by understanding" [135: 75]. Elsewhere, Potebnya, in speaking of understanding, has in mind not so much repetition of the speaker's utterance as its "translation" into one's own language. "Understanding," he writes, "is the simplification of thought, its translation, so to speak, into other language . . ." [135: 79].

A. L. Pogodin, the author of an extensive monograph on the psychology of language, analyzing the importance of inner speech for the process of understanding, calls it "the translator into the language of our thought of that which we hear and which, without the aid of this internal speech of ours, would be devoid of any sense for us" [130: 5]. At the same time he believes, along with a whole succession of researchers in psychiatry, that "somebody else's words are perceived as complexes of sounds, being converted for us into words by our own speech apparatus (meaning the auditory, motor, and visual centers for speech) which, in turn, sets in motion the organs necessary for the utterance of words. Each word which we hear and repeat passes along two pathways: from the external world to our internal speech and from the latter to external speech, or speaking" [130: 30].

The need for the inward repetition of the speech heard to understand it was particularly stressed by P. P. Blonskii in his book *Memory and Thought.* "The hearing of speech is not simply hearing: to a certain degree we, as it were, speak together with the speaker" [29: 451].

To prove this hypothesis, Blonskii cites the simplest test possible, of everyday occurrence but highly interesting. "When I look at something, I am free at the same time both to look attentively and to say something to myself. When I listen attentively to music, I can at the same time think, talk to myself silently. But it is commonly known how difficult it is simultaneously to listen attentively to a speaker and to say something inwardly to oneself: if we listen with attention, we are unable to think or talk silently to ourselves, for instance, recite a familiar verse; moreover, we notice that when listening very attentively, we repeat to ourselves the speaker's words; if, on the contrary, we start to think at this moment, to talk silently to ourselves (not the speaker's utterances), we cease to hear the speaker's words, experiencing something akin to sensory aphasia, roughly that stage of it when words are heard as words but are as yet not being understood: we hear everything that's being said but are unable to repeat anything since the speech hasn't reached, so to speak, our 'psychic' ear. . . The impossibility of speaking inwardly about other matters while listening attentively to speech is explained by the fact that listening to speech is accompanied by its simultaneous reproduction: if this is so, the experiment described above consists in an attempt to have two internal speeches at the same time, which of course is physically impossible" [29: 452].

The evident inference from Blonskii's interpretation of this experiment is that inward repetition of the speaker's utterances (simultaneous reproduction during listening to speech) is a necessary factor in understanding it.* But

---

* L. A. Chistovich [186; 187] too holds that the speech heard has to be reproduced kinesthetically to be understood; she believes that the speech-understanding effect depends chiefly on the reproduction (imitation) of speech.

how correct is this hypothesis which asserts categorically the need for re-producing speech in order to understand it?

Let us turn first to the analysis of factual data. Generally speaking, there are quite a few facts attesting the presence of "listening *cum* enunciation." This repetition of the speaker's words is especially frequent in small children. No one observing the psychic life of children could fail to notice it. As noted by W. Stern, beginning with the second half of the first year of life, the child repeats "all kinds of noises, as well as syllables and combinations of syllables uttered by others" [199: 74]. In child psychology, such a repetition of another's speech has long since been termed echolalia, which is a clinical term but which conveys well the essence of this phenomenon. It is well known, however, that the child does not by any means repeat everything that he hears and understands; many words which he understands remain "beyond the threshold of his speech": while understanding them he is unable to repeat them. This lag of the child's speech behind his understanding of the speech of those surrounding him is in itself sufficient argument against the necessity of repeating words in order to understand them.

Let us consider facts of a different kind.

Everyday school experience indicates beyond any shadow of doubt that listening to a lecture cannot indeed be mere listening; it is, to a considerable degree, also oral or written repetition of the teacher's words. Inward, repetition of some of the speaker's words and phrases is also noticed occasionally in listening to a public address, and so on.

Of interest in this connection are also certain facts pertaining to the psychology of reading. E. Meumann, analyzing the process of reading, points out that "In the majority of people reading is at the same time inward listening and silent enunciation; children and uneducated adults frequently accompany their reading with a soft enunciation, they move their lips and thus reveal the setting in motion of the entire motor apparatus of speech; educated adults, too, unwittingly start reading in an undertone whenever they want to achieve particular concentration in spite of distracting extraneous stimuli or when they read with great interest and excitement (similar phenomena may be observed during writing)" [107: 109].

While pointing to these facts, Meumann at the same time believes this inward enunciation of words during reading not to be necessary for all people to the same extent. H cites his own experience in reading with the eyes alone without enunciating words. To eliminate the enunciation of words in reading, he used to count simultaneously, "One, two, three," etc. Such reading proved to be quite possible for him. He describes this process as follows: "I keep grasping a part of a sentence in a purely visual way; after a small pause I am able to grasp another part, comprehend its meaning and join it to the first part. To be sure, this purely visual reading is difficult, and this indicates that I am accustomed to the inward cooperation between hearing and enunciation" [107: 117].

As pointed out earlier, R. Pintner arrived at similar conclusions.

The problem of "inward repetition" can be approached by still another route. As we have pointed out, Potebnya, Pogodin, and others related the repetition of somebody else's speech to the need for "simplification of thought," its "translation into one's own language." Translation of this kind does indeed occasionally take place, but can it in this case be nothing but mere repetition of the speaker's words? For it is evident that in cases like these understanding ensues as a result of foregoing reflection—comparison, generalization, etc.—so that it becomes unlikely that all that is involved is mere echolalia.

It should be kept in mind that the term "understanding" is, generally speaking, very vague. In some cases, to understand means to remember an old experience, to bring it into proper correlation with what is known. Such is frequently the case with the understanding in the middle of a phrase. The need for coenunciating the speaker's words seems to be completely superfluous in this case. In others, one often has to reread a difficult text twice or thrice before understanding occurs. Understanding comes here via contemplation, reflection. In this case, to understand means not so much to refer new experience to the old as to express it in the form of new inferences, new concepts. Mere repetition of the speaker's words (or rereading of text) is insufficient for understanding, and if repetition of the speaker's words does take place, its role evidently must involve something else.

Apparently, one may speak of different types, or rather different levels, of understanding. We have pointed out two of them here, but conceivably there may be many more.

Therefore we deem it important to investigate the question on the significance of verbal expressions on various levels of understanding. For all practical purposes, this question is related to the mechanism of understanding: does the understanding of other people's speech occur through reproducing, in part or in full, this speech to oneself, or is it restricted to auditory perception? In a more general form this problem may be stated thus: is the perception of somebody else's speech purely auditory or does it involve motor action as well? Actually, two different questions emerge from the viewpoints concerning the role of inward repetition in listening to speech: first, is it necessary for an understanding of speech, and if not, what is its significance all the same; second, if and when inward repetition takes place, is it always verbal, i.e., verbally expressed speaking?

By way of proof of his hypothesis Blonskii, as we have seen, suggests a test which, in his opinion, demonstrates the impossibility of listening to somebody else's speech while enunciating verses learned by heart. But in Binet's experiments, which we discussed earlier and in which inner speech had been eliminated by exactly the same method as that suggested by Blonskii (by reciting verses learned by heart), the subjects did not only understand the questions asked but found answers to them, i.e., they were thinking. Subsequently, Meumann and Pintner, using a similar method to eliminate speech movements from the reading process, also failed to notice any effect of this elimination on the understanding of what was being read. Thus, consideration of this aspect of the problem has not settled the problem either. It was therefore of interest to reproduce those experiments.

In our experiments, the subjects recited rapidly, without pauses, verses well known to them, in a soft voice or in a whisper.

Simultaneously, the experimenter read a text previously unknown to the subjects; later on they had to reproduce its contents.

The main experimental condition was that listening to the text and recitation of verses be simultaneous. This eliminated listening during pauses. In addition, it was very important to avoid acoustic mixing of the experimenter's speech with the subject's. The most suitable technique for this purpose was to enunciate verses in a soft voice or in a whisper. Conditions were thus created which reduced to a minimum the possibility of coenunciation (repetition) of the speech heard.

The test series started with preliminary experiments in which some of the graduate students and I were the subjects. The initial preliminary experiments confirmed Blonskii's conclusions. The enunciation of verses made listening to speech extremely difficult. Under such conditions one indeed experiences something akin to sensory aphasia: words are heard but not understood, sounding like an unfamiliar dialect. Moreover, it was impossible to do both things at once: one could either listen or enunciate verses. When one concentrates on extraneous speech, one begins to grasp the meaning of some of the words, but to make up for it one stops reciting verses, thereby violating the main experimental condition. When, however, these factors coincide, one tends to "flee" from the sounds of speech, the sole aim being to go on with the verse.

To understand speech under such conditions seemed impossible, and to continue with the experiments, fruitless. One circumstance changed the entire situation, however. While listening to the radio one day, I started to count automatically to myself, "One, two, three, four," etc. The result proved completely unexpected: I was able to understand clearly the announcer's every word, but whatever I heard disappeared from memory almost at the same moment. I had the feeling that I was forgetting everything that had been present just a moment before and more than once I felt tempted to break off the count so as to fix somehow the meaning of the speech heard. I was experiencing what might be called "instantaneous amnesia." I have repeated this experiment many times, the result always being the same. It was entirely clear that elimination of speech movements made it extremely difficult to memorize speech.

Wishing to find out just how important repetition of the speech heard was for memorization, I started to repeat the announcer's statements word by word. The result of this experiment too was unexpected. While repeating the announcer's words rapidly, I of course understood the meaning of each word, but I failed to grasp the general meaning and even the meaning of individual sentences. Moreover, I was experiencing "instantaneous amnesia," and this to almost the same degree as in the first case: the words that had just been repeated disappeared from memory. The resulting phenomenon was paradoxical: total repetition of words led to forgetting.

The conclusion from the first experiment was that forgetting of the material understood was due to the impossibility of fixing it by repetition. In the second experiment such repetition was carried out intentionally, yet the extraordinary forgetting remained, resulting in almost complete loss of meaning. It was decided to determine what lay behind it all.

With this in mind, we started to vary experimental conditions in terms of two factors: first, according to the degree of automatization with which the subjects enunciated extraneous material and, second, according to the degree of complexity of the texts which were being presented at this moment. The former was achieved by making the subjects listen to texts not only while reciting verses but also while counting, some of the subjects having been obliged preliminarily to learn the verses by heart for the specific purpose of making their recitation as automatic as possible.

Control experiments were carried out concurrently. They involved understanding a text of the same degree of difficulty, but listening to the text took place under ordinary conditions, that is, without simultaneous recitation of verses or counting.

Thus the following main test series were set up:

First series—listening to texts with simultaneous recitation of verses;

Second series—listening to texts with simultaneous ordinal count ("one, two, three," etc.);

Third series—listening to texts with simultaneous recitation of specially learned verses (at individual stages of learning);

Fourth series—control—free listening (without recitation of verses and counting).

The texts read to the subjects varied in difficulty, both in terms of understanding and in terms of memorizing. One group of the texts contained artistic descriptions of nature, historical events, biographical material, etc., the other group dealt with scientific reasoning; more often than not those were excerpts from the literature on natural science and philosophy, such as exposition of the views of Einstein, Bernard, Kepler, Meillet, and others; excerpts from Kant's *Critique of Pure Reason* or Hegel's *Logik*. The former group we termed, for convention's sake, descriptive; the latter—also conventionally—discursive (the conventionality of these designations was due to the fact that descriptive texts could contain some reasoning, whereas the dicursive ones could have descriptive elements). Some texts consistently developed some single idea; some of the others represented expositions of several more or less isolated ideas.

In each test series one text of each type mentioned above was read. The texts were read in a clear voice and with the usual semantic intonations. The reading of a single text lasted a little over one minute (60 to 80 sec). After the reading, the subjects had to reproduce the text's content.

The subjects were scientific staff members and graduate students from the Institute of Psychology (10 persons) as well as first-year students from a medical institute (5 persons).

About 300 protocols were obtained in these experiments.

2. NEGATIVE EFFECT OF ARTICULATORY INTERFERENCE ON THE UNDERSTANDING AND MEMORIZATION OF SPEECH HEARD

We shall present the results of the experiments according to individual series.

In the first series all subjects listened to texts with simultaneous recitation of verses. The experimenter read four different texts, two descriptive and two discursive. Following the reading of each text the subjects tried to reproduce it.

The first two texts were reproduced by the subjects in a very fragmentary manner, with great lacunae and occasional distortions of meaning. This is particularly true of the first text which dealt with a spring trip of children to the tundra in the far north of the Soviet Union, and with a letter from the schoolchildren of the North to their comrades in Moscow.

Here are some typical samples of the reproduction of this text:

Subject T. "The sun was rising. Some school children and vacations."

Subject Sh. "The subject matter was spring, vacations . . . Apparently not in the Soviet Union because the meaning was—to write to the Soviet Union. I didn't get anything else."

Subject F. "A trip of some kind . . . Children walk together with adults . . . They write something to their comrades abroad . . . There remain also single words: spring . . . air."

To a question as to the locality of the trip he replied: "I don't know . . . Seems to be somewhere in Moscow." Later on this question was put to every subject, and their answers were for the most part incorrect. Some said they "didn't know, didn't hear." Others stated that the trip took place in Moscow, still others believed it had been somewhere abroad. Yet the text stated explicitly that the children's trip took place in the far north of the Soviet Union.

The failure to understand the text manifested itself not only in this instance but in a number of other instances as well. Thus, the text read: "It is already May, yet the weather is still cold." Those subjects who had taken notice of this phrase retold it roughly thus: "The cold weather will pass, it will become warm and May will come." Having failed to comprehend that the story was about the far north of the Soviet Union, the subjects related all the events described in the passage to the climatic conditions in Moscow, which they knew well.

All subjects noted the extreme difficulty of listening while reciting verses at the same time.

The scientific staff members and graduate students from the Institute of Psychology, who acted as subjects, produced very detailed reports.

Subject Sh. stated: "It was very difficult to listen to your speech. My activity was at the center of my attention, whereas listening was peripheral. Sometimes I succeeded in placing in the center of attention the meaning of that which was being read at the moment. Individual words broke through then, and their meaning became generalized; for example, I said to myself mentally: 'Aha, spring . . . a demonstration . . . they are about to write a letter . . . the Soviet Union." This realization was joined by some attempt at memorization, an effort whose futility was being realized at the same moment. Turning my attention to the meaning of what was being read resulted in my stopping verse recitation. I noticed then that about two lines of the first stanza I enunciated without sound. But when I started to really pronounce it I got the feeling that whatever I had grasped in the text read was being erased thereby. I grasped some of the words in transition from one stanza to another, but other words in the moment of reading was well."

Subject T. stated: "It is completely impossible to reproduce. I simply haven't heard it. Not physically (you have a loud voice), but in the way of psychic deafness: you hear it but don't understand a thing. How I nevertheless managed to reproduce one phrase I don't know. At any rate, it was not because of pauses. The words which I have reproduced flashed in my consciousness at the moment of listening. There were a few other words which I would understand but also forget at once."

Although the reports of the students tested provided less detail, they too were quite significant in this case.

Subject Z. said: "It is completely impossible to listen under such conditions. I hear noise of some kind. And the verses too somehow went wrong: I was able to pronounce the first line only, and after that I didn't know what to say. I had to force myself to recite the verses. I heard and grasped only single words, without knowing what they referred to."

Subject R. reported: "While reciting the verses I often went astray and uttered some jumble of words, mere verbiage. I heard the words but they didn't reach my consciousness." Other subjects gave similar reports.

Thus, the subjects all noted the extreme difficulty of listening to speech under such conditions. Not breaking off the verse recitation, deprived the subjects of the ability to listen attentively to the text. Attempts at grasping the meaning of the material read resulted, as a rule, in enunciation defects: in this case they kept repeating the same stanza or even the same line, at times stopping the recitation altogether. In short, the enunciation of verses required no less attention than did listening to speech. As a result, the subjects faced a task consisting more in watching their enunciation process than in listening to what was being read.

Some of the subjects noted, nevertheless, that at times they were able to listen to speech while enunciating verses. This was usually the case while the same stanza or line were being repeated. Such cases were rare, however. Listening in fragments at the moments of transition from stanza to stanza or during stops in recitation was the more frequent occurrence. Hence the fragmentary nature of comprehension noted above.

True, this fragmentariness was not always manifested directly in the account of the text. The narrative was frequently coherent enough, but in such cases connections still turned out to be completely arbitrary: catching individual words and fragments of phrases at different instances, the subjects connected them by mere guesswork, which, as we have seen, was not always correct.

The fragmentary nature of comprehension, masked by the coherence of narration due to the subject's contribution of his own knowledge, was in evidence in subsequent experiments as well, particularly when the second text was presented. This one was more discursive in content than descriptive: it dealt with the changes taking place on the earth's surface because of volcanic activity, earthquakes, and slow uplifts and subsidences of the continents. A knowledge of these phenomena enabled the subjects to grasp the meaning correctly from individual sentence fragments.

Some characteristic results of this experiment follow.

Subject T. again gave a very fragmentary account of the text: "Finland several kilometers from the sea. The land now subsides now rises. Petrified material ... Fossils ... Some cities were mentioned, whose names I became aware of at that moment but have forgotten by now." The subject pointed out that while listening to the passage he did not understand a few phrases but "if the sebsequent phrases were understood, that which had been obscure before became clear in the light of those phrases." At the same time the subject continued to stress the difficulty of recitation. "At those times when I understood phrases (I mean precisely phrases, not words), I would entangle myself in the verse and go astray. The understanding of the narrative made a mess of the verses but considerably less so than last time. It was sheer chaos then, but everything is much more orderly now." The subject pointed out further that he would rapidly forget what he had heard: "I fully comprehended the first sentence of the narrative. There was this thought: I have understood everything, but by the time the reading was over I forgot it. In general, a whole succession of phrases understood would be forgotten toward the end." A more connected and detailed account, as compared with the first, was given by subject Sh. "The subject matter is changes in the earth's surface. Such changes take place not only suddenly (volcanic activity and earthquakes) but also gradually. For example, the city of Vaasa which used to be on the sea coast is now far removed from it. The presence of limestone on land is proof of the constant changes. The land had once been the bottom of the sea." As in the previous trial, the subject noted vacillations in attention between listening to the text and recitation of verses. At the same time he pointed out (and this is very significant) that at times, when the recitation came easy to him, "the meaning of what was being read was fully comprehended." Moreover, in this case the subject found himself having a "third train of thought." For example, while listening to the passage he concluded that this particular text seemed to him easier than the previous one. "I had the idea that this was not a description but a logical narrative and that I knew the meaning of it all." While listening to the part where it was stated that changes may not only be sudden but also gradual, the subject thought: "This is the usual order of exposition: first they talk of catastrophic changes, then of gradual." In addition, the subject stated that "There was no internal articulation of words with any train of thought," noting at the same time the presence of "vague visual images," such as the map of Finland, limestone, the cover of "Volcanoes and Earthquakes," a book with which he was familiar.

Subject M. gave, on the whole, a rather detailed and correct account of the text. She pointed out that listening and recitation were much easier this time than it had been before. "I have understood the subject matter and it looks like I have given a correct account of it. The text was being comprehended without repetitions, simply by ear. It seems to me that I did repeat one sentence, but I don't know exactly how. Nor do I know what sentence it was, I forgot."

The majority of the subjects, however, gave of this text, too, a very fragmentary account. Some of them heard nothing but the beginning and the end of it, others nothing but the middle portion, and so on. Subject B. said: "I do not listen continuously, I listen only at certain moments, and the rest of the time I am busy with the recitation."

Although the subjects continued to point to the extreme difficulty involved in the listening under such conditions, they noted nevertheless that at times, when the recitation was so easy as to proceed "by itself," "without any control," listening would become easy. This circumstance is very significant; it indicates that the task of distributing attention ceases to matter whenever the subjects achieve a more or less automatic recitation of verses. Subsequent experiments confirmed this to an ever-increasing degree.

The third text read in this test series described the Soviet subtropics. Mention was made of the comparatively low temperature in our subtropics and the need, in this connection, for growing frost-resistant varieties of citrus plants.

The subjects for the most part listened to this text almost continuously with continuous recitation of verses. They stated that they heard and comprehended everything, but forgetting was very rapid. This was confirmed by objective data as well: the majority of the subjects gave a correct account of the text's general contents but many details were beyond their recollection.

Subject T. gave the following account: "It's about Soviet subtropics and citrus plants. Then about the temperature in the subtropics and about the growing of lemons. Everything seems to be clear: they talk about the subtropics." The subject was, however, unable to reproduce any details, pointing out that it had been extremely difficult to memorize them. He said: "Subjectively, recollecting these tales of yours is like remembering a dream: just a moment ago there had been some kind of a thing but next it submerged in such a fog that, apart from some chance fragments, nothing can be pulled back out of there."

Other subjects too mentioned the rapid forgetting of the contents. The majority could not remember the details (geographic names and numerical data). Thus, subject M. gave the following account of the contents: "In our Union there are subtropics. In Sukhumi and Batumi citrus plants are cultivated—lemons, oranges, but they do ripen . . . I forgot just when they ripen, though I heard it distinctly. Somewhere else . . . I forgot, where exactly—I forgot again . . . they ripen in January-February. We are interested in cultivating lemons. We have to develop frost-resistant citrus varieties." In her report she stated: "I had trouble with memorizing things. I felt that I was losing the trend of your narrative. I clutched at the general meaning only: subtropics, cultivation of citrus plants, the value of lemon. I remember vaguely that there was something else but I forgot what precisely it was about."

We asked this subject: "What countries, besides the Soviet Union, were mentioned in the text?" She answered: "I don't know, I don't remember." We then asked her to listen to this text without reciting verses. Having done so, she was amazed: "But I have heard all of this the first time too. I heard distinctly about Florida and even tried to memorize it at the time but, as you see, I forgot. My auditory impression about California was less distinct."

Subject B. stated that she perceived this text as a whole and piecewise, in fragments as previously: "I heard a vague unity but it was very hard to memorize it. In order to remember it somehow, I had to resort to certain techniques. I felt like fixing some of the things in images, in spatial schemata, but there was no time because the articulation interfered with it. I comprehended what was being read to me, I wished to fix this understanding in memory, but the techniques of fixing were being interfered with by articulation. Words of some sort were being reproduced acoustically; a single word then became a fixation point, the carrier of the general meaning."

Subject Sh. said that while listening he on purpose formulated the meaning of the text: "I was listening and telling myself, so to speek, Aha, it's about the subtropics. I have to remember that there are moist and dry subtropics, and so on. I was comprehending the rest but without formulation or repetition, and this was being forgotten."

Thus, in listening to text read the problem clearly was not so much to understand as to memorize. This finding was in fairly good agreement with the results of the preceding experiments. The subjects comprehended the text clearly enough, yet that which had been understood was forgotten at almost the same instant. We are dealing here with "instantaneous amnesia" evoked experimentally.

The last text of this series described briefly the vivisection controversy (mention was made of Simon's arguments in favor of vivisection at the Second International Conference of Physicians in London in 1881).

While stating correctly the general meaning of the text, the subjects all pointed out that a considerable portion of the contents "disappeared from memory instantly," there remaining nothing but the "general, undifferentiated meaning." Attempts at contextual fixation of phrases produced delays in the recitation of verses; in such cases the subjects would start repeating the same line over and over again, but even so the contextual expressions were very hard to fix.

While giving a correct account of the general meaning of the text, the subjects did not reproduce the dates and names mentioned there. Yet some of them had been making special efforts to memorize this part. Subject M., for example, repeated for this purpose the date of the conference and Simon's name mentally. But this mental repetition proved insufficient for memorization: the date of the conference was stated incorrectly, and Simon's name was forgotten altogether. The subject said, moreover, that she caught herself repeatedly thinking: "It would be nice if they stopped reading right here, I could remember it then."

In summing up the results of this test series, we have to admit the fact of fragmentary listening in those cases when verses were not recited automatically, i.e., when the recitation required special attention on the part of the subject (this occurred with particular frequency in the first two experiments). The subjects then indeed experienced something like "sensory aphasia": the words sounded to them just like any noise. It was only at the moments of more or less automatic recitation that they were able to comprehend the meaning of individual phrases and then make a more or less correct guess as to the text's general meaning. This "guessing" type of listening was easier for our subjects in the case of discursive texts and more difficult for descriptive ones.

With habituation to the experimental setting (third and fourth trials of this test series) the majority of subjects began to listen continuously, being capable, likewise, of continuous concurrent recitation of verses. But, even at this stage, memorization of the speech heard was extremely difficult. The elimination of speech movements from the listening process resulted in very rapid forgetting: the subjects heard everything, comprehended it, and forgot most of it in almost the same instant. Speaking in clinical terms, there is no sensory aphasia here but there is instantaneous amnesia. Rapid forgetting of this kind could not fail to lead to fragmentary reproduction. As a result of very rapid forgetting the subjects could not, of course, achieve total understanding either, but at the moment of hearing they felt that they were understanding.

Because of the trouble with memorization which arose in these experiments, the subjects began to make attempts at fixing the speech heard with the aid of visual and auditory images. Subject Sh. noticed the presence of rather vivid visual images, usually absent in ordinary listening. Subject B. tried to fix individual ideas of the speech heard with the aid of auditory images by making them "carriers of the general meaning." Concerning the auditory images it must be said, however, that initially, in the absence of comprehension of speech, they did not result in memorization; at that time they did not establish logical connections and were forgotten at once, although individual words and phrases did have "internal ring" to them (this apparently was the appearance of the so-called primary auditory images). For example, subject T. pointed out in the first trials that for him, many phrases "rang inside and vanished from memory at once, one auditory image being erased by the next."

Some of the subjects tried to fix separate elements of speech with the aid of movements of various kinds: some moved their feet, others flexed their fingers, etc.

Thus, these experiments have demonstrated the great significance of speech movements in memorization: their elimination resulted in "instantaneous amnesia." They showed also that the task of distributing attention, mentioned by the subjects in the first trials, is eliminated as soon as the recitation of verses becomes more or less automatic. The comprehension of meaning was facilitated most precisely during automatic recitation in spite of the fact that at this moment the organs of articulation were maximally engaged (at these times recitation proceeded without any stumbling or pauses). This allowed us to hope that as the recitation of verses became increasingly automatic, the comprehension of speech would grow accordingly. Subsequent experiments have fully confirmed this assumption.

3. APPEARANCE OF FRAGMENTARY INNER SPEECH WITH AUTOMATIZATION OF SPEECH MOVEMENTS AND DURING MICROPAUSES IN ARTICULATORY INTERFERENCE

In the preceding experiments we have seen that the subjects possessed individual characteristics. While for some the preoccupation of the speech machinery with recitation constituted no hindrance to listening, others faced the very difficult task of distributing their attention. In that case the subjects used to say that they would become aware of "two different semantic series"—perception of the speech heard and control over the recitation of verses—which tended to displace each other. As a result, the subjects indeed experienced sensory aphasia of a sort. Even these subjects noticed, however, that occasionally, when recitation proceeded automatically enough, the fact that the speech apparatus was busy ceased to be a hindrance to listening. This provided grounds for assuming that the difficulties involved in listening to speech arose not so much because the speech apparatus as such was busy, as that this stage of the business was insufficiently automatized.

This was also indicated by preliminary experiments: counting to twenty produced no sensory aphasia; in this case the subjects understood speech quite well but forgot most of what they heard.

In the next test series too the recitation of verses was replaced by counting. The perception of speech under these conditions was found to become so easy that the subjects were able not only to listen but also to think about what they heard.

Thus, subject T. stated repeatedly in his reports: "It is possible simultaneously to count, listen to your story, and in addition to think about something. When you read, for example, about Moscow's picturesque surrounds, I thought, Could this be from Turgenev? Turgenev has something similar in his "On the Eve." Then I decided. No, it's not from Turgenev, it's from the literature on natural science."

In the course of these experiments many of the subjects were able to establish at will various associations to better memorize the material heard. For instance, subject R. stated that when one of the texts referred to springtime she thought: "It's winter now, winter is opposed to spring," etc. Subject M. called her activity during listening and simultaneous counting, "multilevel work." She said: "I can, while I count, at the same time listen, understand and in addition think about the material heard, none of these things interfering with each other."

Thus we are dealing here with inner speech; moreover, it is speech which occurs under conditions that maximally preclude its articulation.

Further tests showed that, along with the appearance of inner speech in the subjects, the above-mentioned phenomenon of instantaneous amnesia began to disappear.

In the first two counting experiments the subjects noted numerous cases of instantaneous amnesia, but with each new trial the reproduction of texts by the subjects becomes ever more complete; as early as the third trial, the instances of instantaneous amnesia were rare. Here are some relevant findings.

The subjects had a text read to them, in which Einstein's views on matter and energy were presented. The text continued the following words of Einstein: "There is no dualism in nature. The world is built of a single entity. If the primordial elements appear in a concentrated form, it's matter; if they are in a rarefied form, it's energy." This part of the text was stated almost literally by every subject. Many subjects, however, forgot the beginning, where Einstein's theory was said to be independent of Kaufmann's experiments and the studies of radium.

Subject T. reproduced this text as follows: "The theory of relativity was presented. It was stated that matter and energy are not diametrically opposed things. The world is a unity, it is built of a single essence. If this essence is rarefied, it is energy; if it is concentrated, it's matter. This was stated in Einstein's own words." The subject said further: "I understood everything but was unable to memorize many things, there was no way of fixing them. Apart from Einstein's there were no proper names or, perhaps, there were some, I just couldn't remember them. Sometimes I obviously tried to repeat some of the propositions in order to memorize them, I also reproduced them, but the manner of reproduction was such that I felt it wouldn't be of any use. Metaphorically speaking, this took place somewhere on a level above the mouth, approximately on the eye level."

In this case there were no gross omissions in the reproduced text, with the exception of Kaufmann's name which meant little if anything, and the independence of Einstein's theory from the study of radium rays.

The reproduction of the text by subject B. was even more comprehensive. She stated in her report: "It was very easy to listen. There was a unity of thought so that thoughts fell into a fixed place of their own accord. I caught some of the figures of speech when it was stated, for instance, that matter and energy are not opposed like good and evil are. At this moment I visualized two points which had to denote the polarity of good and evil."

The majority of other subjects too described the contents in detail, with the exception of those who had had no previous knowledge whatever either of Einstein or the relativity theory in general. These subjects termed the text difficult despite the fact that during the reading it did not seem incomprehensible to them. One of this class of subjects described the contents as follows: "Independently of some scientist's experiments and of the discovery of radium and beta-rays, the scientist (I don't remember his name) has advanced a brilliant idea. He said that there is no dualism in the universe, that matter and energy are one in essence. Then something was said about this unity but I can't remember exactly what."

After listening to this text for a second time without the count, this subject stated: "I heard all of this the first time too, only I forgot much of it. I recognize well the entire text."

Subsequent experiments revealed that forgetting was decreasing progressively. Thus, the last text in the series, which described the characteristic features of old historical novels, was reproduced by all the subjects as fully as with ordinary listening, i.e., listening without the count.

Subject T. stated concerning the listening process: "The count proceeded automatically, I took care to articulate all the numbers well. Understanding and memorization proceeded without a hitch. There were associations of my own: Richard the Lion-Hearted—"Talisman," Elizabeth—"Kenilworth," etc. These titles of the novels occurred to me spontaneously. There was psychological leisure. It was even easier to listen this time than the last. I knew that counting wouldn't be any hindrance."

Subject B. stated in her report: "It was not difficult to listen. I noticed, moreover, that I was fixing the contents somehow. This was no reproduction of words, I couldn't reproduce them, yet some voluntary fixation of thoughts did take place. There was a squeezing out of thoughts of some kind, a thought complex was formed, which then was reproduced in a very condensed form without articulation and without any muscular effort being experienced."

Subject M. said: "I operated in three or four ways of some sort—I was listening, understanding, counting, and thinking about the text's contents. I thought that the text had been composed in a special way, containing as it did many names, and that it would be interesting to see how well they would be remembered. When the story of the *Captain's Daughter* was being read, I thought, 'What a shame, I forgot the names of the heroes of Pushkin's novel,' and tried to keep them in my mind after I had heard them. The work proved to be on several levels. It seems to me that somehow I did articulate some of the words, such as Richard, Louis XI, though I did not stop counting" (the experimenter noticed that when the historical characters of Sir Walter Scott's novels came to be mentioned, the subject repeated the same numbers twice, although without any interruption in the count).

Other subjects too mentioned mental repetition in this case; it caused hesitation in counting in some of the subjects and none in others. For example, subject R. stated that when she repeated mentally the names of Elizabeth, Richard, and Louis, she lost count. However, other subjects stated that counting "does not interfere with the mental repetition of the material heard."

Thus, despite the fact that in these experiments the organs of articulation had been continuously busy enunciating extraneous material (listening with simultaneous counting), the subjects were able not only to understand but also to memorize the material heard.

Moreover, under conditions which eliminated speech movements as much as possible, inner speech put in an appearance and, as a result, instantaneous amnesia disappeared.

Such are the principal findings obtained in this test series.

They indicate that in the preceding experiments the possibility of listening, understanding, and memorizing was directly dependent on the degree to which the enunciation of extraneous material was automatized. Counting was a much more automatic operation than was recitation of verses, which accounts for the ability of the subjects to listen to and memorize material simultaneously.

If this is so, if the most important factor here is not that the speech machinery be busy but that the activity it is engaged in be highly automatized, the vacillations in attention noticed at the moment of listening to extraneous speech and concurrent enunciation of verses should disappear as soon as the verses have been learned by heart.

To test this assumption, we continued with the experiments for the next 5-7 days. Participating were six subjects who had not previously achieved sufficient automatization of verse recitation and had frequently noticed vacillation of attention on their part.

Prior to the beginning of this new test series the subjects had to make special efforts to learn verses by heart, repeating them 50 times a day. The subjects discovered as soon as the first day that their recitation had become much more automatic and that contents of a text were being reproduced more fully than before. The subjects described correctly the principal ideas (which had not always been the case previously) of discursive texts, yet they still failed to reproduce the details of description.

Introspective data continued to indicate great difficulties involved in memorization while reciting. The subjects stated that it was mostly the "logical skeleton" of the text that remained in their memory, whereas everything not constituting the logical base was subject to as quick a forgetting as before.

The reproduction of descriptive texts suffered most, although in terms of understanding they presented no difficulties, whatsoever. Owing to this, the reproduction of descriptive texts remained for a long time much more fragmentary than that of discursive texts.

To illustrate this point, we adduce the reproduction of discursive and descriptive texts by subject F., a student.

The discursive text first mentioned Baer's discoveries in embryology, and then went on to describe Baer's attitude towards Darwin's theory of evolution. It should be noted that this subject had never heard Baer's name or known anything of his discoveries. In spite of this, she reproduced the text correctly and in considerable detail. She said: "Baer made a number of major discoveries in the field of embryology. He discovered the notochord, brain vesicles, and he showed that the anterior vesicle develops into the organ of vision. After the publication of Darwin's book Baer read it but made no comments. He was then questioned directly about it. He said that changes do occur but they are exceptions and predetermined."

In describing the contents, the subject omitted the concluding words of the text, which dealt with Baer's attitude toward Cuvier's views. We asked her to tell us what she knew about Cuvier. She replied: "When you were reading about Cuvier, I understood what it was about and was even trying to memorize it; still, I forgot. Somehow I always forget the end; while I try to remember the beginning, I forget the end."

The text describing woods in the fall was reproduced by the subject in a very fragmentary manner. The description, which consisted of 14 sentences, was reproduced by her as follows: "The picture of the 'Indian summer' in the forest is very beautiful. Rowan tree . . . Can't remember what was said about the rowan tree. A young oak . . . Can't remember about it either. I remember now: it has not shed its leaves but all around . . . I don't remember what there was all around, although I heard it all quite distinctly. I would hear and forget."

Subject B. was able to reproduce only the following from this text: "It's about fall. It seems to be fall: the rowan is bare, everything is being shed. In general, it's a description of nature. Can't say anything sensible." The subject mentions difficulties she always encounters while listening to descriptive texts: "I retain to a greater extent not the descriptions but a complex of thoughts, whereas what matters here is sequential accumulation of details, which is very difficult to do while reciting verses at the same time. The fixing of details impairs the recitation of verses—it makes me lose my footing much more often than while listening to a discourse."

In the next few days the recitation of verses progressed steadily in terms of automatization, so that in the end the subjects would state: "I don't hear any verses at all, I don't understand them—they are being articulated by themselves" or: "As far as I am concerned the words of the poem have become meaningless sounds, so that when I stop I don't know where I stopped; I then have to start from the very beginning."

The subjects who had achieved this degree of automatization in reciting the poem, would reproduce the contents of texts for the most part as fully as they would for ordinary listening, without recitation. This refers to both discursive and purely descriptive texts.

As an illustration, here is the way subject F. reproduced the description of a summer morning from Tolstoy's *Youth*, which we presented on the last day of trials and in regard to which the subjects used to say that it was almost as easy to listen to as it was "without the poem." "Each day I used to get up early in the morning, take my towel and a French novel, and go off to bathe in the river. The river seemed violet, the rays of the sun illumined the trunks of the trees ... Something else was described but I forgot what ... When the sky was overcast, I would stroll over the fields, imagining myself the hero from a novel I had read."

As can be seen, subject F. reproduced this text in much greater detail than she had the description of the autumn forest quoted above. Formerly fragmented in the extreme, reproduction now became much more full and connected.

Thus, with increasing automatization of recitation of the poem the subjects became capable not only of continuous listening to but also of memorizing the material read to them. At this experimental stage instantaneous amnesia was not as pronounced as before. If in some cases it did occur, its intensity was no greater than with listening under ordinary conditions, that is, when the listeners do not have a special set for memorization.

Eventually the subjects became so used to the experimental setting that they ceased completely to regard it as a hindrance to listening. As in the counting experiments, they reported the presence of an "additional train of thoughts," that is, thoughts concerning the textual contents.

In what manner were the subjects able to implement the fixation of the speech heard?

The initial reports contained no definite indications on this point. The subjects stated only that memorization of the material heard was very difficult. Later on, they began to point out that, in attempting to memorize some particular spot of a passage, they used to repeat or mark its contents mentally. They did not succeed at first in this mental repetition, for it produced confusion in recitation or counting. Subject F. noted in the first trials: "I tried to memorize it, repeating mentally some passages, but then my recitation would become confused." Later, when the recitation of the poem became fairly automatic, this subject said: "The poem no longer hinders my repeating mentally the things I hear, but it used to before." Subject R. stated that she "repeated inwardly the main ideas of the text, and this was no hindrance in the recitation of the poem." Subject B. pointed out that during listening she was continually aware of a "tendency to repeat in my mind those points which it was necessary to memorize."

Other subjects too made similar statements.

Thus, it turned out that in our experimental setting, i.e., conditions maximally excluding the coenunciation of the speaker's words, internal word reproduction did take place at times. In other words, inner speech proved to be possible even when great efforts had been made to eliminate speech movements.

This fact deserves much attention and, before we interpret it in some way or other, we shall try to find out what exactly the subjects did reproduce and how they succeeded in doing it at a time when the speech apparatus was busy.

As just noted, in trying to fix the material read, the subjects used to repeat or mark mentally textual contents. They indicated that the mental repetition was in an extremely abbreviated form: the textual contents were fixed in the mind with the aid of a few key or generalizing words. Moreover, even these words, the subjects reported were not pronounced by them—rather, they were borne in mind, implied, or thought, occasionally arising as auditory images.

Subject B., for example, used to point out repeatedly that she "fixed thought complexes with a single generalizing word." Speaking of the difficulty of memorizing descriptive texts while reciting, she indicated that they have "no points of reference to fix the meaning and for this reason they are difficult to memorize." Another time subject B. stated that she reproduced the textual contents on the basis of principal semantic landmarks which she used to note the meaning of speech. "I tried to correlate everything with semantic landmarks, to link it up into some meaningful connection, into a single semantic content—a semantic scheme." In this connection she added that fixation of this kind required some additional psychic act: "One has to comprehend it to the end, concentrate, bring it into focus, whereupon it is easy to develop a thought."

Other subjects made similar statements. Subject M. said that, while listening to our texts, she constructed in her mind a "scheme of the material. With the aid of this scheme," she said, "I fix the sequence of material: this comes first, that comes next, etc." Such a scheme would sometimes be fixed with the aid of an image of some kind, but more often than not it was a word, "rather, some kind of a hint at a word—a thought about a word."

It should be noted that even this schematic fixation of meaning was so indefinite under the conditions of our experiments that the subjects used to reiterate: "I didn't repeat the word, I merely thought it!"

Schematic fixation of this type is, as we have seen, nothing but generalization of a meaning and its expression in a single mental, or internal, word. We are dealing here, therefore, with true thought activity, implemented under conditions of maximum elimination of speech movements and, hence, impossibility of articulating words to a more or less full extent.

* * * * *

This being the case, what could be the meaning of the expressions "mental word," or "internal word," encountered so often in our subjects' reports? Could it be merely an ordinary word enunciated without sound?

The latter possibility was eliminated completely in our experiments: the recitation of a poem made it impossible to articulate anything besides the poem. And yet, as we have seen, inner speech, inward repetition, did take place.

Perhaps those were auditory or visual word images? Ordinarily, when speaking of inner speech, one has in mind not only the motor but also the auditory and visual images of words. Had they been present in our subjects, and, if so, what role had they played?

Some of the subjects did indeed have auditory word images. Three of them stated definitely that in their consciousness words were reflected as "auditory echoes," two of them, moreover, having been able to produce them voluntarily. As for visual images of words, our subjects noticed none. Occasionally they made mention of the visual images of objects, never those of words.

Let us note, however, that neither the auditory images of words nor the visual images of objects resulted, in themselves, in comprehension or fixation of the speech heard. The images were found to be very fleeting and fragmentary, never creating an integrated picture. In addition, even if such images were noticed, it was always at the moment of listening and almost never during reproduction, since by that time most of them turned out to have been lost.

For example, subject T. stated in one of the first trials that he had "clear-cut auditory images of the material read and no comprehension of any kind." His images were not interlinked and became lost. Subject M., too, frequently noticed having auditory word images. She said that "some kind of an echo is formed," but she was at a loss to say what precisely it was that rang in her ears.

Ordinarily, images became a means of fixation for our subjects only when they were preceded by consideration, generalization, etc., i.e., when they became carriers of the general meaning of the text. In this case images did not so much arise of their own accord as they were created at will by the subjects. But then, it was no longer mere echo, no mere succession of images in general—these were images created as a result of generalization, i.e., these were generalizing images.

Here let us recall that fixation of meaning required from our subjects a "certain additional psychic act—one has somehow to comprehend it to the end, concentrate on it, bring it into focus." In this case the images, if they indeed became a means of fixation, could not fail to expand their original meaning after becoming the carriers of the general meaning of the passage. Thus, during listening to a text describing the characteristics of the vegetation cover of a ravine (excerpt from A.K. Timiryazev's *The Life of Plants*), the image of ferns evoked in the subjects became the carrier of the text's general subject matter: the vegetable kingdom of past geological epochs.

Introspective data collected from different subjects are in good agreement on this point: if the images arising during listening had no logical connection with the text, they were, in all cases, of no use for the fixation of general meaning. Something more was required for this purpose, namely, construction of a logical scheme for the material heard; whereas everything which was not included in this scheme, was not marked with semantic landmarks, would be quickly forgotten. It was at such moments that instantaneous amnesia would set in.

It is important to emphasize, moreover, that instantaneous amnesia owed its origin not so much to the fact that the subjects were unable to repeat the text as to the fact that they failed to link individual passages together. Instantaneous amnesia could, therefore, be found even when the subjects became aware of inner speech but used it to reproduce only separate passages of the text instead of reproducing the general meaning in it.

On such occasions, the subjects used to say frequently on repeated listening to texts: "After you had read this phrase I repeated it without stopping the recitation of the poem; I repeated it many times and still I forget it."

We have a paradoxical phenomenon before us: that which was repeated in this manner would frequently be forgotten, nevertheless. We termed this phenomenon "paradoxical forgetting." It inevitably took place whenever the subjects tried to memorize individual phrases or facts separate from the general text. A different train of thoughts, having no bearing on the general contents of the text, would arise.

The most graphic illustration of paradoxical forgetting was offered by subject M. when she listened to a text titled "Hegel." The text stressed the significance of Hegel's work in psychology and psychopathology but in the beginning it also told of the circumstances of Hegel's death. Having correctly reproduced the text's general contents, the subject said nothing, however, about the cause of Hegel's death. To our question, "What has Hegel died of?" the subject replied: "He caught cold and, as a result, there is mention of adynamia," thus avoiding direct answer. The experimenter prompted her then: "How about the cholera epidemic?" The subject: "Oh! But this is what it started with, I even repeated it several times and, imagine that, forgot, having become distracted by what came next."

Similar examples of paradoxical forgetting also occurred in control experiments. These involved listening to a text without recitation of a poem. Much would be forgotten because images would be repeated without being generalized or because the general relationships within the text would not be established first; the direct cause of instantaneous amnesia was the absence of a logical scheme from the material. This is why we relate the disappearance, or at any rate attenuation, of instantaneous amnesia in our experiments, to the appearance of inner speech. Inner speech enables one not only to repeat but also—and this is more important—to generalize that which is being heard. And, indeed, in our experiments inner speech was a means of fixation not so much because it enabled one to reproduce the speech heard as because it generalized it, creating a logical scheme of material and fixing thereby the contents of the speech heard.

In what manner could such a logical scheme be constructed in the conditions of our experiments?

We believe that, despite the impossibility of complete articulation in our experiments, a logical scheme was nevertheless set up with the aid of words, but words in an extremely abbreviated form, at times hardly perceptible hints at words. To be more precise, there were no words here in a grammatical sense; instead, there were certain elements of articulation that assumed the role of carriers of general contents. This assumption, it seems to us, is supported by numerous data.

As already pointed out, some of our subjects definitely noticed the presence of articulatory movements *in embryo,* which entailed irregularities in recitation. These irregularities did not consist in pauses, however; for the most part the rhythmicity of recitation or counting was disturbed, usually resulting in a repetition of the same numbers or the same words of a poem. Such a brief disturbance in the speech rhythm was, of course, insufficient for the full articulation of a word, but it was quite sufficient for its partial articulation.

Of particular interest in this respect is the introspection of subject B. Having at first denied any possibility of an inward enunciation of words (except by way of their auditory images), at the end of the trials she said: "Sometimes it is good to repeat what you hear, to say it in words. No, you don't have to say it, I don't articulate in an unfolded form, it's in the form of a tiny hint, so faint that I am not sure whether a repetition has taken place or not."

Subject R. noticed that sometimes, while reproducing textual contents, she pronounced to herself just the first one or two letters of a word. For example, while listening to a list of M. M. Antokol'skii's sculptures in one of the texts, she fixed them in memory either visually (e.g., the "Ivan the Terrible" sculpture) or by means of a word fragment (Socrates as So . . . Peter as P . . ., etc.). In the last case there are no words; a word is abbreviated to one or two letters. Inwardly, the word ceases here to be a word in its grammatical sense, although it not only preserves but even intensifies its generalizing function, not infrequently becoming the carrier of a text's general contents.

4. INSUFFICIENCY OF FRAGMENTARY INNER SPEECH FOR AN UNDERSTANDING OF DIFFICULT TEXTS–THE NEED, FOR UNFOLDED ARTICULATION OF WORDS

Thus, if someone listens to a text and simultaneously articulates a series of extraneous words, he will be unable to reproduce correctly the contents of the speech heard. However, partial fragmentary reproduction of it is possible with the aid of fragmentary articulation of certain generalizing words during the micropauses in articulatory interference. We have no grounds whatsoever for ignoring the possibility of embryonic or fragmentary articulation of the words bearing on the contents of a text being perceived by ear, the more so since many of the subjects have found this to be the case.

Of no lesser importance in this connection is the fact that our subjects were capable not only of listening to and comprehending extraneous speech but also of generalizing it, of accumulating introspective observations, and not infrequently, of an extra train of thought which arises by way of association during listening to speech. The subjects thus often performed intellectual work on several planes, and this all with maximally reduced speech movements, too. How could this be understood if each of the processes mentioned above actually involved the articulation of words? The chaos which in this case would reign in the subjects' heads is hard to imagine. Yet the subjects became accustomed to the experimental setting to such an extent that in the final trials they noticed no substantial difference between listening to a text with or without simultaneous recitation of a poem. The only assumption possible therefore is that the process of listening was not intimately related to the unfolded motor-speech enunciation of words. The need for the articulation of words arose essentially in two cases: either when unfamiliar names, family names, numerical data, etc. had to be memorized, or when things had to be juxtaposed, compared, related, or generalized. In either case, moreover, both the experimenter and the subjects readily detected small irregularities in the recitation of verses.

We shall now adduce supplementary data which confirm this proposition.

In one of the last trials, i.e., when the poem was recited with maximum automatization, subject A. noticed that "inward repetition of the name Meillet disrupted the poem." An identical observation was made by subject R. when she tried to memorize the unfamiliar names of Claude Bernard and Magendie as well as numerical data.

But the subjects faced even greater difficulties when they had to listen to texts of an abstract nature. In such cases deautomatization even of well-learned poems could always be observed. For instance, even the not-too-abstract passage from Hegel's *Logik*, describing the difference between arithmetical and geometrical quantities, brought about drastic deautomatization of poem recitation. This passage could more readily be understood under simultaneous counting, but even here the ensuing phenomenon of instantaneous amnesia resulted in a fragmentary reproduction of textual contents. Long sentences were forgotten at once. Thus, in this case too, comprehension was far from complete.

The report of subject M. is of interest in this regard. She stated in connection with this text: "I could understand many individual phrases, but I was unable to unify them into a single whole, and they were forgotten. No matter how I tried, I did not succeed in producing connected thought."

Other subjects, too, made the same observations. All of them could understand the meaning of individual words, but there was no understanding of the text's general contents.

Even with free listening, i.e., listening without simultaneous counting, the comprehension of this passage was far from complete. The reproduction of this text by the majority of subjects was very diffuse in this case as well; they attributed this to the difficulty of understanding abstract ideas by ear. We then asked some of them to read the passage aloud and to vocalize all the reasoning in relation to textual contents.

Subject S. reads the text aloud.

"Spatial and numerical magnitude are generally considered as two different species, the distinction being understood as follows ... (A pause. The subject rereads the text and says: "The spatial and numerical magnitudes are different. What is the difference?") ... This distinction is interpreted to mean that, taken by itself, a spatial magnitude is as much determinate as is the numerical one ... (A pause. "In themselves, these magnitudes are generally considered to be equally determinate. Very well!") ... According to this viewpoint, their distinction is only in the different determinations of continuity and discreteness ... ("Aha, one magnitude is continuous and the other discrete") ... but as a determinate quantum they rank equally ... ("I don't understand. They are different: one, the spatial, is continuous, the other, arithmetic, is discrete, and yet they are equal." The subject rereads the text) ... but as a determinate quantum they rank equally. Geometry, in spatial magnitude, generally has continuous magnitude for object ... ("Of course, for instance, a triangle or a square, but even their spatial magnitude can be expressed as the number of square units") ... and arithmetic, in numerical, has discrete magnitude for an object" (This is clear: arithmetic is one, two, three, five, ten. These are units, but units too can continue to infinity—a million units, a trillion units"). Eventually the subject arrives at the following conclusion: "Spatial and ari..imetical magnitudes are different magnitudes. The spatial magnitudes are continuous, the arithmetical magnitudes are discrete. Both are, however, determinate magnitudes."

This is a description of the process of understanding an abstract text by repeating individual phrases and generalizing them to a single idea. This process required that words be articulated in an unfolded manner. And conversely, the simpler the text the more abbreviated would be its reproduction. Only a few generalizing words, a brief textual scheme, are fixed when a text is simple. This is not enough when a difficult text is to be understood; a more unfolded form of its reproduction is required here. The latter was impossible in the conditions of our experiments, and this is what made understanding difficult.

So far we have emphasized the abbreviated character of inner speech. Generally speaking, however, this rather common statement is not always in accord with reality. Inner speech is not always abbreviated to the extent mentioned earlier. At times it may occur in a very unfolded form. For instance, this is the case when we reason or argue with ourselves. Occasionally, the name of the subject of speech is all that is omitted then, all the rest

articulated almost in full. Precisely this type of unfolded inner speech wa
required for an understanding of difficult texts. But in our experiments
unfolded inner speech was eliminated, hence the difficulties in understanding
abstract texts.

Thus this experiment had demonstrated that, by blocking verbalization,
the elimination of speech movements renders the understanding of abstract
texts more difficult, and that in order to understand them the subject has to
reread them. This is a common phenomenon: to be comprehended, a difficult
book has to be read two or three times. What, then, is the mechanism of
understanding and what role is played in it by repeated reproduction of text?

Upon the first reading of difficult texts, understanding commonly is
very vague, diffuse and may be termed "understanding in general terms."
Thus, following the first reading of the above-mentioned passage from *The
Science of Logic,* all that the subjects understood was that the text dealt with
a difference of some kind between spatial and numerical magnitudes; they
missed completely the moments regarding their unity. Rereading resulted in
the material being broken down into its components, the subjects beginning to
consider carefully not only each sentence but also the meaning of individual
words. Characteristically, the subjects not infrequently ignored, for a while,
subordinate clauses, focussing their attention for the most part on the
principal ones; having understood these, they turned to subordinate clauses.
Individual sentences were thus broken up and the most essential elements
were singled out.

Yet this procedure was not enough to understand the text's general
contents. A new thought-process was needed here: a process of joining
disconnected thoughts into a single whole, a process of generalization, without
which it was impossible to formulate a general conclusion. Approximating
individual concepts and notions was the first step toward generalization. In
reading the text, the subjects kept returning to the portions read, and this
enabled them to link sentences together.

The enunciation of words during reading or listening retarded
understanding, thus preventing the diffuse, indefinite grasping of meaning.
Unfolded articulation, while retarding understanding, at the same time divides
the material into portions, thereby allowing the most essential of them to be
marked off and fixed.

If we take into account this need to divide difficult material into parts
and generalize them later in order to understand it, we shall also see why the
abbreviated form of inner speech proved to be insufficient for an
understanding of difficult texts. The abbreviated form of inner speech is but a
scheme for the verbal expression of thoughts, this is but a hint at the few
generalizing words which, representing semantic complexes, can be unfolded
should one wish to do so. With the aid of these allusions, we can mark what
is already more or less known; we can also use them for generalizations if

such generalizations as, for instance, "sudden" ideas (the *"Einsicht"* of German authors), have at any time been preceded by analysis. But something which is completely unknown cannot be analyzed by means of such a verbal scheme. What is necessary is unfolded inner speech and, at times, even explicit articulation of words. Both were eliminated in our experiments, and this made the understanding of complicated texts more difficult.

Reproducing material heard is not the only role of articulation. Of no lesser significance is the fact that the motor speech reproduction of words fixes material in the memory, and in many cases this could well be of decisive importance to understanding, as well. For, to establish connections and relationships of some kind between two sentences being comprehended separately, both of them must be kept in mind. Without a fixation of the preceding sentence it cannot be linked to the next. Each generalization requires that ideas or concepts be linked together. Long ago Hegel wrote that the association of ideas is a *"subsumption* of individual ideas under the *general"* which links them together [50: 261].

We thus arrive at the conclusion that hindering the unfolding of inner speech and rendering completely impossible external speech makes the understanding of abstract material difficult for two reasons: first, it deprives a person of the possibility to analyze material, i.e., to single out the most essential parts and generalize them later on; second, it does not allow one to fix this material with the aid of speech movements.

Certain findings of psychopathologists are of interest in this regard. As a rule, motor aphasia is not known to result in a loss of understanding of speech. The inability to comprehend speech is usually related to sensory aphasia. P. Marie believed, however, that some of the motor aphasics, too, suffered from loss of understanding of speech, this fact escaping the researchers' attention for the simple reason that the tasks the patients are usually asked to perform during diagnosis are too simple (e.g., close one's eyes, show one's tongue, etc.); but if the instructions are more involved, the patients immediately display an impaired understanding of speech. To detect this impairment, Marie used the following techniques on motor aphasics.

1. After placing in front of a patient three pieces of paper differing in size he gave the subject the following task: "Out of the three shreds of paper lying in front of you, give me the largest, keep the small one, and the medium-sized one you must crumple and throw to the floor."

2. "Get up, approach the window, knock three times with your finger against the window pane, then return, go around the table and sit down."

Motor aphasics were unable to carry out these complex instructions. Marie concluded from this that motor aphasia involved symptoms characteristics of sensory aphasia and that in both cases speech disturbances were caused not by motor phenomena but by a drop in the intellectual level (feeblemindedness).

It is well known that the majority of psychopathologists were quite unsympathetic toward Marie's hypothesis, though they did not put forward any convincing arguments against it. M.I. Astvatsaturov, from whom we have quoted the description of Marie's viewpoint, replicated Marie's experiments in V. M. Bekhterev's laboratory. In analyzing his experiments, he notes the correctness of Marie's statement concerning the inability on the part of all aphasics to carry out the complex instructions listed above. However, Astvatsaturov notes the fact that motor aphasics did not carry out complex instructions if they were given all at once, yet they were fully able to cope with the tasks when they were presented in parts. "This fact," Astvatsaturov points out, "gives us reason to believe that we are dealing here not with impaired understanding but rather with difficulties in memorization" [18: 49].

This conclusion seems to us to be quite justified. Indeed, even a person not suffering from motor aphasia would find it difficult to carry out tasks like these at once. To read them cursorily once, and even less so to hear them read, is not enough for memorization, since each word is understood separately but the sequence of the individual parts cannot be fixed immediately, of which each reader can convince himself if he so desires. To memorize such instructions, they must be enunciated rather slowly, the individual parts singled out and fixed. For motor aphasics the act of articulation is known to be difficult, and this may be the real reason why they don't understand "complex instructions."

Let us recall that in many cases our subjects too felt that they were "comprehending quite well," yet very rapidly forgot most of what they heard. The exclusion of speech movements manifested itself initially in forgetting. After repeated trials, however, the subjects were given the opportunity to test the sense of textual contents by reproducing them in a generalized way. The latter factor seems to have been related to the rudimentary articulation of generalizing words.

Those experiments made it clear that articulation of words of itself was insufficient even for memorization. The experiments in which the subjects deliberately reproduced the material in full, word by word, were particularly indicative in this respect. Introspective data of these subjects showed convincingly that forgetting was very rapid under these conditions because it was impossible to make generalizations about the material (there was no time to do this). That which was not generalized and logically related often turned out to be quickly forgotten despite verbalization.

Is not the quick forgetting of dreams due perhaps to the fact that we have here only a picture of images, a picture where one image is superimposed on another without any generalizations? It is a different matter when, on awakening, we recount the dream. In recounting, we partition the fused unity of the whole, thereby generalizing the parts singled out and fixing them in memory.

By partitioning thought, speech helps us to separate the essential from the nonessential, to detect a contradiction in thinking and, by the same token, to develop it. "The word generalizes"—this is indisputable; and it does this because it expresses the unity of verbal analysis and synthesis.

When we listen to someone speak—listen truly attentively—we single out the main items in his speech and generalize them. While listening to something more or less familiar or commonplace, we often limit ourselves to an undifferentiated grasping of the whole. In this case, to understand means to grasp something in a cursory manner and relate the perceived to what had already been known. No unfolded speech is required for an understanding of this kind; the speech may be abbreviated in the extreme, abbreviated to a few hints, for this kind of understanding presupposes much to be known. But, such understanding does not extend beyond that which is familiar. To understand something new, however, is to express it as a new idea or concept, and this must be preceded by an inward processing of material, its analysis.

Thus we are dealing here with the different stages of the process of understanding—from an undifferentiated grasping of the whole to its differentiation, the singling out of individual parts, and, thence, to a formulation of a general conclusion in the form of new concepts.

The experimental data cited here indicate beyond any doubt that the role of verbal expressions varies depending on the stage of understanding. It is at a minimum when the sense is grasped in an overall manner. In this case the principal role of verbal expression consists in memorization. When material needs interior processing—analysis and synthesis—the role of speech is at a maximum. Any obstacle to the verbal expression of thoughts, in this case, signifies obstructed understanding.

The adherents of the "inward repetition" hypothesis believe, as we have seen, that speech cannot be understood without being repeated. From this viewpoint, to listen means to repeat. We have attempted to show that a mentally developed person usually does not engage in such word-for-word repetition and that such repetition is of no significance even for the fixation of speech heard, since fixation requires something more—generalization of material. Yet such repetition, accompanied by an interior processing of material, may take place where something new and difficult must be comprehended. In this respect, the proposition "to understand means to repeat" contains truth, but only a particle of it, because the essence of the matter here lies not in repetition as such, but rather in an analysis of material and subsequent generalization of it.

5. INNER SPEECH AS A MECHANISM OF SEMANTIC GROUPING

It seems to us that on the basis of our study we may draw some general conclusions concerning the structure and development of inner speech. These conclusions ensue, first of all, from the indubitable fact that suppression of articulation by enunciating material learned by heart (a poem, counting, etc.) did not deprive the subjects of inner speech. We have seen that they did not limit themselves to the auditory perception of material read, but noted within it essential points, and partitioned and generalized it, not infrequently creating thereby a logical scheme. In other words, they continued to think even with articulation suppressed.

Was this perhaps thinking without words?

In analyzing experimental data we arrived at the conclusion that the suppression of speech movements in our experiments did not preclude the possibility of fragmentary or abbreviated articulation of words. It is certain that some of the words were inwardly reproduced by the subjects, though, to be sure, instead of words those were rather hardly-perceptible hints at words, expressed in some elemental form of articulation. But the role of these inwardly reproduced words was enormous: by marking off the primary sense of the speech heard, they became condensed expressions of large semantic groups.

Images too at times became generalized expressions of sense, but in that case they carried not the concrete meaning but the general sense assigned to the words by subjects in connection with a given context. Thus we are faced here with an extraordinary expansion of the meaning of words and images which we use in inner speech.

Condensation of word sense also takes place in external (oral and written) speech. Thus, in many colloquial turns of speech one word not infrequently replaces an entire group of words. In philology such turns of speech are called ellipses. L. Borovoi cites many examples of the use of ellipses, encountered in modern colloquial and literary speech. One such example, from Vs. Ivanov's *Parkhomenko,* is:

> "I wish you," said Alexander, touching the horse and moving off. "I wish you," replied Ivan, and everyone present understood what it was that the brothers were wishing each other; and the peasants said with one voice, "We wish you!"

Entire links have been left out in this logical chain and yet, as later on noted correctly by Borovoi, "this is not simplified, but very complex speech; it presupposes quite active participation on the part of him to whom it is addressed" [33].

Even formal logic, which insisted that thinking was always developed in syllogisms, had to admit the existence of the so-called enthymemes— abbreviated syllogisms in which one of the premises is omitted if it is considered to be generally recognized or evident. Formal logic regarded this, however, as an exception rather than a rule.

In real life laconism, brevity of thought expression, is ever present. Colloquial language does not tolerate long sentences. But laconism is even more feasible in our inner speech. Hints at a few words suffice here to make it clear what it is about. That which is being reproduced in our inner speech is nothing but a very abbreviated verbal scheme whose elements, carriers of generalized sense, become, metaphorically speaking, quanta—condensed particles of thought.

Owing to such an abbreviated expression of thoughts, inner speech is capable of a rapid approximation and comparison of various word groups; out of this comparison and generalization there may arise, in a single "imperceptible" moment, new ideas and new semantic complexes. The suddenness and rapidity with which thoughts appear—which usually seems so mysterious—becomes possible precisely because of the presence within us of large thought complexes, expressed through slight verbal hints. In conveying our thoughts to others, we unfold them, using these semantic complexes as support, and, depending on the situation, impart to them a more or less full verbal expression.

The process of external speech needs, however, much more time than does inner speech to express thoughts. The conciseness of semantic complexes in inner speech allows for their separation, comparison, generalization, and like intellectual operations, even at the moment of unfolding of oral or written speech. The illusion is then created that the flow of thought forestalls speech, that thought precedes words. But this is nothing but an illusion. Thought can indeed be antecedent to oral or written speech since both develop relatively slowly; it also can forestall inner speech if the latter involves reasoning, but it never forestalls the abbreviated form of inner speech which expresses the semantic complexes described here.

As for the sensorimotor processes of inner speech, no matter how imperceptible they would seem, they undoubtedly take place. E. Jacobson's experiments leave no doubt as to the connection between inner speech and the activity of the organs of articulation. It is of course possible that the motor elements, i.e., rudimentary articulation of words, are not always manifested in as definite a manner as they were in Jacobson's experiments. Individual differences may be expressed in a predominance of visual and, in particular, auditory images of words. But even if it were always possible inwardly to see words as written, or to hear them inwardly, rudimentary articulation still would take place, if only as the so-called ideomotor act.

In our analysis of inner speech we have always departed from two of its forms or stages: unfolded (inner talking) and abbreviated (operating with allusions to words). In connection with this we attempted to demonstrate—and the experiment involving understanding of difficult material did demonstrate it—that the abbreviated form of inner speech (thinking in allusions to words) arises only on the basis of preceding thoughts consisting in verbal reasoning. In speaking of the development of inner speech, none of its forms should therefore be ignored. While engaged in thought, we constantly pass from thinking-reasoning to thinking in allusions to words.

Unfolded inner speech is what Plato called "silent speech expressed verbally," a talk with oneself. In its further development inner speech departs ever farther from vocal, audible speech. The abbreviated character of verbal expression results in an ever increasing condensation of sense into a single word or, even, hint at a word; inner speech thus begins to represent the highest synthesis of individual word meanings; it turns into a language of semantic complexes.

No matter how abbreviated a verbal expression is in inner speech, it does not cease to be speech. The semantic complexes with which we operate in the thought process are complexes of our concepts, arising as a result of man's and mankind's practical activity and reflecting real objects and phenomena. No matter how abstract our concepts or how abbreviated their expression in inner speech, they are related to real things and phenomena. Even the concepts of pure matter, as Engels pointed out, have been adopted from the real world: "The ten fingers on which men learnt to count, that is, to carry out the first arithmetical operation, may be anything else, but they are certainly not a free creation of the mind. Counting requires not only objects that can be counted, but also the ability to exclude all properties of the objects considered other than their number—and this ability is the product of a long historical evaluation based on experience" [3: 37]. The fact, Engels continues, that real material "appears in an extremely abstract form can only superficially conceal its origin in the external world."

Representing the extreme stage of abstraction and generalization, the abbreviated expression of sense in inner speech becomes possible only on the basis of a prolonged evolution of the thought process, a process the initial stages of which consist in operating with real objects and phenomena, real differentiation (analysis) and no less real generalization (synthesis) of them. It is only on such a material basis that man is able to idealize in his imagination the objects and phenomena of the external world and to acquire knowledge about their connections and relationships, expressing the latter in the form of general concepts.

The inexpressible, however, is not yet thought. It may be a feeling or an emotional attitude (for example, a sensation of familiarity, a sensation of difference or similarity, etc.) but not thought, if by the latter we mean an expression of the universal. Hegel aptly characterized sensations of this kind by the phrase "was ich nur meine." "That which I only *wish* to say, that which I fancy, is *mine*, it belongs to me as this particular individual; but if language expresses only the universal, I cannot say that which *I only fancy*" [49: 45-46].

By expressing the universal, language becomes at the same time a means of social intercourse and the "basic element of thought, an element," as Marx put it, "in which the life of thought is expressed" [2: 630].

Chapter V

Comparative Effect of Various Articulatory Conditions on the Processes of Perception, Memorization, and Thought

1. TESTING THE EFFECT OF VERBAL AND NONVERBAL MOTOR INDUCTION

From the psychophysiological point of view it is obvious that the method of speech interference (enunciation of extraneous word series or syllables during simultaneous auditory perception of speech) used in the preceding experiments was based on the effect on the nerve processes of negative induction which arose in the speech areas of the cerebral cortex as a result of an incoming flow of afferent kinesthetic and auditory impulses due to extraneous verbal stimuli. This technique made it possible to elucidate the role played not only by external (overt) but also by internal (concealed) articulation in the process of mental activity and, moreover, not only at the peripheral but also on the central (cerebral) level.

That a state resembling "sensory aphasia" set in during the early stages of those experiments apparently indicates that the normal activity of both motor speech and auditory speech analyzers was impaired, because the subjects had simultaneously to watch the correctness of their articulation and to listen to material read to them. When, subsequently, a motor-speech stereotype for the articulation of these word series became stable enough, the need for auditory control over correct enunciation was no longer necessary or, at any rate, it diminished considerably. At the same time, the "sensory aphasia" mentioned above either disappeared or diminished: the subjects began to understand the sense of phrases but quickly forgot it because it was impossible to fix it in memory with the aid of articulation which was busy enunciating extraneous words not belonging to the given text. In those cases, however, when the subjects succeeded in fixing the speech heard by articulation, there occurred irregularities in the tempo and rhythm of the enunciation of extraneous words. The irregularities in the tempo and rhythm of speech interference thus served as an objective indicator of a hidden speech activity arising at moments like these and related to the perception and comprehension of heard speech.

We carried out additional experiments to determine whether the enunciation of extraneous speech material renders impossible the articulation of words related to performance of the main intellectual activity, and the effect of nonverbal motor induction (e.g., squeezing a rubber balloon with a definite force) on the performance of mental activity, since in this case there also arises a focus of excitation in the motor analyzer of the cerebral cortex?*

To answer the first question we used kymographic recording of laryngeal movements with the aid of a small laryngograph fastened to the laryngeal region of the neck with a rubber band. The laryngograph recorded only the extraneous words and syllables ("speech interference") which were vocalized, but by observing changes in the tempo and rhythm of their enunciation it was possible, as stated above, to assess also hidden articulation or the attempts at it, should such be made.

Fig. 4a shows a laryngogram of mental solving of arithmetical problems without simultaneous enunciation of extraneous words or syllables. We see a completely smooth, straight line which makes an upswing only when the results of calculations are vocalized. When, however, arithmetical calculation problems and textual problems were being solved with simultaneous articulation of extraneous syllables, there appeared on the laryngograms heterogeneous oscillations of varying intensity and duration, whose frequency increases particularly toward the end of the solving process (Fig. 4b and 4c). The duration of problem solving is indicated by the time marker.

Fig. 5a shows laryngeal movements recorded during vocalization of "la-la" syllables for 30 sec without simultaneous arithmetical calculations. The laryngogram shows clearly the up- and downswings of the recording pen when each syllable is pronounced. In addition, it may be seen how, at times, these oscillations cease when two deep respiratory pauses 0.6 to 0.8 sec in duration take place. The respiratory character of these pauses is confirmed by the simultaneous recording of respiration with a pneumograph: each pause on the laryngogram has a corresponding moment of inspiration precisely recorded on the pneumogram (Fig. 5b).

Thus, continuous (without prolonged respiratory pauses) articulation of syllables or words can be maintained effortlessly for 8 to 10 sec, which is quite sufficient for performance of short mental tasks. This time can be

---

* Scientific staff members, N. K. Indik and E. D. Lyubimova, graduate student M. V. Matyukhina, and students working on their thesis-L. L. Babalova, V. T. Ivankov, R. Martinez, and M. B. Mikhalevskaya from the Department of Psychology of Moscow University helped conduct these experiments.

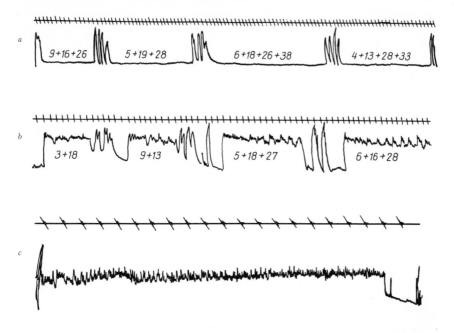

Fig. 4. Laryngograms taken during mental solution of arithmetical problems and a textual problem: a) problem solving without articulation of extraneous syllables; b) problem solving with loud articulation of syllables "la-la" (the problems were read by the experimenter); c) solution of a textual arithmetical problem in three steps: "48 kg of apples were collected from an apple tree and put into three baskets. The first basket received 6 kg of apples; the second, four times more than the first; and the third basket, all the rest of apples. How many kilograms of apples were put into the third basket?" (The text of the problem was read by the subject himself). Time marks (upper line) on the first and second laryngograms, 0.2 sec, on the third laryngogram, 1 sec.

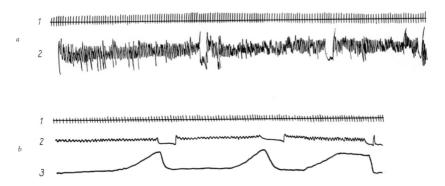

Fig. 5. Laryngograms taken during vocalization of "la-la" syllables and respiratory pauses: a) with a loud vocalization of syllables; b) with a soft vocalization of the same syllables. 1) Time marks at 0.2 sec; 2) laryngograms; 3) pneumogram.

increased by means of voluntary prolongation of deep inspirations and expirations up to 15 sec and more; in that case, longer mental operations, such as arithmetical problem solving involving a combination of addition, subtraction, and multiplication, arithmetical problems in several steps, etc., can be carried out without any noticeable pauses.

The solving of problems involving a large number of operations is accompanied by short respiratory pauses.

Let us note the following, however, concerning the respiratory pauses. First, usually there is no articulation of words during inspiration (we articulate words on expiration and not on inspiration). Second, the respiratory pauses noted are of such a short duration that, even should we articulate words on inspiration, it would still be impossible to articulate them to a more or less full extent.

But even if we assume that hidden (suppressed) articulation can take place during respiratory pauses or that parallel functioning of some other muscle groups of the speech apparatus, not engaged in the enunciation of particular words or syllables, is possible, we still have to admit the possibility of performing certain mental operations even with the speech organs being maximally engaged in articulating extraneous words or syllables. A more detailed analysis of speech mechanograms discloses in this case, too, a number of changes in the intensity, tempo, and rhythm of enunciation of extraneous words and syllables, which evidently indicates an activation, in these moments, of articulatory mechanisms for incomplete (abbreviated) articulation of words in the process of problem solving. These changes are noticed both during the auditory perception of a problem's conditions and during the subsequent solution of the problem (Fig. 6).

The second question to be elucidated involved comparison of the effect of verbal and nonverbal motor induction on the performance of appropriate

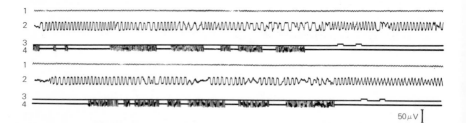

Fig. 6. Movements of the tongue during the enunciation of the syllables "la-la" while listening to conditions of an arithmetical problem and its solution. 1) Time marks in 0.2 sec intervals; 2) mechanogram of tongue movements; 3) marks indicating problem solution; 4) phonogram of experimenter's speech while reading aloud the text of arithmetical problems. Movements of the tongue were recorded with the aid of Kratin's horseshoe electrode placed under the tongue (see Fig. 18b).

mental operations. For this purpose M. B. Makhalevskaya carried out experiments in which adult subjects had to perform arithmetical calculations under four different conditions: 1) with free articulation (performing calculations silently); 2) with a mechanical obstruction to articulation (by compressing the lips and clamping the tongue between the teeth); 3) with simultaneous recital of a poem (Pushkin's "The Snowstorm Covers the Sky with Darkness"); 4) while pressing with the hand (with some force) on a rubber balloon connected via pneumatic transmission to a kymograph. Arithmetical calculation problems were presented visually, with the aid of Ranschburg's apparatus. The time of problem solving was recorded with an electrical timer to within 0.01 sec; the time of the hand's motor reaction was recorded with a Jacquet watch within 0.2 sec.

The experiments showed that mechanical retardation of articulation (compressing the lips and clamping the tongue between the teeth) has a very small, short-term negative effect on arithmetical problem solving. In experiments on adults, mechanical retardation of articulation leaves the hidden articulation of words related to solution of the problems presented almost unaffected. Only occasionally, when the lips and tongue are very strongly compressed, does there arise noticeable negative induction (time delay in problem solving). Negative induction due to lip compression may, moreover, turn out to be stronger than that due to the clamping of the tongue between the teeth, which seemed to have been due to the different intensity of the effects of this kind of interference.

Negative induction much stronger in intensity and longer in duration is produced by recital of a stanza of verse. In this case the time of arithmetical problem solving increases by 150-200% and more. Nonverbal motor induction (due to pressing on a rubber balloon with the hand) has almost no effect on the simplest of calculation problems (adding two, three, and four two-digit numbers). When calculations are made more complex (adding five two-digit numbers), the speed with which they are solved slows down compared to that in control experiments (from, approximately, 11.8 to 15 sec, i.e., by 27%). Data from these experiments is introduced in Fig. 7.

The slowing down of the speed of problem solving observed in these experiments, when addition of five two-digit numbers is involved, in comparison to the time of solution of analogous problems in control experiments, can probably be explained by the fact that mental activity of greater complexity is always associated with the functioning of a large group of nervous connections. As a result, there takes place spatial approximation of foci interacting through mutual induction, and intensification of negative induction.

The intensity with which the rubber balloon was squeezed was nonuniform only in the initial experiments, fluctuations occurring both during problem solving and in the intervals between problems (Fig. 8a). In

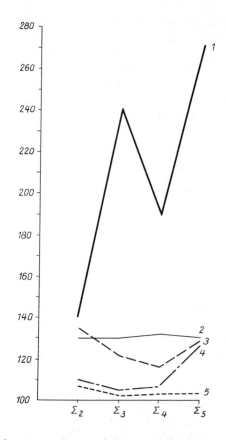

Fig. 7. Effect of verbal and nonverbal motor induction on the mental solution of arithmetical problems. Along the abscissa, problems involving addition of two, three, four, and five two-digit numbers; along the ordinate, time in percent, relative to control experiments. 1) Recital of a poem; 2) mechanical retardation of articulation; 3) enunciation of syllables; 4) squeezing of a balloon with visual control over the force of squeezing; 5) squeezing of the balloon without control over the force of squeezing.

subsequent trials these fluctuations stopped and the graph became smooth (Fig. 8b), which apparently was related to the greater concentration of the excitation process setting in when the balloon is squeezed, since the subjects constantly kept the uniformity of squeezing not only under kinesthetic but also under visual control, being guided by the tracing recorded on the kymograph; and the arithmetical problem solving became increasingly automatized.

Thus, in setting up and analyzing further experiments involving negative induction, both the intensity and complexity of acting stimuli must be taken

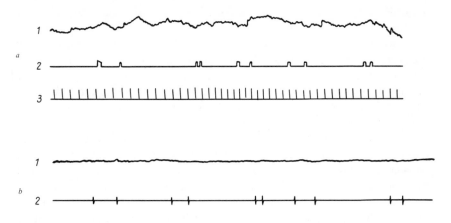

Fig. 8. Kymograms recorded during the squeezing of a rubber balloon with the hand while doing arithmetical calculations mentally: a) in initial trials; b) in final trials. 1) Kymogram of balloon squeezing; 2) indication of the beginning and the end of problem solving; 3) time intervals, 0.2 sec.

into account, keeping in mind that an "excitatory process at one point of the brain induces inhibitory states at the rest of the points, to a greater or lesser degree" [122: 171]. It is evident that the stronger the stimuli and the closer spatially the points stimulated, the stronger and more stable is the negative induction originating there. Hence the stronger inhibitory effect of extraneous speech kinesthesis as compared to that of nonverbal motor induction.

2. THE SCOPE AND ACCURACY OF VISUAL PERCEPTION UNDER VARIOUS CONDITIONS OF ARTICULATION

In the next group of experiments we examined the effect of retardation of external and internal articulation on the visual perception of various objects. It may be assumed that of primary importance here is not only the degree to which articulation is inhibited, but also the character of the objects perceived (drawings, letters, words, etc.) as well as the age of subjects, since the accumulation of temporary connections (associations), their systematization and consolidation increase with age.

Experimental confirmation of this hypothesis was undertaken by V. T. Ivankov. Experiments were performed on adults and children—third-graders from a primary school (aged 9 to 10 years). There were 10 subjects, five adults and five children. Drawings and concrete, abstract, or uncommon words served as objects of visual perception. Objects were presented (with the aid of a tachistoscope) with exposure times of 0.2 sec for adults and 1 sec for children.

Words were printed on a card, in two columns of four words each. The drawings depicted objects well known to the subjects, such as a tree, a key, fish, teapot, house, table, a suitcase, etc. New words and drawings were used in each experiment. Whenever a card was presented, the subject had to note what, and in what order, was depicted (or written) on the card and to report this to the experimenter after exposition.

The experimental setup was as follows. Control experiments were carried out first; they involved perception of the above-mentioned objects with free articulation. This was followed by experiments involving perception of objects with simultaneous retardation of lip and tongue movements and continuous enunciation of the "la-la" syllable and a stanza from "The Snowstorm Covers the Sky with Darkness." This was followed by experiments performed under conditions of speech interference (visual perception of objects while listening to the experimenter say phrases such as "children are playing ball," "mountains could be seen in the distance," "snow has fallen today," etc. At the end of each test series, control experiments with free articulation were carried out. The data were averaged over the initial and final control experiments, and this average served as a basis for comparison of all the remaining experiments.

In processing the data obtained, two principal indices were taken into consideration: the scope of perception, i.e., the total number of correctly perceived stimuli, and its accuracy, i.e., the number of objects which were reproduced by the subjects in the same order (succession) in which they had been presented during exposure. All calculations were made in percentage in relation to the results of control experiments which were carried out under conditions of free articulation (without interference). The results are given in Tables 2 and 3 and in the diagram, constructed on the basis of these tables, showing the levels to which the scope and accuracy of drawing and word perception had dropped under the influence of speech interference of various kinds (Fig. 9).

These data make the following perfectly clear:

1. The maximum effect of negative induction from extraneous motor speech and verbal auditory stimuli is manifested in relation to the perception of abstract and uncommon words. It is somewhat less for perception of words having concrete meanings—lesser still for perception of drawings. The accuracy of perception is affected most.

2. The scope and accuracy of visual perception in the presence of speech interference are affected to a greater degree in children than they are in adults.

3. Acoustic interference (listening to phrases unrelated to visual perception) has an effect as negative as that exerted by articulation of

TABLE 2. Visual Perception under Various Articulation Conditions*

Subjects	Drawing			Concrete words			Abstract words		
	Mechanical retardation	Extraneous articulation	Auditory interference	Mechanical retardation	Extraneous articulation	Auditory interference	Mechanical retardation	Extraneous articulation	Auditory interference
Adults									
A	66	83	66	66	75	100	50	75	33
B	200	175	200	50	75	50	100	100	100
C	66	83	66	75	112	100	100	63	100
D	66	83	66	50	63	100	100	75	100
E	100	100	50	200	125	100	75	50	100
Mean	100	105	89	88	90	90	85	72	86
Children									
I	63	63	75	100	75	100	0	100	100
J	100	83	66	75	87	100	75	50	50
K	100	100	100	66	50	33	50	37	50
L	83	83	100	50	50	50	50	50	100
M	150	100	50	75	75	50	75	37	0
Mean	99	86	78	73	67	66	50	55	60

*In percent of data from control experiments.

extraneous words, which indicates that all speech analyzers are interlinked with each other.

4. There are considerable individual differences as regards the effect of speech interference on the perception of drawings and words. For some of the subjects, extraneous speech stimuli have a strong negative effect on the scope and accuracy of visual perception. For others, the effect is negligible, occasionally being altogether absent. This may be due to typological differences in the relationship between the two signal systems.

5. It should also be noted that there were cases where the scope and accuracy of visual perception not only did not diminish with suppressed articulation but was, on the contrary, found to be slightly higher as compared to controls with free articulation. This phenomenon was found much more frequently in adults than in children. One may see from Table 2 that the scope of perception under mechanical retardation of articulation, while enunciating and listening to extraneous words, remained unchanged in 14

TABLE 3. Accuracy of the Visual Perception under
Various Articulation Conditions*

Subjects	Drawings			Concrete words			Abstract words		
	Mechanical retardation	Extraneous articulation	Auditory interference	Mechanical retardation	Extraneous articulation	Auditory interference	Mechanical retardation	Extraneous articulation	Auditory interference
Adults									
A	50	75	0	50	70	66	33	56	0
B	100	100	200	0	50	0	0	0	0
C	100	100	100	100	170	200	50	0	100
D	0	100	100	0	25	0	0	0	0
E	200	125	0	100	50	0	50	0	100
Mean	90	100	80	50	73	53	27	11	40
Children									
I	0	62	75	0	0	0	0	0	0
J	100	66	66	100	150	200	0	0	0
K	100	100	100	66	33	0	0	0	0
L	83	83	100	0	0	0	0	0	0
M	150	87	0	50	75	0	50	0	0
Mean	87	79	68	43	52	40	10	0	0

*In percent of data from control experiments.

cases for adults and in 12 cases for children; increased in 6 cases for adults and in one case for children (and even then for the perception of drawings only); decreased in 25 cases for adults and in 32 cases for children. Similar results were also obtained from an analysis of the accuracy of perception (see Table 3).

6. The experiments with extraneous articulation showed an increase in assimilative errors when, for instance, the word *zavet* [behest] was perceived by the subjects as *zavod* [works] or even as *zima* [winter]; the word *tiran* [tyrant] as *tetrad'* [exercise book], etc. Errors of this type were approximately twice as frequent in the experiments with articulation of extraneous words than they were in control experiments where articulation was free, and for the most part in children (despite the fact that their exposure to words was five times longer than that of adults).

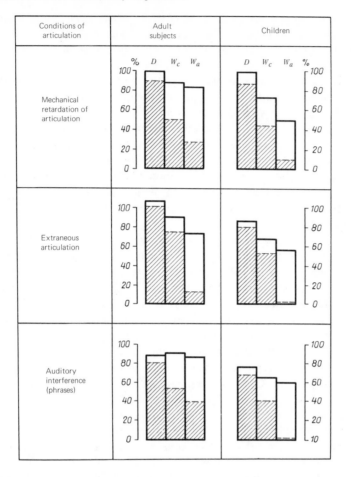

Fig. 9. Decrease in the level of the scope and accuracy of visual perception of drawings and words in adults and children under the influence of verbal interference of various kinds (in percent of data from control experiments without verbal interference). D) drawings; Wc) words, concrete; Wa) words, abstract. Blank spaces together with shaded portions, scope of perception; shaded portions alone, accuracy of perception.

3. MEMORIZATION AND REPRODUCTION OF DRAWINGS AND WORDS UNDER VARIOUS CONDITIONS OF ARTICULATION

In order to elucidate the effect of the various conditions of articulation on memorization and reproduction of material, experiments were carried out by the paired association method. Pairs of drawings (depicting objects) and pairs of concrete and abstract words were selected to serve as stimuli. The pairs were chosen in such a way as to make their association into a meaningful whole difficult. This was done to enable us to trace the effect of different conditions of articulation on the formation of relatively new connections.

The subjects were instructed to memorize each pair of drawings or words and to reproduce the missing member of a pair upon presentation of its mate. The drawings were projected onto a screen, the time intervals between the pairs being equal. Words were presented by means of a Ranschburg apparatus, and the exposure of words was regulated by a metronome. The latent period of reproduction was measured with an electrical stopwatch which was switched on upon presentation of the first member of the stimulus pair and turned off automatically via a microphone or a laryngophone (in experiments with drawings) upon reproduction by the subject of the second member of the pair.

In N. K. Indik's experiments the number of correct answers (after three presentations of appropriate pairs of drawings or words); and the magnitude of the latent period of reproduction (i.e., time elapsed between the presentation of stimulus and the subject's verbal response) were the factors taken into account. The latent period was measured in hundredths of a second. The time of exposure was two seconds for each pair of drawings and one second for each pair of words.

In R. Martinez' experiments account was taken of the time necessary for complete (correct) reproduction of stimuli presented and the latent period of their reproduction. Each pair of drawings or words was exposed for three seconds.

As in the preceding experiments, articulation was studied under various conditions (mechanical retardation of articulation by compressing the lips and clamping the tongue between the teeth, as well as charging the motor speech analyzer with the enunciation of syllables and verses). Martinez also investigated in his experiments the effect of verbal-auditory interference on the memorization of drawings and words. For this purpose, the subjects, while visually perceiving drawings and words, had at the same time to listen to texts read by the experimenter and reproduce their contents at the end of the particular experiment.

The results of experiments involving suppressed articulation and acoustic interference were compared with those of two control experiments, where articulation was free and which were performed at the start and at the end of each series.

Indik worked with 12 subjects. Each test series involved the presentation of ten pairs of drawings or words. Martinez worked with seven subjects, and in each test series 20 pairs of drawings or words were presented. All the subjects were adults (students and scientific staff members).

Table 4 shows the average indices of reproduction under various conditions of articulation obtained in Indik's experiments. Let us analyze them.

TABLE 4. Average Indices of Reproduction of Drawings and Words under Various Articulation Conditions

Articulation conditions	Number of correct answers			Latent period of reproduction		
	Drawings	Concrete words	Abstract words	Drawings	Concrete words	Abstract words
Mechanical retardation of articulation:						
1. Compressed lips	83	86	77	118	141	113
2. Clamped tongue	82	77	74	128	142	121
Group average	82.5	81.5	75.5	123	141.5	117
Enunciation of extraneous verbal material:						
1. Articulation of syllables	83	66	77	128	160	82
2. Recital of verse (first day of trials)	81	57	57	137	145	98
3. Recital of verse (second day of trials)	89	79	81	120	123	89
Group average	84.3	67.3	71.6	128.3	142.7	89.6

When these experiments are assessed on the basis of averaged data, mechanical retardation of articulation, and particularly the enunciation of extraneous verbal material, are found to affect adversely the memorization and reproduction of drawings and words. Moreover, the enunciation of extraneous verbal material (especially that of a poem) has a greater negative effect on the memorization and reproduction of words than it has on the memorization and reproduction of drawings. No substantial difference was found between the memorization of concrete and abstract words, which apparently indicates that in this particular group of subjects (students and scientific staff members) both concrete and abstract associations were equally stable.

The latent period of the reproduction of drawings and concrete words increases in comparison to control, especially with the reproduction of concrete words. The latent period for abstract words is reduced slightly, which seems to be due to diminished negative induction as a result of previous exercise (the experiments with abstract words followed those with concrete words).

Martinez' experiments yielded similar results (Table 5). They are of interest because they include a number of additional test series in which drawings and words had to be memorized in the presence not only of motor speech but also of verbal-auditory interference. As seen from these experiments, mechanical retardation of articulation (clamping the tongue between the teeth) has almost no effect on the time of memorization both of drawings and words, while the latent period of word reproduction is even slightly decreased.

Articulation of extraneous verbal material (enunciation of syllables and verses) increases memorization time considerably. Memorization during simultaneous listening to a text is inhibited particularly strongly when the subjects are warned that they would have to memorize not only word pairs (or pairs of drawings) but the text read as well. Listening to a text without being warned that it would have to be reproduced later has a relatively small inhibitory effect.

Average data from both experiments are represented graphically in Fig. 10, where it may be seen that mechanical retardation of articulation has almost no effect on memorization time, but it affects noticeably the scope of reproduction. Extraneous articulation, however, affects negatively both the time of memorization and the scope of reproduction. Also, it is typical that this speech interference manifests itself with the memorization and repro-duction of not only verbal but also graphic material (drawings).

There are individual cases where extraneous verbal stimuli slightly improve the memorization and reproduction of the material presented instead of inhibiting them. Thus, of Indik's 144 trials involving memorization of drawings and words with simultaneous enunciation of extraneous syllables or

TABLE 5. Average Indices of Memorization Time for Drawings and Words under Various Articulation Conditions*

Articulation conditions	Memorization time			Latent period of reproduction		
	Draw-ings	Concrete words	Abstract words	Draw-ings	Concrete words	Abstract words
Mechanical retardation of articulation (clamping the tongue)	100	103	101	100	92	91
Enunciation of extraneous material						
1) syllables	133	135	133	127	143	93
2) recital of verse	160	156	150	161	146	107
Listening to text without being warned that it will have to be reproduced	110	117	117	115	110	90
Listening to text with a warning that it will have to be reproduced	190	191	166	170	152	104

*In percent of control experiments.

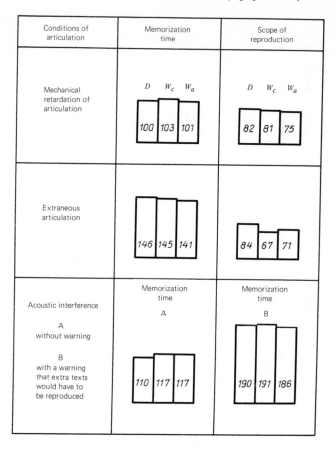

Fig. 10. Effect of various articulation conditions on the time of memorization and scope of reproduction of drawings (D) and words, both concrete (Wc) and abstract (Wa) (in percent of control experiments where memorization occurred without verbal interference).

words, in 13 there was no interference whatever with the memorization of drawings and in 10 with that of words. In 8 other trials the memorization of drawings and words was even slightly improved. On the average, there were roughly 20% of such cases in Indik's experiments involving enunciation of extraneous verbal material and about 23% in experiments involving mechanical retardation of articulation. Analogous cases were also noted in Martinez' experiments.

It is of interest to compare these data with the subjects' reports concerning the techniques they used for memorization when articulation was suppressed. The subjects point out that in such cases they had various visual images appearing before them, images that were usually absent in the tests involving free articulation. For example, one of the subjects reports that in memorizing the word pair "atom, mole" he "imagined a very small mole in the form of an atom model"; another subject, in memorizing the word pair "rifle, fish," imagined a man taking a rifle shot into the water (Martinez' experiments).

Occasionally the subjects also noticed similar images while memorizing words of a more abstract nature. For instance, while memorizing the words "battle, smoothness" one of the subjects imagined "a battle of sailing ships in progress on the smooth surface of the sea." In some cases the subjects have images of the letter structure of words. Thus, a subject stated about the memorization of the word pair "instant, viscosity": "We have here one long word and another consisting of three letters" [instant is "mig" in Russian] (Indik's experiments).

In other cases the subjects memorized abstract words presented by means of thoughts linking them together. Thus, in order to memorize the words "extremity, courage" in Martinez' experiments, subject K. combined them into the phrase "extreme courage"; and to memorize the words "sonorousness, savagery" he made use of a quite complex train of thoughts which he later expressed as the following chain of judgments: 1) musical sounds underwent historical development; 2) their elements were present in the beginning; 3) "beginning, savagery."

The visual perception of words apparently activated the verbal connections previously formed and imprinted in the cerebral cortex, which by virtue of their state of consolidation could be reproduced even while the speech apparatus was busy articulating extraneous series of words or syllables.

It is also evident that the basis for the memorization and reproduction of words under conditions of suppressed articulation are not only the visual word images as such but also the past motor speech images fixed in the cortex. It is this circumstance, it seems to us, that makes the memorization of words possible under conditions of suppressed articulation.

4. SOLUTION OF ARITHMETICAL CALCULATION PROBLEMS UNDER VARIOUS CONDITIONS OF ARTICULATION

In these experiments the subjects—scientific staff members and students—were instructed to solve mentally arithmetical problems involving addition, subtraction, and multiplication under conditions of free and suppressed articulation. The solution time was recorded by means of an electrical stopwatch calibrated in hundredths of a second. The stopwatch was switched on simultaneously with the presentation of problems by means of a Ranschburg apparatus; it was switched off when the subject uttered the result of calculations into the microphone in front of him.

Control experiments consisted in solving analogous problems under conditions of free articulation. These experiments were repeated thrice: at the beginning, in the middle, and at the end of each test series. The arithmetic mean from the three control experiments was compared with the results of all the rest of the tests, the quantitative data of which was calculated in percent in relation to the arithmetic mean.

Seven subjects took part in the experiments. Each subject had 280 problems to solve, apart from the control problems (80 problems with mechanical retardation of articulation and 200 problems with enunciation of extraneous verbal material).

The results of these experiments are summarized in Table 6.

This table clearly shows that arithmetical calculations are slowed down by all kinds of verbal interference, particularly by the recital of a poem. The magnitude of the delay in calculation varies, however, from subject to subject: it is smaller in the case of the first four subjects and greater in the last three, and this too is particularly pronounced with the recital of a poem.

Further, it was established that, as calculations became more involved, the negative induction from extraneous verbal activity was intensified, being smallest during the addition of two numbers and greatest during the addition of five numbers and multiplication of a three-digit number by a one-digit number (Table 7).

TABLE 6. Average Time for Arithmetical Problem Solving under Various Articulation Conditions*

	Types of verbal interference†						
Subjects	Compressing the lips	Clamping the tongue	Enunciation of syllables	Enunciation of individual words	Enunciation of verse		
					First day	Second day	Third day
A.	141	100	138	124	134	160	100
N.	111	111	103	132	102	123	110
K.	115	105	111	107	115	104	107
P.	96	112	117	136	152	132	119
R.	137	130	116	134	141	130	149
E.	100	103	158	243	309	191	134
I.	114	136	100	118	249	311	387
Mean	116	114	120	142	172	164	158

* In percent of control data.
† Nonverbal motor induction due to rhythmical clenching and unclenching of the fist lengthened the time of arithmetical problem solving by 113%-115% in these experiments; that is, to the same extent as in the case of the mechanical retardation of articulation.

TABLE 7. Solution Times of Arithmetical Problems of Varying Complexity

Arithmetical problems	Types of Verbal Interference	
	Mechanical retardation of articulation	Enunciation of extraneous verbal material
Addition of two numbers	124	127
Addition of three numbers	126	157
Addition of five numbers	112	173
Multiplication of a three-digit number by a one-digit number	104	168

On the other hand, of no lesser importance is the fact that, no matter how great the delay in calculations in the case of suppressed articulation, arithmetical calculation problems eventually would be solved by all the subjects—quicker by some, slower by others, but solved nevertheless. This means that stereotyped and well consolidated mental operations such as arithmetical calculations are possible with delayed or suppressed articulation.

In addition, as in the preceding experiments, there were cases in these experiments when interference with articulation had no negative effect whatever on arithmetical problem solving: in 380 trials (i.e., about 20% of the 1960 experiments conducted under conditions of verbal interference) arithmetical problems were solved a little faster than in the control experiments, where articulation was free, "to oneself." This was experienced by every subject. The results are summarized in Table 8.

The number of similar instances of accelerated problem solving under suppressed articulation grew as the subjects became more experienced in arithmetical calculations; i.e., as the operations became increasingly stereotyped. Thus, on the first day of trials involving the recital of a poem there were 30 cases of this kind among the subjects; on the second day, 55; on the third day, 60; and the number of delayed solutions decreased correspondingly (Table 9).

The solution of arithmetical problems usually was accelerated by 10-20% with respect to the time required to solve similar problems in control experiments. In some instances it was even as high as 30-40%.

In analyzing the data cited, that subjects A. and K. belonged to the group of fast calculators must be taken into account. When solving 15 control problems involving addition, subtraction, and multiplication under articulation, A. spent 15.48 sec, K., 20.73 sec. Subject N. also belonged to the fast calculators: she needed 17.4 sec to solve these problems.

TABLE 8. Total Number of Delayed, Equivalent, and Accelerated (Compared to Control) Problem Solving with Verbal Interference

Subjects	Delayed solutions		Equal in duration to controls		Accelerated solutions	
	Mech. retard.	Extraneous syllables, words	Mech. retard.	Extraneous syllables, words	Mech. retard.	Extraneous syllables, words
A.	45	160	–	–	35	40
N.	65	160	5	5	10	35
K.	60	110	–	10	20	80
P.	50	180	–	5	30	15
R.	75	165	–	–	5	35
E.	40	190	15	5	25	5
I.	60	170	–	5	20	25
Total	395	1135	20	30	145	235
Percent of total number of solved problems for a given verbal interference	70.5	81.2	3.5	2.1	26	16.7

With subjects E. and I., slow calculators who spent 32.28 and 40.35 sec, respectively, on solution of 15 control problems the number of accelerated solutions with suppressed articulation was considerably less than with the first three subjects (Table 8), their maximum speed-up not exceeding 10-20%, while in the first three it reached 30-40%.

This indicates that the speed of calculations, while the speech apparatus is continuously preoccupied with enunciating extraneous verbal material, is a

TABLE 9. Gradual Increase in the Number of Accelerated Solutions of Arithmetical Problems According to the Day of Trial

Articulation condition	Day of trial	Accelerated solutions	Solutions equal in duration to control	Delayed solutions
Recital	1	30	5	245
of a	2	55	–	225
poem	3	60	5	215

direct function of the stability of the verbal connections formed previously and which are necessary for the execution of corresponding arithmetical calculations.

As regards the slow calculators, negative induction from extraneous speech kinesthesis extremely slowed down the process of problem solving because the verbal connections necessary for arithmetical calculations were not established firmly enough in them. For example, subject I. displayed considerable delay in problem solving even on the third day of trials involving recital of a poem (the delay was even greater than on the first two days of trials, reaching up to 387% of the time required to solve control problems with free articulation). It is evident that in this case verbal associations necessary for arithmetical calculations were thoroughly inhibited under the influence of extraneous verbal stimuli.

Verbal reports of the subjects indicate that in solving problems they, while reciting a poem or enunciating syllables, at the same time attempt "somehow to articulate" the calculations as well, but at first such attempts were unsuccessful because the fluency of recitation at once became disturbed. The subjects started to confuse the words, the increasing auditory control over the correctness of poem recitation enhancing still more the negative induction. The subjects noticed, moreover, two difficulties of a subjective nature: they found it difficult to carry out an appropriate arithmetical operation and to retain (fix) the intermediate result if the operations numbered more than one. Some of the subjects reported that they were able to retain the intermediate result visually, yet they were still unable to perform addition, subtraction, or multiplication in a purely visual fashion, for this at the outset required that the resulting figure somehow be named.

Also, it must be pointed out that replacement, under these conditions, of speech kinesthesis with some other kind of kinesthesis, even one intimately related to it, does not improve the situation to any appreciable extent. Thus, the suggestion was made to the slow calculators to "write down" the results of intermediate calculations in the air with a finger in the course of experiments with poem recital. The improvement in calculations observed in these cases turned out to be insignificant. In subject E. the delay in answer decreased from 204 to 194%; in subject I., from 538 to 446%, remaining in both cases very high.

Lastly, let us note that in transition to arithmetical operations of a novel type, the great majority of the subjects, including the fast calculators, found themselves facing difficulties almost as great as those encountered in the initial problems (which by the final trials they solved routinely, without any appreciable delays). Thus, subjects who had been solving, without any delays, problems on adding five two-digit numbers, once again experienced considerable difficulties when they had to switch to subtracting a simple number from a two-digit one. This same phenomenon was observed in the transition to multiplication problems (Table 10).

**TABLE 10. Increase in the Solution Time of Arithmetical Problems
on Transition from One Type of Problem to Another
in Poem Recital Experiments**

Subjects	Addition of five numbers*	Subtraction of one number from another	Multiplication
A.	94	110	140
N.	87	132	116
K.	97	104	143
P.	95	171	120

* These experiments were preceded by problem solving involving the addition of two, three, and four two-digit numbers.

The difference between fast and slow calculators depends, in this respect, upon the fact that in the fast calculators the negative induction, due to extraneous speech kinesthesis, disappears very quickly when problems of the same type are repeated, whereas in the slow calculators it persists for a long time, especially in the case of extraneous articulation (Fig. 11).

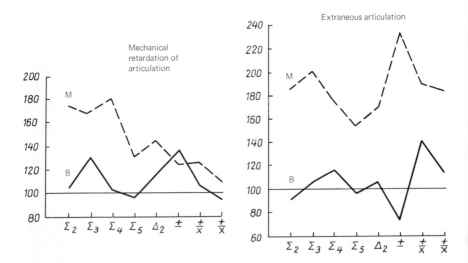

Fig. 11. Effect of verbal interference on the solution time of arithmetical problems of identical and different types. Abscissa: summation (Σ) of two, three, four, and five numbers, subtraction of two numbers (Δ), combined operations with addition and subtraction ($\pm$); addition, subtraction, and multiplication ($\frac{\pm}{x}$). Ordinate: solution time in percent of controls. B) fast calculators; M) slow calculators.

E. D. Lyubimova carried out experiments with 8 first- and third-graders, using the same techniques and simple arithmetical problems involving addition, subtraction, and multiplication within the range of 50 (the experiments were carried out at the end of the school year). Mechanical retardation of articulation and extraneous verbal interference were found to delay solution of these problems in first-graders only. Third-graders displayed only isolated cases of such delays, in a number of cases solving problems even quicker than in control experiments with free articulation. On the average, however, as may be seen from Table 11, neither mechanical retardation of articulation (compressing the lips and clamping the tongue between the teeth) nor extraneous speech kinesthesis had any appreciable negative effect on the third-graders.

These results are completely straightforward: the third-graders had had much more experience with similar arithmetical exercises at school than had the first-graders, and delayed articulation and verbal interference had therefore no effect on their solving problems as simple as those involved. The first-graders had had less experience, hence the considerable delay in problem solving under conditions of suppressed articulation and verbal interference. Here too, then, the possibility of solving arithmetical problems with delayed articulation depends on the degree to which the previously formed verbal connections have been stabilized.

M. V. Matyukhina compared in her experiments the effect of motor speech and verbal-auditory interferences on the process of arithmetical problem solving. She also determined the effect of their concurrent action. Auditory interference consisted of reading, while arithmetical problems were being presented, by the experimenter or via a tape recorder of texts whose contents had to be reproduced later by the subjects (who were warned of this in advance). The concurrent action of motor speech and speech-auditory interference during problem solving was achieved by continual enunciation of "la-la" syllables and listening to the texts read by the experimenter. Eight adult subjects took part in these experiments.

TABLE 11. Average Solution Times for Arithmetical Problems of First- and Third-Graders under Varying Articulation Conditions*

Articulation Conditions	First grade	Third grade
Mechanical retardation	129	100
Enunciation of extraneous material (syllables and words)	144	101

* In percent of control experiments.

Extraneous speech auditory stimuli were found to have as negative an effect on problem solving as had the extraneous speech movements during the recital of a poem (Table 12).

The data cited are of considerable interest. They indicate that auditory perception of speech entails interaction on the part of the auditory and motor speech analyzers, and that it is precisely because of this that the auditory perception of speech inhibits arithmetical calculations and the latter inhibit the auditory perception of speech. In other words, listening to texts is not mere listening; to a certain degree it is also concealed (inward) articulation of their principal content. Any interference (inhibition) with the action of normal connections of the motor speech and speech auditory analyzers results inevitably, therefore, in an incomplete and faulty perception (and subsequent faulty reproduction) of texts, and this is consistently found in Matyukhina's experiments. The reproduction of texts is found to be very fragmentary in these cases and the solution of problems is delayed, also.

Concurrent action of motor speech and verbal-auditory interference has approximately the same effect, although in this case one might have expected even greater intensification of inhibition. And it does indeed become more intense, but only with respect to the perception and memorization of the texts listened to: their reproduction becomes still more fragmentary than in the experiments with auditory interference alone.

It is also important to note that as little as 5.7% of cases were noted where arithmetical problems took less time to solve with auditory interference than they had in control experiments, in the case of extraneous motor speech stimuli the figure is 7.9%, and with mechanical retardation of articulation, 28.5% (Table 13).

The data cited attest to the great significance of auditory analysis in the process of concealed (inward) articulation of words and the constant interaction between the motor speech and auditory analyzers during the

TABLE 12. Effect of Extraneous Motor Speech and Speech Auditory Stimuli on the Solution of Arithmetical Problems*

Test Series	Condtiions of Articulation	Average time of Problem Solving
I	Free articulation (control experiments)	100
II	Enunciation of "la-la" syllables	112
III	Recital of verse	156
IV	Listening to a text	150
V	Listening to a text and enunciation of "la-la" syllables	145

* In percent of control experiments.

TABLE 13. Total Number of Cases of Delayed, Equivalent, and Accelerated (in Comparison to Controls) Solution of Arithmetical Problems under Conditions of Motor Speech and Speech Auditory Interference

Subject	Delayed solution				Equivalent				Accelerated			
	Mech. retard.	Extraneous speech	Listening to a text	Text syllables	Mech. retard.	Extraneous speech	Listening to a text	Text syllables	Mech. retard.	Extraneous speech	Listening to a text	Text syllables
V.	1	16	4	5	1	3	–	–	3	1	1	–
M.	1	14	4	4	1	1	–	–	3	5	1	1
K.	4	19	5	5	–	–	–	–	1	1	–	–
O.	3	17	5	4	1	–	–	1	1	3	–	–
S.	5	18	5	5	–	2	–	–	–	–	–	–
L.	4	16	5	5	1	3	–	–	–	1	–	–
N.	3	20	5	4	–	–	–	–	2	–	–	1
Total	21	120	33	32	4	9	–	1	10	11	2	2
Percent of the total number of solved problems for a given interference	61.1	85.7	94.3	91.4	11.4	6.4	–	2.9	28.5	7.9	5.7	5.7

formation and functioning of all second signal connections. We are of the opinion that this fact is a sufficient evidence for the interaction of the motor speech and speech auditory analyzers in the process of mental activity, which seems to account for the emergence of an "inner sonority" of speech kinesthesis as a basal component of the second signal system.

5. TRANSLATION OF TEXTS FROM FOREIGN LANGUAGES UNDER VARIOUS CONDITIONS OF ARTICULATION

The purpose of a new test series was to trace the effect of inhibited articulation and of extraneous verbal kinesthesis on the translation of foreign-language texts—an activity incomparably more complex than solving elementary arithmetical problems.

As noted in Chapter III, the comprehension and translation of foreign texts is a very complex activity. The initial step in any kind of translation is to determine the meanings of words, which includes, first, assignation of words to definite objects and real phenomena; second, determination of syntactic connections of words; third, differentiation among the shades of word meanings in relation to a given context. The comprehension of a text's contents is at its fullest when every aspect of word meanings–lexical, syntactical, and contextual–is unified into a single meaning ("sense") which represents a complex group of joint associations.

The unification of word meanings into the common sense of a phrase or a paragraph is usually achieved in two ways: either by singling out the most significant components of the verbal complex (principal, or key, words) or by gradually linking the words together syntactically, followed by a linking together of their meanings, which eventually leads to a choice of the most significant words.

The "direct," or "instantaneous," comprehension which occasionally takes place is none other than the closing element of the comprehension process, the final synthetic operation which unites the results of the preceding analysis into a single whole, a general idea or context. The translation of foreign texts is thus connected with mental activity in an unfolded form–perception and recognition of words, analysis of the syntactic structure of sentences, comprehension of the general sense of phrases, idioms, etc. This is demonstrated frequently by beginners in the study of a foreign language, who for a long time experience great difficulties with translations–reflected in the process of their reading of a foreign text: they usually read or translate aloud, in a whisper or, at least, with the aid of lip and tongue movements. This phenomenon is analogous to that found in children learning to read and write in their native tongue.

It is evident that for people who are in the initial stage of mastering a foreign language, inhibition of articulation should represent a substantial obstacle to their translating of foreign texts. In the present case it should be kept in mind, however, that we are dealing here not only with the degree to which a foreign language is mastered (i.e., with the volume and stability of the appropriate vocabulary and grammatical connections), but also with the degree to which articulation is being inhibited. L. L. Babalova's investigation, described below, was structured around the variations in these factors.

English texts were used in the experiments which were divided into two series: the first consisted of adapted texts, i.e., of short stories and tales from special issues of foreign literature intended for the first years of English studies and therefore as semantically and grammatically elementary as possible. The second series consisted of excerpts from fiction, in the form of an author's discourse on the actions or character of his heroes, often presented as aphorisms unfolded to a greater or lesser extent. The texts of this series were taken in their entirety from Hardy's *Tess of the D'Urbervilles* and represented complex semantic units containing a large amount of abstract concepts. Grammatically they consisted of complex sentences with participial and gerundial constructions and subordinate clauses. In the first (adapted) series the texts consisted of 100 words; in the second (advanced), of 50 words.

Eleven students from the Department of Philology of Moscow University—six first-year and five fifth-year students—were enlisted as subjects. In the first year English was studied as a general subject four hours a week; in the fifth year it was studied ten hours a week as a special subject. The texts belonging to the second series were presented to the fifth-year students only.

The subjects had to read texts of equal complexity under three different conditions of articulation: 1) with free articulation in control experiments; 2) with mechanical retardation of articulation (clamping the tongue between the teeth); 3) in the presence of extraneous speech kinesthesis (enunciation of "la-la" syllables and of a stanza from Pushkin's "The Snowstorm Covers the Sky with Darkness . . .").

For the purpose of analysis, the experimenter, prior to tests, divided each text into semantic units, that is, individual sentences or parts of sentences representing a more or less independent semantic unity. The number of semantic units, translated by each subject in the two control experiments where articulation was free (as always, the control experiments were carried out at the beginning and at the end of each test series), was assumed to represent 100%, and the percentage of semantic units translated under various conditions of articulation was calculated accordingly.

Since the subjects were apt to encounter unfamiliar words in a number of instances, they were warned by the experimenter that in the course of translation they had to point to these words with a pencil silently, and the experimenter would translate them at once. The number of such cues was recorded by the experimenter and taken into account in the analysis of the results (on the average, it took from one to two seconds to translate such words).

The subjects were instructed to read the text under varying conditions of articulation and then to recount its contents in as great detail as possible. The time of translation was registered with a stop watch. The total number of trials was 266.

Table 14 gives a summary of these experiments. The results indicate that for the first-year students, mechanical retardation of articulation (clamping the tongue) and enunciation of a syllable affect the results of translation to a very insignificant degree.

The recital of a poem affects the translation adversely as far as all the subjects are concerned, which manifests itself in an increase in the time required for translation and a decrease in the number of semantic units translated correctly. Moreover, the subjects found it particularly difficult to establish logicogrammatical connections whenever the need arose to do so. They would report: "Individual words are clear, but when one tries to connect them somehow into a single whole, the poem gets in the way terribly; one becomes confused and has to return to the beginning."

TABLE 14. Translation of English-Language Texts under
Varying Articulation Conditions

| Articulation Conditions | Adapted text | | | | Complicated text | |
| | First-year students | | Fifth-year students | | Fifth-year students | |
	Trans-lation time	Semantic units translated	Trans-lation time	Semantic units translated	Trans-lation time	Semantic units translated
Mechanical retardation (tongue clamped)	102	105	105	111	97	100
Enunciation of extraneous material						
1) articulation of syllables	100	89	102	96	107	88
2) recital of verse	134	87	112	99	161	85

For the fifth-year students, mechanical retardation of articulation and enunciation of syllables had almost no effect on the translation of adapted texts. The negative effect of the poem recital also was considerably smaller. With advanced texts, however, the enunciation of syllables, and the recital of a poem in particular, changed the results for the worse.

Here, as in the experiments involving other types of mental activity, there are cases where retardation of articulation and enunciation of extraneous verbal material not only did not reduce the quality of translation in comparison to controls but, on the contrary, accelerated it slightly.

However, such cases occurred only with the reading of the adapted texts. With the reading of advanced texts, they are found for the most part in the case of mechanical retardation of articulation. By way of illustration, here are the results of a fifth-year student (Table 15).

Thus, here, as in all the preceding experiments, the ensuing stereotyped activity results in gradual diminution of negative induction due to suppressed articulation and extraneous speech kinesthesis. This seems to be explained by the fact that in the first-year students the verbal connections (which are necessary for translation of foreign texts) are few and unstable; sufficiently strong verbal kinesthetic stimuli are needed to form new connections and to "revive" (reproduce) the connections which have just become established and which are as yet not "well-trodden" enough; this is only possible when the articulation of words is more or less complete. If partial exclusion of articulation by mechanical suppression of tongue movements is not a sufficient obstruction, the more complete elimination of the possibility of

TABLE 15. Improvement in the Quality of Translation after Training under Various Conditions* (Subject B)

Conditions of articulation	Number of exercise	Translation time	Semantic units translated
Tongue clamped	1	142	100
	2	117	116
	3	80	116
	4	100	108
Mean		109.7	110
Enunciation of a syllable	1	158	90
	2	117	95
	3	85	95
	4	90	102
Mean		112.5	95.6
Recital of poem	1	212	100
	2	182	100
	3	132	107
	4	125	125
	5	112	116
Mean		152.8	109.6

* Indices calculated in percent of control experiments.

interior articulation of the text during the recital of a poem leads to difficulties in the comprehension and translation of a foreign-language text.

On the other hand, well habituated to reading and translating easy (adapted) texts, fifth-year students need no extensive articulation to read advanced texts. According to their statements, they used to "grasp the text with their eyes and enunciate the words inwardly, largely at the moment of the grammatical and logical unification of the words in the text."

Whereas the first-year students usually accompanied their comprehension of foreign words with their translation into the native tongue, the fifth-year students read easy texts without translating them. Specifically, this is indicated by the fact that these subjects frequently would include foreign words as synonyms for Russian words while recounting the contents of a text in Russian. For instance, in translating a text, the subject says: "One day the *rabbit* [using the English word for rabbit] met the fox" or "There were many trees there and *among them* ["among them" in English] an oak and an apple tree."

It goes without saying that associating foreign words with corresponding objects and phenomena in such a direct fashion, bypassing their Russian designations, facilitates the task of translation under conditions of inhibited articulation. But with translation of difficult (nonadapted) texts containing complex logicogrammatical structures, where such direct associations are still absent, verbal interference rendered the translation more difficult by hindering the articulation of the words of the text.

This means that operating with abstract concepts in the presence of insufficient consolidation of the corresponding verbal connections is bound up with an intensified activity of speech kinesthesis of various kinds, so that any inhibition directed at it not only delays the translation but also makes it imprecise and fragmentary.

6. PRINCIPAL CONCLUSIONS FROM THE SPEECH INTERFERENCE EXPERIMENTS

Let us summarize the main results of the experiments described.

1. Mechanical retardation of external articulation (speech movements of lips and tongue) has an insignificant effect on the performance of mental tasks by adults; in many cases it has no effect at all. In children, the mechanical retardation of articulation has a noticeable negative effect.

2. Extraneous motor speech and verbal-auditory stimuli have a strong adverse effect on the performance of mental tasks, lowering the scope and accuracy of the perception, memorization, and reproduction of both concrete and, especially, verbal material. The solution of arithmetical calculations and problems and the reading and translation of foreign texts are slowed down. This is found in both adults and children. As tasks of the same type are repeated, however, negative induction due to extraneous verbal stimuli grows weaker and the tasks presented begin to be performed without any noticeable delay (and in some cases even slightly faster than in control experiments, where articulation was free). Moreover, the less the auditory control over the enunciation of extraneous words or syllables, the less is the inhibition of principal mental activity. The enunciation of syllables has therefore a much smaller inhibitory effect than has the recital of a poem.

3. The most difficult observation to explain physiologically is the fact that loading the speech apparatus with extraneous activity, as well as forced listening to extraneous verbal material, is far from always having a negative effect on the mental operations under study, occasionally even accelerating slightly the execution of those tasks. Cases like these were usually observed during performance of relatively uncomplicated, stereotyped tasks (i.e., if

mental operations become stereotyped they may be performed with the motor speech analyzer being in a more or less inhibited state). This experimental finding is also in accord with everyday experience. It is, for instance, well known that many thoughts occur to us during conversations with other people or while reading books or listening to lectures, that is, while the speech apparatus is busy performing its natural function of articulating other words.

How, then, is the thought process implemented? Do these facts mean that in this case thought activity is being implemented without speech kinesthesis?

In view of the data presented above, the following assumptions may be made concerning the speech mechanisms underlying thought activity during inhibited articulation.

It should be remembered that the articulation of words is not only a motor speech process but, at the same time, an auditory process. This, in particular, is what explains the onset of a negative induction which is equally strong during the action of both motor speech and verbal-auditory extraneous stimuli, and the diminution of negative induction as the auditory control over the enunciation of extraneous word series weakens if the latter begin to be articulated more or less automatically. The presence of a constant coupling and interaction on the part of the motor speech and speech-auditory analyzers permits us to assert that every kind of speech kinesthesis is "wired for sound," i.e., linked with auditory speech stimuli, whereas auditory (and, in reading, visual as well) perception of words is linked with speech kinesthesis. When speech movements are inhibited, residual kinesthetic impulses are capable, therefore, of activating verbal connections in the auditory analyzer despite their weak intensity, compensating thereby for inhibited speech movements.

Further, it must be kept in mind that retarded articulation did not, in our experiments, exclude the possibility of replacement of certain muscle groups of the speech apparatus with other muscle groups not participating at a given moment in the articulation of extraneous syllables or words. In such a case, even if their activity is very weak (attenuated), substituting verbal kinesthesis of this kind may be quite sufficient to carry out more or less stereotyped thought operations based on well-stabilized verbal connections. When the verbal connections necessary for implementation of given tasks are unstable (all the more so if they are absent), concealed speech kinesthesis may turn out to be insufficient for the functioning of thought activity. In this case thinking becomes possible only by switching to external articulation or articulation in a whisper, this fact being invariably noted in child education and underlying the educational importance of reading aloud and of the spelling out of words difficult to write, etc.

Finally, along with concealed (inhibited) articulation, of great importance in the thought process may be trace excitation due to speech kinesthesis and auditory and visual perception of words (during listening to speech or during reading). As do stimuli in general, verbal stimuli possess a trace effect—an aftereffect—of shorter or longer duration. "As for trace stimuli," Pavlov wrote, "there is no room for perplexity here. Each stimulus leaves a trace in the nervous system for a while; we encounter the phenomenon of so-called aftereffect in all divisions of the nervous system" [122: 49].

The existence of trace phenomena in the nervous system permits the assumption that in the process of human thought activity or, speaking in a broader sense, intellectual activity, there may be functioning two different forms of verbal stimuli and, correspondingly, two different forms of inner speech—the ongoing inner speech and that in the form of traces, constantly interacting with each other. In that case, the trace stimulation due to movements of the speech organs, lasting for some time, is capable of generating in the cerebral cortex a succession of many different associations. It is also possible, moreover, that the aftereffect due to previous verbal stimuli may coincide in time with the ongoing verbal stimuli, so that this kind of a simultaneous action of two or several verbal afferent volleys may be experienced subjectively as a flashing of thoughts.

All the aforesaid points to the enormous complexity of the speech mechanisms in human intellectual activity. That which in psychological analysis is being described as "inner speech" represents, from the physiological point of view, an interaction of different speech mechanisms: motor, auditory, and visual. If this is so, it is quite probable that attenuation of the motor speech component can take place in inner speech only under the condition of complete preservation or even intensification of its other components, auditory and visual verbal stimuli (both ongoing and trace). The functioning of these hidden speech mechanisms is to be assumed to be responsible for making thinking possible in the form of an internal speech process, a process of verbal abstraction and generalization of concrete stimuli.

As for the slight acceleration of thought operations occasionally observed in our experiments at the moment of automatized enunciation of extraneous syllables or words, it appears that it might be explained by the overall activation of the brain's speech centers, taking place at times like these, and by an increase in their working tone in virtue of the rhythmic articulation of the words being enunciated with retention of definite microintervals between them, during which very rapid and abbreviated implementation of other thought processes becomes possible. This kind of a rhythmic organization of two different speech processes facilitates and accelerates their differentiation, lowering or even abolishing temporarily thereby the inhibitory effect of extraneous verbal stimuli.

Part Three

Electromyographic Studies of Inner Speech

Chapter VI

Electromyographic Study of Inner Speech and an Overview of Electromyograms Revealing Hidden Articulation

1. ELECTRICAL ACTIVITY OF THE SPEECH MUSCULATURE AS AN OBJECTIVE INDICATOR OF HIDDEN SPEECH PROCESSES

It is known from neurophysiology that action potentials are generated in muscle fibers when the latter become excited, and that these potentials precede muscle contraction, being indicators of the concealed (latent) phase of the excitation of muscles by motor neurons of the spinal cord and of the medulla oblongata. The motor neurons are in turn connected with the overlying, suprasegmental divisions of the brain, up to the subcortical ganglia and cerebral cortex. One of the most important regulatory mechanisms of movements resides in the muscles proper: while contracting, the muscles generate in their receptors (muscle spindles) proprioceptive impulses which proceed via afferent fibers to the various divisions of the brain.

This regulation of motor impulses on the part of proprioceptors is known as "return afferentation" [10] or as a system of "automatic control of excitation of motor neurons by means of feedback" [57]. It is also known that this system is not autonomous, being constantly exposed to the effects of central innervation. Thus, recent morphophysiological investigations [251] have established that muscle spindles are innervated by the fine myelin fibers of anterior roots—the so-called gamma-efferents which affect the excitation threshold of the muscle spindles and thus, so to speak, attune them to delivering proprioceptive impulses of a certain intensity. It has also been found that the spinal nuclei innervating the muscle spindles are, in turn, under the influence of the suprasegmental divisions of the nervous system [61; 216; 223; 224].

The foregoing attests to the rather complex nature of the nervous regulation of muscle tensions by both central and peripheral organs. Despite the fact that the action currents in muscles reflect directly only the fluctuations in potential related to the excitation of motor end-plates and muscle fibers [202], it still is evident that indirectly they reflect the entire system of neural control over muscle contraction, including the central influence exerted on them by the cerebral cortex. These notions are also in accord with the presence, in the motor analyzer of the cerebral cortex, of both efferent (kinetic) and afferent (kinesthetic) motor neurons.

In this case the opinion should be considered as justified that the electromyogram (recording of muscle potentials) represents "the outcome of a succession of processes unfolding consecutively in the central nervous system, which find a correspondence in the alternate processes occurring in muscle elements" (advanced [136: 67] by V. V. Pravdich-Neminskii, one of the pioneers in the modern electrophysiology of the brain and muscles). In other words, the electromyogram is an integrated expression of all neuromuscular processes, including those in the cerebral cortex. The above remarks concerning the complex nature of the nervous regulation of voluntary muscle contractions and their summary reflection in the electromyogram also pertain to movements of the speech organs with both overt (aloud) and concealed (soundless) articulation of words. Of great interest in this regard is an electromyographic analysis of inner speech during execution of various mental operations.

First investigations in this direction were carried out by E. Jacobson [342; 245] and later by L. Max [256]. Using oscillographic recording of action currents in the speech musculature (tongue and lips; finger muscle potentials were also recorded in Max's experiments on deaf subjects), they found hidden muscle tensions in the majority of their subjects while the latter were engaged in solving mentally problems of various types. Subsequently, similar experiments, involving electromyographic recording of the tone of various muscles during mental work or while performing imaginary operations, were carried out by a number of other researchers as well (Shaw [265]; Aserinsky and Kleitman [204]). Along with the specific (local) tension of individual muscles or muscle groups directly involved in speech, visual, or specific proprioceptive activity, there was observed also an overall increase in muscle tone, e.g., in the hands and neck (Davis [218]), which seemed to point to a manifestation of diffused excitation on the part of the sympathetic division of the autonomic nervous system (Woodworth and Schlosberg [282: 816-817]). Subsequent experiments increasingly convinced the researchers, however, that, unlike the diffused autonomic innervation, the action potentials of speech musculature were bound up directly with the phonation and articulation mechanism of speech.

L. Gould's [235; 236] experiments are of particular interest in this respect. Gould used electromyographic recording of the tone of the lower lip and chin to study verbal hallucinations in schizophrenics. He found the verbal hallucinations of his patients almost always to be accompanied by a hyperactivity of vocal musculature, whereas in the nonhallucinating patients it was observed much less frequently (in the first case, in 83% of patients; in the second, in only 10 out of 100 patients examined). Occasionally the hyperactivity of speech musculature was so intense in hallucinating patients that the emerging subvocal speech could be heard with the aid of a stethoscope and a sensitive microphone. Here is one of such examples of subvocal (soundless) speech in a hallucinating patient: "Something worse than this ... No, certainly not ... Not a single thing. It certainly is not. Something is going on. That's all right. Anything around. Not very much. Something else. Looks like it isn't?" Interestingly, the patients themselves did not notice their subvocal speech at all and used to deny having uttered anything to themselves when hearing haunting voices. In this case it is quite evident that the hyperactivity of speech musculature is directly related to the hidden articulation of words, and this was a definite indication of the specifically verbal character of recorded potentials.

In the years that followed, the interest in electromyographic studies of speech reactions attending mental activity became still greater in connection with studies on the functioning of the brain stem reticular formation and the general (nonspecific) activation of behavior, or the arousal reaction, elicited by it. Of great interest in this regard is the work of a group of Canadian electrophysiologists (A. Smith, R. Malmo, and C. Shagass [267]; H. Wallerstein [278]; A. Bartoshuk [207]) who found appreciable increase in electrical activity in the muscles of the forehead, chin, and hands during attentive listening to texts, during conversations, and while executing certain motor tasks. After discussing their experiments the authors conclude that the action potentials generated in the above-mentioned muscle groups are indicators of attention and verbal activity related to the comprehension of verbal material during attentive listening to a text.

Even more definite data on the locality of the tonic changes taking place in speech musculature can be found in the writings of Soviet neurologists and neuropathologists, who have devoted special attention to this problem in connection with clinical investigations into various speech disturbances. Thus, discussing the results of their electromyographic studies of speech disturbances in aphasics, F. B. Bassin and E. S. Bein [22] arrive at the conclusion that electromyographic recording of the tone of speech muscula-ture is directly related to the innervation processes of articulation, so that in this respect speech electromyograms are substantially different from recorded autonomic reactions (e.g., vascular and galvanic skin responses); the latter can be related to speech activity only secondarily (via the mechanism of conditioned reflex), whereas electro-myographic speech reactions are a necessary link in the mechanism of speech articulation proper. The electromyographic speech reactions are analyzed in considerable detail also in the work by Yu. S. Yusevich [201; 203] and L. A. Novikova [113], who have confirmed the selective localization of motor speech activity in intellectual processes.

In Novikova's experiments, simultaneous intensification of electrical activity was found both in tongue muscles and in hand muscles of deaf children who had been taught oral and dactylic (finger alphabet) speech, during execution of mental problems. This, in Novikova's opinion, points to formation in those children of a unified functional speech system, embracing both tongue kinesthesis and finger kinesthesis. A functional speech system of this kind is also formed in the nondeaf who had been taught dactylic speech, but in them the leading role ("triggering afferentation") is retained by tongue kinesthesis which, judging from electromyograms, joins the speech process before the hand kinesthesis does.

Further material on the localization problem of speech musculature in the processes of phonation and during silent reading of texts were obtained by K. Faaborg-Andersen [226] and Faaborg-Andersen and A. Edfeldt [227]. Using needle electrodes inserted into the intrinsic and external muscles of the larynx, these authors found that not all laryngeal muscles were equally active electrically during phonation of speech sounds. At the moment of phonation, m. vocalis is active electrically, while in the m. cricoarytaenoideus posterior the electrical activity is suppressed at this time, being detected only after cessation of phonation. This is explained by the fact that these muscles perform different functions in the mechanism of phonation: the vocal muscle constricts the glottis and relaxes the vocal cords, whereas the posterior cricoarytenoid muscle, on the contrary, draws the glottis apart and tightens the vocal cords. This reciprocal activity on the part of the laryngeal muscles mentioned above is noticed not only during the phonation of speech sounds but also during a silent reading of texts and may, therefore, be regarded as direct proof of the selective localization of their operation in both external and internal speech. Since the authors used needle electrodes, they were able to obtain very well-defined electromyographic records, indicating that when inner speech is in progress (during silent reading of texts) the potentials generated are much higher (200-500 μV) than those recorded by surface electrodes.

The authors also noticed strong electrical activity at the moment of phonation and silent reading in the m. mylohyoideus.

Lastly, the speech and vocal specificity of laryngeal muscle stress during silent verbal activity is evidenced also by the recent spectrographic studies conducted by E. Kurka [252; 253].

To prove the underlying motor basis of inner speech, Kurka recorded the sound spectra of control tones intoned before and after an activity which involved prolonged utilization of inner speech (work of typists and typesetters). He observed appreciable changes in the sound spectra of control tones, brought about by fatigue of the speech musculature during execution of the above-mentioned work.

The data cited clearly indicate that electromyographic recording of the tonus of speech musculature (provided the recording apparatus is sensitive enough) may be quite a reliable index of concealed motor speech reactions, although they, like all the rest of man's voluntary reactions, are affected by activation on the part of the autonomic and reticular systems.

2. MICROMOVEMENTS OF THE TONGUE IN INNER SPEECH

Taking into account the enormous complexity of the problem of electromyographic analysis of inner speech, we began our investigation with preliminary experiments and, moreover, experiments in their simplest form—electrical recording of mechanograms of micromovements of the tongue. In addition, the latter task was of interest in its own right, since in this manner it was possible to investigate the most intense form of inner speech, verging on its transition to speech in a whisper or vocal speech. Subsequently the obtained mechanograms of tongue micromovements were correlated with the electromyograms of action potentials, which facilitated considerably their analysis and permitted, at the same time, the pinpointing of a number of common factors in their dynamics.

The micromovements of the tongue were recorded with the aid of a special transducer which transformed the mechanical vibrations of the tongue into electrical pulses. This transducer was designed by A. M. Fonarev [185]. It was cross-shaped and consisted of four closed cylindrical capsules filled with carbon powder. The capsules were connected in pairs by copper-wire rods whose flattened tips entered the capsules and established surface contact with the powdered carbon, so that the slightest vibrations of the rods were reflected in the electric conductivity of the carbon powder in which a weak electric current was circulating (provided by a flashlight battery). After amplification the current was fed into an electromagnetic recorder whose oscillations were recorded on a kymograph. The circuit diagram of the transducer is shown in Fig. 12.

The pickup was placed on the anterior part of the tongue and responded to both longitudinal and transverse vibrations of the tongue. In order to eliminate chance (nonverbal) movements of the tongue, the subjects received preliminary training in fixing the tongue (with the pickup in place) in a state of rest; it was only after a quite even baseline had been obtained that the subject was given pertinent tasks (arithmetical calculation problems and texts for reading and listening).

The kymograms of tongue micromovements obtained with the aid of this device indicate that initially the execution of mental operations, including

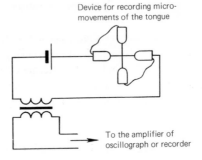

Fig. 12. Diagram of an experimental device to record micromovements of the tongue.

those of a very elementary nature, such as adding two or three numbers (consisting of one or two digits) mentally, is accompanied by well-defined tongue movements. These become less and less marked, being damped as it were, with subsequent solution of problems of the same type (Fig. 13).

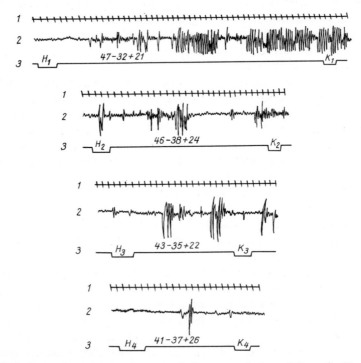

Fig. 13. Kymograms of micromovements of the tongue during solution of arithmetical problems of the same type, involving addition and subtraction. The gradual damping of those movements may be seen. 1) time intervals, 0.2 sec; 2) kymograms of tongue micromovements; 3) marks indicating the beginning (H) and the end (K) of solution, with the problem shown above the line.

The movements of the tongue become intensified (Fig. 14) with transition to more complicated problems (multiplying a simple number by a three-digit one).

Distinct micromovements of the tongue and their gradual damping are quite marked also when a text is read "to oneself": at first the movements are very intense and numerous, but later on they become increasingly weaker and less frequent, without, however, disappearing altogether (Fig. 15). But if the subject had been given a preliminary instruction to read a text and then to reproduce it to the experimenter, the tongue movements became intensified and increasingly frequent (Fig. 16).

During listening to texts, the intensity and frequency of the micromovements of the tongue diminish in comparison to those observed during reading, but in a reduced form they are retained even here (Fig. 17).

Micromovements of the tongue of an appreciable magnitude are also observed when texts are read with the tongue clamped between the teeth. This indicates that mechanical retardation of tongue movements inhibits external (vocalized) articulation only, while the micromovements of the tongue, involved in reading the text "to oneself," continue to persist. It is precisely because of this that in our preceding experiments with speech interference, mechanical retardation of speech had a very small inhibitory effect on mental operations, frequently there having been no effect at all.

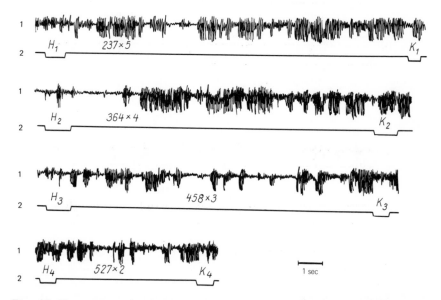

Fig. 14. Kymograms of micromovements of the tongue during multiplication of three-digit numbers by simple numbers: 1) micromovements of the tongue; 2) indication of the beginning (H) and end (K) of solution of the problems involved.

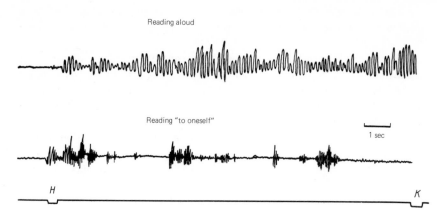

Fig. 15. Kymograms of micromovements of the tongue while a text is being read aloud and "to oneself."

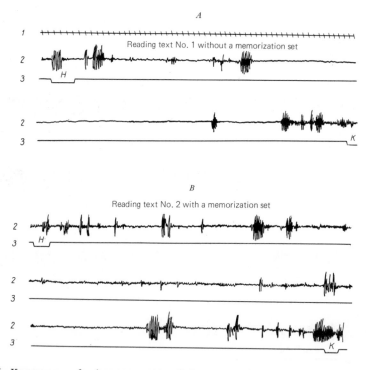

Fig. 16. Kymograms of micromovements of the tongue during reading of a text "to oneself": A) without a set for memorization; B) with a set for subsequent reproduction of text. 1) time marks; 2) micromovements of the tongue; 3) indication of the beginning (H) and end (K) of reading.

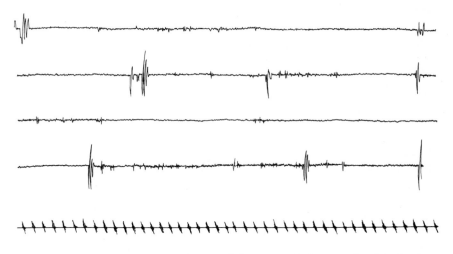

Fig. 17. Kymograms of micromovements of the tongue during attentive listening to a text (description of a transformer). At the bottom, time intervals at 0.2 sec.

Thus, recording of the micromovements of the tongue confirms in a graphic manner the occurrence of motor speech reactions during execution of mental operations and their gradual damping as those operations become stereotyped. Subsequently this regular pattern had to be tested with the aid of electromyographic techniques.

3. METHODS OF RECORDING ACTION POTENTIALS OF SPEECH MUSCULATURE

In our experiments (A. N. Sokolov [153-157; 159; 160; 269]), the electrical activity of speech musculature was for the most part recorded with an eight-loop (8- unit galvanometer type) photooscillograph driven by conventional electroencephalograph amplifiers. The remaining recordings were made with a four-channel ink-writing electroencephalograph. The electrodes were connected to the amplifier input via small condensers (25,000 pF).

Muscle potentials were detected by surface electrodes. The electrical potentials of tongue muscles were led off by means of L. A. Novikova's [113] suction electrodes or silver horseshoe electrodes of Yu. G. Kratin's [92] design. The latter type of electrode was placed under the tongue, within the arc of the lower jaw, enabling us to record potentials from both tongue muscles and the mylohyoid muscles which form the floor of the oral cavity and work in unison with the vocal muscles of the larynx. To detect muscle potentials from the tongue, the second electrode was placed on the earlobe or, to obtain greater frequency in the record, on the teeth. To detect muscle potentials from the lower lip, use was made of cup electrodes 9 mm in diameter, made of pure silver or pure tin, filled with conducting paste and affixed to the lower lip surface with leucoplast. In this case the detection of potentials was bipolar, the distance between the electrodes being about 2 cm. The outward appearance of the electrodes described is shown in Fig. 18.

The electromyographic experiments were carried out under the usual conditions: the subject was placed in a chamber screened from all external electrical interference. He received preliminary training in the voluntary relaxation of various muscle groups of the face, hands, and feet, and the orienting reflexes to the experimental setting were extinguished. In order to eliminate extraneous movements, the subjects had to lie supine or recline in a chair. Besides the speech electromyograms, potentials in the extensor digitorum communis muscle and the galvanic skin response (GSR) were recorded. In addition, in some of the test series continuous EEG recordings were made of potentials from over the occipital and Rolandic areas.

The subjects were students, scientific personnel, and young school-children. They were given various verbal and graphic-visual tasks which they had to perform mentally, e.g., arithmetical calculations, reading texts in their own and in foreign languages, listening attentively to texts read by the experimenter and reproducing their contents, memorizing series of drawings, and solving chess problems, etc. The problems were for the most part transmitted via an audio system connecting the experimenter's room with the subject's booth. In part the tasks were given to the subjects typewritten. At first all the tasks were performed silently; then, for comparison's sake, some of them were performed in a whisper or louder.

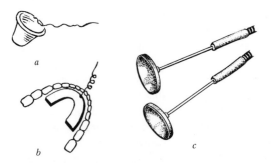

Fig. 18. Electrodes used for derivation of electrical potentials from the muscles of the tongue and lower lip: a) suction electrode for the tongue (see text); b) sublingual horseshoe electrode (see text); c) surface electrodes affixed to the lower lip with leucoplast (DISA design).

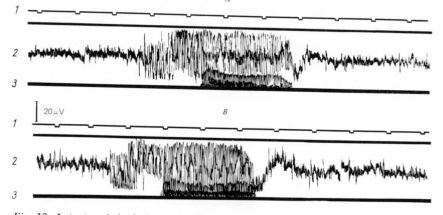

Fig. 19. Latent period of phonation (time elapsed from the onset of muscle potentials in the lower lip, prior to appearance of sound). Subject P., student, 24 years old, pronounced aloud the sound "o." A) first phonation with a latent period of 440 msec; B) second phonation with a latent period of 380 msec; 1) Time interval, 0.25 sec; 2) EMG of lower lip; 3) microphone recording of sound.

Twenty students from Moscow State University took part in the preliminary experiments considered in this chapter. The results are recorded on 2000 frames of various lengths, the scanning rate being 25-50 mm/sec for the loop oscillograph and 30 mm/sec for ink-writing oscillograph.

4. GENERAL CHARACTERISTICS OF THE ELECTRICAL ACTIVITY OF SPEECH MUSCULATURE WITH VOCALIZED AND SILENT ARTICULATION OF WORDS

In the rest state, the electrical activity of speech musculature usually did not exceed 5 μV, but even while listening to a problem in many cases it increased to 10-15 μV, and during subsequent mental execution of tasks (depending on their complexity and novelty) it increased still further, not infrequently being accompanied by "bursts," or "volleys," of impulses which reached 50 μV or more in intensity.

The differences in the intensity of motor speech impulses enable us to separate in the electromyograms two principal components: a tonic component, characterized by slow, low-amplitude potentials, and a phasic component, characterized by fast, high-amplitude bursts of electrical activity, which evoke micromovements in the speech organs.

From the electromyograms it can be established that loud enunciation (phonation) of discrete speech sounds and words, the action potentials of speech musculature are antecedent to phonation by approximately 350-700 msec (Fig. 19).

In preschool children this latent (anticipatory) period is even longer, reaching 500-1000 msec (Fig. 20). With repeated phonation of the same speech sounds and words, its latent period diminishes slightly. Nevertheless, taking into account tonic electrical activity, it remains fairly long. Apparently, it is precisely during this period that there arise the prephonation movements of speech organs, observed by N.I. Zhinkin while making x-ray films of the speech organs during phonation [64: 321-324], [284: 400-402]. It is quite evident that this prephonation electrical activity of the speech musculature is the final link in the neuromuscular activity of the mechanism of phonation

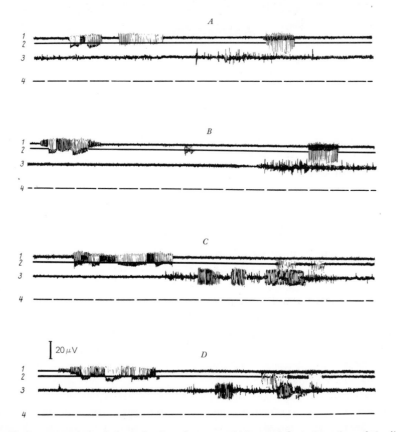

Fig. 20. Latent period of phonation in a four-year-old boy. A) first phonation of the "i" sound (750 msec); B) third phonation of same sound (620 msec); C) first phonation of the word "mama" (1000 msec); D) second phonation of the same word (870 msec). The duration of the latent period, expressed in milliseconds appears in parentheses. The microphone registers first the experimenter's instruction and after that the subject's phonation: 1) microphone registration of the experimenter's instruction; 2) microphone registration of the child's voice; 3) EMG of the child's lower lip; 4) time intervals, 0.25 sec.

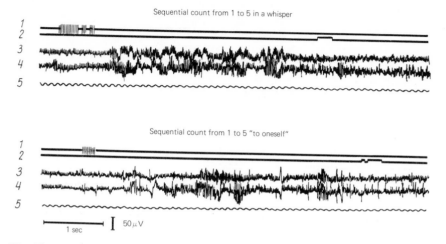

Fig. 21. Simultaneous onset of electrical activity in muscles of the tongue and lower lip during sequential counting from 1 to 5 in a whisper and silently: 1) microphone registration of the experimenter's instruction; 2) subject's signal that the task has been completed; 3) tongue EMG; 4) lower lip EMG; 5) time interval, 0.1 sec. Photographic recording with the aid of a loop oscillograph.

and articulation which generates voiced speech. With rapid enunciation of words and phrases, however, these transformation processes converting hidden articulation to voiced speech are considerably abbreviated and are super-imposed upon each other, so that a much greater scanning rate is required for the electromyograms recorded.

When action potentials from two different divisions of the speech musculature (tongue and lips) are recorded simultaneously during soundless enunciation of words, their activity is found to be synchronous in the majority of cases—simultaneous intensification and attenuation of potentials—which undoubtedly points to a common source of their excitation, the innervation of these muscles being different* (Fig. 21). However, with wide scanning, the motor speech impulses from the tongue and lips can also be found to be slightly desynchronized in electromyograms. In experiments involving the soundless enunciation of vowels, the difference in the intensity of muscle potentials during silent articulation of labialized and nonlabialized vowels (Russian sounds "o" and "i") is particularly pronounced, correspond-ing to the difference in the articulation of these sounds aloud (Fig. 22). This phenomenon is additional evidence for the local specificity of the muscle potentials recorded from the tongue and lips not only during voiced but also during silent articulation of words.

---

* Muscles of the tongue are innervated by the hypoglossal nerve (n. hypoglossus); the lips by the facial nerve (n. facialis) and the buccal nerve (n. buccalis).

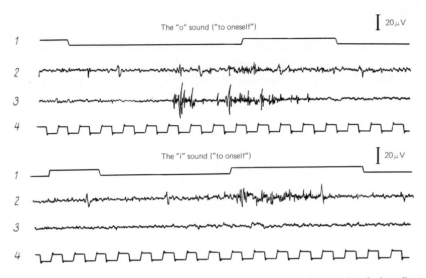

Fig. 22. Difference in the action currents of the tongue and lip muscles during silent enunciation of a labialized ("o") and a nonlabialized ("i") vowel: 1) experimenter's signal to the subject to enunciate the appropriate vowel; 2) tongue EMG; 3) lower lip EMG; 4) time interval, 0.25 sec. Recording was done with an ink-writing oscillograph.

Comparison of the numerous electromyograms from the speech and nonspeech musculature, described below, indicates that when the hands are at rest electrical activity begins to increase in their muscles only in the presence of relatively prolonged mental activity—at any rate, later than in the speech musculature. For short-duration mental activities, muscle potentials of the hands did not change (Figs. 37 and 40). In view of this, it may be concluded that the increase in hand muscle potentials accompanying prolonged mental stress is a secondary phenomenon, a result of the wide generalization of excitation which probably takes place under the activating influence of the brainstem reticular formation.

It should not be overlooked, that in some of cases the hand musculature may be directly involved in a speech process as, for example, when writing or when normal speech function is impaired (in the deaf or aphasics). In this connection it should be noted that terms like "speech" and "nonspeech" musculature are in general quite arbitrary, since it is not just the musculature of the tongue, lips, soft palate, and larynx that directly participates in the acts of phonation and articulation, but also the entire respiratory musculature (of the bronchi, of the lungs, and of the diaphragm) and the related postural musculature of the pectoral region, shoulders, and the neck, participating in the rhythmic articulation of speech sounds [175; 271].

Also, it is of interest to compare the spectra of action potentials of the speech musculature when the same words are pronounced aloud, in a whisper, and silently. The spectrograms shown in Fig. 23 indicate that during silent articulation of words (sequential count) the range of recorded frequencies is considerably narrower than that observed in loud and whispered enunciation of these same words, and the amplitudes recorded are lower. However, the bandwidth range of the medium and maximum amplitudes does not change much, remaining between 30 and 200 Hz.

5. ELECTROMYOGRAMS OF HIDDEN ARTICULATION DURING "MENTAL ARITHMETIC"

The motor speech impulses are of a rather dynamic nature in "mental arithmetic" (solution of arithmetical problems in "one's head"): at some

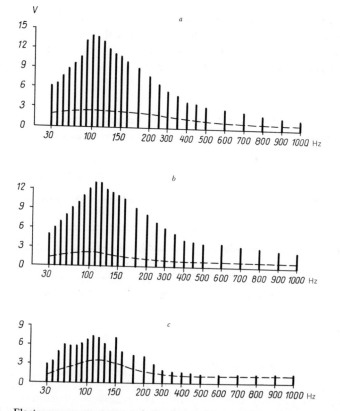

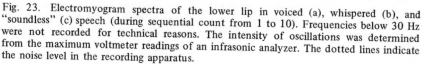

Fig. 23. Electromyogram spectra of the lower lip in voiced (a), whispered (b), and "soundless" (c) speech (during sequential count from 1 to 10). Frequencies below 30 Hz were not recorded for technical reasons. The intensity of oscillations was determined from the maximum voltmeter readings of an infrasonic analyzer. The dotted lines indicate the noise level in the recording apparatus.

moments it is intensified, at others it decreases, occasionally becoming even indistinguishable from the background (electrical activity at rest). These changes in the dynamics of motor speech impulses may be found during performance of arithmetical counting "to oneself" from 1 to 10 and a subsequent count-down from 10.

As may be seen from the electromyograms shown in Fig. 24, the start of counting is marked by rather intensive bursts of motor speech impulses; thereafter, their intensity gradually diminishes. Simultaneously, the time of enunciation of each individual number "to oneself" also is reduced, despite the fact that [in Russian] the sound content of the numbers last in sequence (eight, nine, ten) was much greater than that of the first numbers of the series (one, two, three). With repeated counting "to oneself" the amplitudes of motor speech potentials decrease even further, but they increase again whenever the adopted speech stereotype (in this case, the countdown) is at all disturbed.

Individual differences are linked to habituation in arithmetical calculations: motor speech impulses are much less marked in fast calculators than in slow ones, and when the arithmetical problems are simple enough, the electromyograms of fast calculators reveal no visible changes. In slow

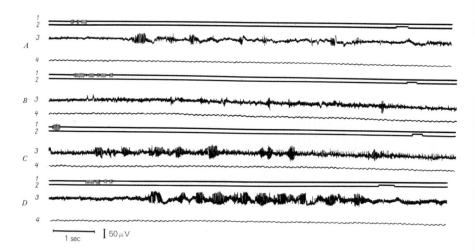

Fig. 24. EMG of the lower lip during sequential count from 1 to 10 "to oneself" and in. a whisper. Subject V., a student: A) count "to oneself"; B) repeated count "to oneself"; C) reverse count "to oneself" (from 10 to 1); D) count in a whisper (for purposes of comparison with preceding electromyograms); 1) experimenter's instruction; 2) subject's signal about completion of the task; 3) EMG of the lower lip; 4) time interval, 0.1 sec. With repeated counting "to oneself" there is a reduction in motor impulses, but with reverse count "to oneself" it becomes intensified, approaching in intensity counting in a whisper.

calculators, motor speech impulses certainly did arise during the solution of the same arithmetical problems (Figs. 25 and 26).

Correlation of the electromyograms of hidden articulation with the data contained in the subjects' verbal reports permits us to elucidate the effect of the individual moments of the problem solving process on the dynamics of motor speech impulses. Of interest in this respect are the electromyograms shown in Figs. 27 and 28. The former is of a subject's lower lip while he was mentally dividing 216 by 3. In this case a slight increase in the amplitudes of

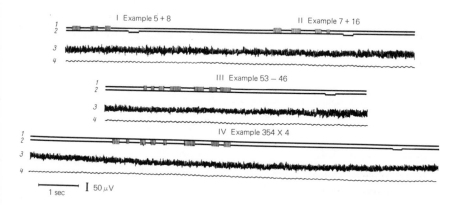

Fig. 25. EMG of the lower lip during mental solution of arithmetical calculation problems without noticeable motor speech tensions. Subject B. (a good counter): 1) experimenter's instruction; 2) subject's signal concerning the beginning and completion of the task; 3) EMG recording; 4) time mark.

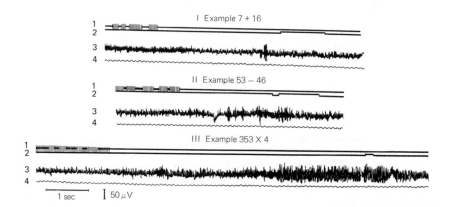

Fig. 26. Increase in electrical activity in the muscle of the lower lip during solution of arithmetical calculation problems of gradually increasing complexity. Subject M. Legend as in Fig. 25.

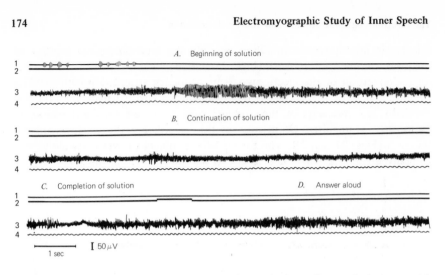

Fig. 27. Dynamics of changes in electrical activity in the lower lip muscle during mental division of 216 by 3. Subject R., a student. Legend as in Fig. 25.

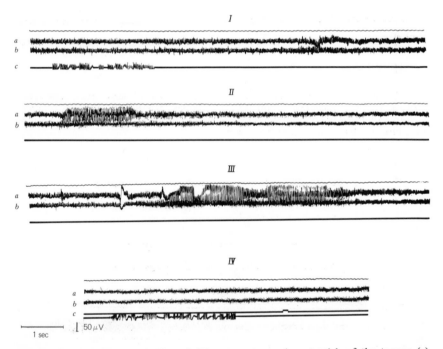

Fig. 28. Electromyograms I, II, and III represent muscle potentials of the tongue (a), lower lip (b) during mental extraction of the square root of 190 (with an accuracy to 0.1); electromyogram IV, mental extraction of the root of 225. Subject K., a student. He calculated the root of 190, whereas that of 225 he "simply remembered"; c) photogram of the experimenter's instruction.

lip muscle potentials is noticed during listening to the problem; during the next two seconds the amplitudes increase sharply, whereupon they decrease gradually to the base level, with subsequent individual discharges which become particularly intense toward the end of solution, when an answer appeared in the subject's mind, announced aloud after a pause of some duration.

If this picture of the muscle stresses within the speech apparatus is compared to the subject's description of the solution process, it will be found that the initial burst of amplitude had been brought about by the motor-speech fixation of the task (the subject reports that he repeated several times to himself, "216 by 3"), the subsequent increase in amplitude corresponding to the abbreviated train of thought ("21 by 3 ... 7 ... 70 ... , 6 by 3 ... 2 ... 72"). The discreteness of the course of reasoning is evidently correlated here with the intermittence of muscle tension in the lip, which becomes intensified when the conditions of the problem are being fixed, during the performance of calculations, and when the final answer is being formulated in the mind.

Just as interesting are the electromyograms recorded while another subject was extracting square roots of 190 and 225 (Fig. 28). In the former case the square root was calculated with an accuracy of 0.1, which required a number of intermediate mental operations and a verbal fixation of their result, and this accounted for the increase in the electrical activity of the speech musculature. In the latter case, however, no calculations whatsoever were done since the square root of 225 was known to the subject, hence no noticeable changes in the electromyogram.

When habituation to arithmetical calculations is insufficient, all mental operations with numbers are accompanied by motor speech impulses, which is particularly marked in preschoolers when they are taught how to count (Fig. 29). This apparently signifies that the increased electrical activity of speech musculature is an index of word articulation in an unfolded form, a diminution of electrical activity being an index of the formation of thought stereotypes, functioning with a minimum of motor speech stimulation.

6. ELECTROMYOGRAMS OF HIDDEN ARTICULATION WHILE READING TO ONESELF AND LISTENING TO SPEECH

Whereas mental arithmetical operations were largely based on the kinesthetic components of speech, reading "to oneself" and listening to someone else's speech must, to a greater extent, be based on other speech components—namely, on the visual (while reading) and auditory (while listeing to speech) components. Having been unable to record visual and auditory reactions directly, in these experiments, at the moment of reading and

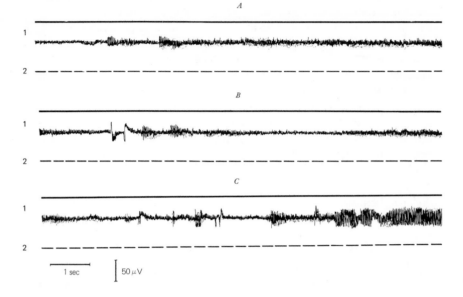

Fig. 29. EMG of the lower lip of a four-year-old boy during mental count of the number of chess figures shown to him: A) counting three white figures; B) counting two black figures; C) total count of white and black figures and answer aloud; 1) EMG of the lower lip; 2) time interval, 0.25 sec.

listening, we were, nevertheless, able to form an indirect judgment about them by the changes in motor speech tensions occurring on visual and auditory presentation of tasks to be performed.

The experiments performed showed that the reading of short phrases to oneself was not accompanied by an observable increase in electrical activity of speech musculature, whereas reading of grammatically complicated phrases brings about the appearance of motor speech potentials attesting to hidden articulation of these phrases or of some of their individual word components during reading (Fig. 30).

The best demonstration of this feature is provided by comparison of the electrical activity in the speech musculature during reading of texts in one's native language and in a foreign language insufficiently mastered. In Fig. 31 recordings are shown of muscle tensions in the tongue and lower lip during reading "to oneself" a Russian text (excerpt from I. S. Turgenev's short story "Bezhin Meadow") and two English texts (an adapted excerpt from M. E. Dodge's "The Silver Skates" and a nonadapted one from O'Henry's "Squaring the Circle"). As may be seen from the oscillograms, the difference in muscle tensions of the speech apparatus is quite appreciable in these cases. As the

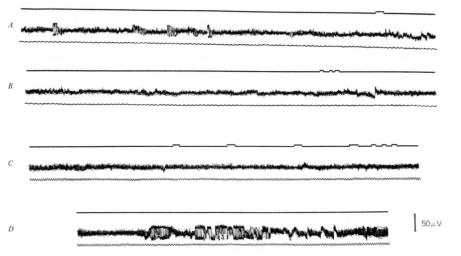

Fig. 30. EMG of the lower lip in reading individual phrases silently (simple and complex sentences): A) "Apart from the boys, there was no one in the boiler room"; B) "Whispering to one another, the boys stood beside the pipe into whose orifice Pet'ka had stuck his head"; C) text consisting of four simple sentences: "There is not enough sunshine. The snow is everywhere. The trees are without leaves. Flakes of snow hang on them"; D) mental reproduction of the preceding text ("Winter"). Subject M., a student. On top, indication of the beginning and conclusion of the reading of each phrase; beneath, time intervals of 0.1 sec. Calibration of potentials is common to all EMGs.

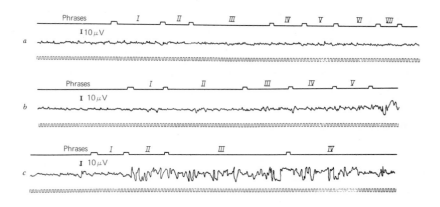

Fig. 31. Micromovements of the tongue, recorded with a sublingual horseshoe electrode during silent reading: a) a Russian text; b) an adapted English text; c) a complicated English text. Time intervals, 0.25 sec. The end of the reading of each phrase was marked by an upswing of the recording pen on the upper oscillogram tracing. The recording was made with an ink-writing oscillograph without low-frequency filtering.

Russian text was read without any noticeable motor speech tensions in the tongue and lips, the English texts (especially the nonadapted one) were attended by considerable motor speech tensions. An analogous phenomenon is also observed during the reading of Russian texts by inexperienced readers and during the reading of phrases which had been "coded" in Latin-alphabet transliteration.

The appearance of strong motor speech impulses when foreign texts are read by people with insufficient mastery of the foreign language involved (or when inexperienced readers must deal with complicated phrases in their native tongue) indicates that the visual components of speech can predominate only in the presence of stable connections established between them and motor speech stimuli in the course of previous experience. Only in such a case will the instantaneous visual signals be sufficient to actuate appropriate motor speech and verbal-auditory connections which are necessary to perceive the meaning of the words and phrases being read.

It seems paradoxical, however, that attempts at reading with eyes alone, without articulation, in our experiments often led to a diametrically opposed result: instead of a reduction they resulted in an intensification of the electrical activity of the speech musculature (Fig. 32). The explanation seems to lie in the fact that in such cases the motor speech impulses were evoked not so much by reading as by the retardation process of articulation proper which, just as any other voluntary acts of man, could be implemented only under the influence of an active retardation of speech movements. Hence the paradoxical intensification of motor speech impulses during the implementation of a given instruction.

Let us now consider the oscillograms of motor speech tensions, obtained while the subjects were listening to somebody else's speech. Even a cursory

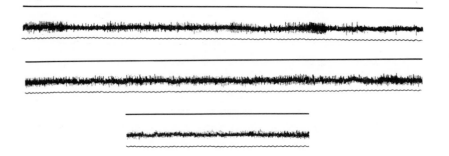

Fig. 32. EMG of the tongue during an attempt to read without enunciating words inwardly ("with the eyes only"). Subject K., a student, reads the phrase: "The wolf stopped on the knoll and listened with his ears pricked up." The reading was very slow (lasting over 25 sec), yet, in spite of this, there was no cessation of motor speech impulses. Time intervals, 0.1 sec.

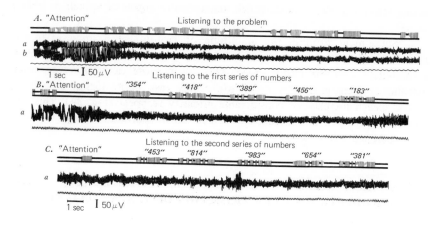

Fig. 33. Onset of strong discharges of electrical potentials in the speech musculature with the first preliminary signals, "Attention!," and their subsequent extinction upon repetition of these signals. EMG of the tongue (a) and lower lip (b) with the first perception of "Attention!" and the task that followed (A). The same with a repetition of the signal "Attention!" (B and C).

examination of the oscillograms makes it clear that motor speech tensions appear during listening, chiefly in two instances: the moment of intense attention to the speaker's utterance and its fixation and whenever difficulties are experienced as regards comprehension of the speaker's utterance and its subsequent logical processing.

Fig. 33 shows electromyograms obtained while the subjects were listening to the conditions of a problem and while they were watching number series presented to them for memorization. In the first two electromyograms one's attention is drawn by the large increases in amplitude occurring when the subjects are addressed with the words, "Get ready! Attention!" Thereupon the amplitudes drop to the baselevel and remain there for the remainder of the listening period. Characteristically, these initial increases in amplitude fade gradually when the subjects are repeatedly addressed with the words, "Get ready! Attention!" and may disappear completely, which is what is recorded in the lower electromyogram in this figure.

Observation of the subjects and examination of their reports permit the assumption that these initial increases in amplitude are a manifestation of the organism's general orienting reaction arising as a result of formation of a dominant focus of excitation in the auditory analyzer of the cerebral cortex. At first glance here, too, only the fact of the intensification (and not that of attenuation) of motor speech stimuli may appear paradoxical, but it can readily be explained by the abrupt arrest of speech movements (as of any other kind of movement), and their orienting inhibition implemented through strong tension in the muscles which maintain the organs of speech in a state of rest.

Subsequent drop in the amplitude of motor speech impulses to the baselevel makes it quite obvious that in this case the verbal-auditory stimuli predominate over the motor speech stimuli. In those cases, however, when listening is accompanied by a fixation of the task or its logical processing, motor speech impulses of considerable intensity reappear (Fig. 34). This was particularly marked during auditory perception of individual foreign words in our experiments (Fig. 35).

7. ELECTROMYOGRAMS OF HIDDEN ARTICULATION DURING MENTAL REPRODUCTION AND RECOLLECTION OF VERBAL MATERIAL

The electromyograms presented below show clearly that mental reproduction and recollection of verbal material, e.g., the reproduction of phrases just heard or read, of familiar names or terms, the recollection of yesterday's or last week's events is accompanied by rather strong motor speech tensions, alternating with periods when the motor speech organs are at rest (Figs. 36 and 37).

The electromyograms of motor speech potentials also clearly reflect the dependency of recall on the stability of previously formed connections. When the connections are not stable enough, recall is known to turn into a more or less prolonged process of reconstructing that which had been forgotten, where the elements of reasoning acquire great importance.

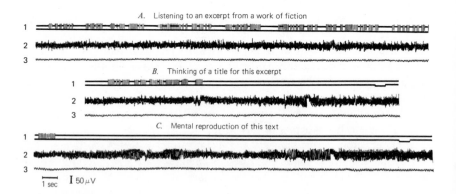

Fig. 34. Increase in the electrical activity of tongue muscles as the tasks become more complex: listening to (A), generalization of (B), and mental reproduction of (C) an excerpt; 1) microphone registration of the experimenter's speech; 2) EMG of the subject's tongue; 3) time interval, 0.1 sec.

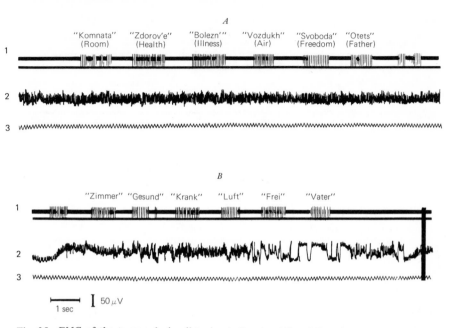

Fig. 35. EMG of the tongue during listening to Russian (A) and German (B) words. In the latter case there arise micromovements of the tongue. Subject Sh., a student. Legend as in Fig. 34.

This is illustrated very well by the following experiment. Subject K., who had been visiting the laboratory for a long time, was asked to remember on what floor she was at the time. This turned out to be difficult for her, and she had, in her words, "to count the floors in her head" in order to answer

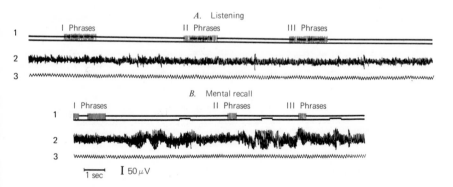

Fig. 36. EMG of the tongue: A) while listening to individual phrases ("The sun is not too bright"; "The trees have no leaves"; "Snowflakes hang from them"); B) while mentally recalling these phrases later on. Legend as in Fig. 35.

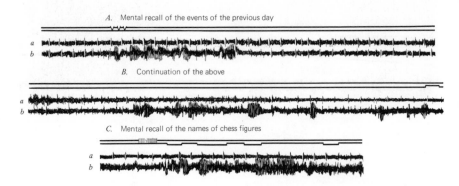

Fig. 37. EMG of the right hand (a) and tongue (b) during mental recall. Volleys of electrical discharges are observed in the tongue muscles, while in the hand muscles they are either absent or very weak (only electrocardiographic impulses are present in a well-defined form).

the question; the amplitude of muscle potentials in the tongue and lips increased sharply at that moment in the oscillogram. Characteristically, the same question asked suddenly four days later did not produce any noticeable increase in motor speech potentials (Fig. 38).

In this case we have exactly the same picture as that obtaining when the subject had to give a mental answer to the question: "Try to figure out on what day of the week will September 1 of this year fall." Initially, the answer to this question was accompanied in the subject by a very large increase in the amplitude of motor speech potentials in the tongue and lips (the subject counted in her head the days of the week); the same question asked again, four days later, produced no increase in the amplitude of motor speech potentials (Fig. 39).

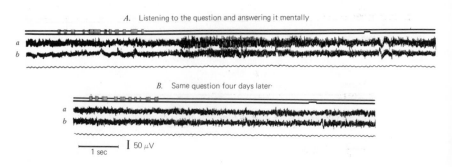

Fig. 38. EMG of the tongue (a) and lower lip (b) while giving a mental answer to the command "Try to remember on what floor you are now" (A) and while answering the same question mentally four days later (B).

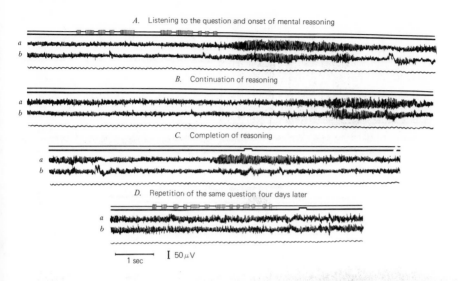

Fig. 39. EMG of the lower lip a) and the tongue b) during mental reasoning provoked by the question "... On what day of the week will September 1 of this year fall?" (A, B, and C) and when the same question was repeated four days later (D).

8. ELECTROMYOGRAMS OF HIDDEN ARTICULATION DURING MANIPULATION OF GRAPHIC-VISUAL MATERIAL

In this series of experiments we recorded motor speech potentials while the subjects performed the following tasks:
1. Imagining objects visually (with the eyes shut);
2. Memorizing a series of drawings on a sheet of paper;
3. Solving a maze problem (visual search for an exit from the maze).

It was found that at the moment of realization of the visual image of an object there was no increase in motor speech tension. Thus, in all cases when the subjects were asked to imagine some object (e.g., a ship), no appreciable change in amplitude was noted on speech oscillograms (Fig. 40A).

Visual memorization of a series of drawings reveals all subjects to be divided into two categories, the "visual type" and the "motor speech type." In subjects of the visual type memorization of a series of drawings is not accompanied by any noticeable increase in muscle tension of the speech apparatus (Fig. 41A).

In the subjects of the motor speech type the muscle tension increases (Fig. 40B).

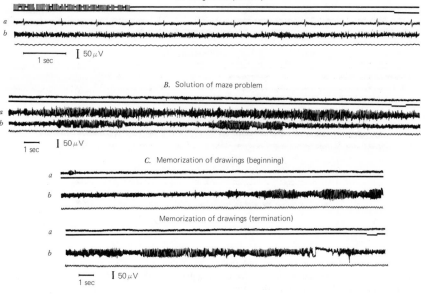

Fig. 40. EMG of the hand a) and tongue b) during visual imagining and maze solving problem. Subject R. When a ship is imagined visually, there is a slow increase in the tone of tongue muscles. The hand EMG shows at this moment nothing but electrocardiographic impulses. When the maze problem is solved visually (the subject had in front of him a maze drawing and was to find the exit, bypassing the dead-ends), electrical activity is seen to take place both in tongue muscles and in hand muscles. The electrical activity of tongue muscle increased markedly when this subject was memorizing a series of drawings.

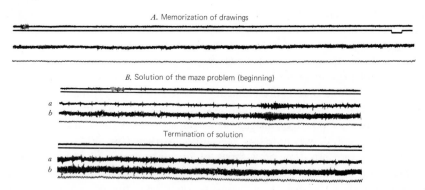

Fig. 41. A) EMG of the tongue during memorization of drawings by subject M. There are no visible changes in the tongue electromyogram during the execution of this task. B) EMG of the right hand (a) and tongue (b) during solution of a maze problem by the same subject. In this case impulses are noted in both the tongue muscles and the hand muscles.

Solution of a maze problem was accompanied by an overall increase of muscle tone in all subjects.

In the experiments of this type the subjects were shown a maze diagram, and they had to point the exit with a pencil. Simultaneously, muscle potentials were recorded from the tongue and the right hand.

9. PRINCIPAL CONCLUSIONS FROM PRELIMINARY EXPERIMENTS

By correlating the data obtained in the different series of experiments, we can draw the following main conclusions concerning the dynamics and functions of inner speech (hidden articulation) in man's intellectual activity.

The kinesthetic speech impulses of hidden articulation, recorded by electrophysiological devices, in the majority of cases do not act continuously or with the same intensity; they act in "volleys," or "bursts," of varying intensity, separated from each other by intervals of greater or lesser duration, when motor speech impulses are either attenuated or absent.

The emergence of strong motor speech impulses of hidden articulation is linked with the verbal fixation of tasks, logical operations on them, retention of the intermediate results of those operations, and the formulation of the final result mentally. All of these facts come to the fore with particular clarity when the tasks to be performed are difficult, i.e., nonstereotyped and multicomponent in composition: arithmetical calculations and problems involving several operations; reading and translating texts in a foreign language by persons without an adequate knowledge of the particular language; paraphrasing of texts (restating them in one's own words); memorization and recall of verbal material; stating thoughts in writing, etc.—that is, in all those cases when the mental activity being performed necessarily involved detailed verbal analysis and synthesis, requiring, therefore, an intensified excitation of the speech centers.

Reduction (diminution) of motor speech impulses occurs during execution of stereotyped tasks, especially if they do not require that intermediate results be kept in one's mind, and during mental replies to the experimenter's questions if they relate to information well known to the subject. Considerable reduction of motor speech impulses is observed when texts are read in one's native tongue, which may be explained, undoubtedly, by the dominating role of the visual components of speech in this case (graphic images of letters and words). The reduction of muscle tensions in the speech apparatus observed in the course of inner speech is thus a complex phenomenon with numerous underlying causes. It can arise as a result of: 1) generalization of mental operations and formation on this basis of verbal and thought stereotypes characteristics of condensed inferences; 2) replacement of the motor speech components by other speech components (auditory, in the case of listening to speech, and visual, in the case of reading); 3) appearance of pictorial components of thought (images of perceptions and ideas).

Appreciable individual differences are found in the functioning of motor speech impulses in inner speech: in some subjects they are quite pronounced, in others, on the contrary, quite weak; they may increase, however, during solution of difficult problems.

It may be assumed on the basis of the material presented that the principal physiological role of motor speech stimuli (proprioceptive afferentation) in the process of intellectual activity probably consists in setting up excitation in the second signal system, which can be regulated voluntarily, thereby maintaining the system's working tonus (speech "dominant") which is necessary for the normal functioning of thought processes. Associated with this is another, mnemonic function of motor speech afferentation, consisting in voluntary fixation of perceived stimuli with their subsequent retrieval from memory with the aid of efferent motor speech impulses.

The aim of subsequent investigations is quantitative analysis of these propositions in greater detail.

Chapter VII

Integrated Electrical Activity of Speech Musculature as an Indicator of Verbal Thought Processes

1. METHOD OF RECORDING AND MEASURING INTEGRATED ELECTRICAL ACTIVITY OF THE SPEECH MUSCULATURE

Despite the fact that modern electromyographic devices make it possible to record very weak muscle action potentials, analysis of electromyograms involves great difficulties, particularly when muscle potentials are detected by means of surface (cutaneous) electrodes. Recorded here is a summated electromyogram, representing the result of excitation interference from the numerous muscle fibers which may be in different phases of excitation and generate impulses of various intensities and frequencies.

The quantitative analysis of electromyograms is usually restricted to approximate comparison of the amplitudes of recorded potentials with those of calibration impulses and a description of the overall picture of the time distribution of recorded impulses. In some cases (with an expanded sweep of electromyograms) it becomes possible also to estimate the number of oscillations. It may be observed, moreover, that the number of oscillations and their amplitudes increase as muscle contractions become stronger. On account of pulse interference, however, the picture may become considerably more complicated depending on the degree of synchrony or asynchrony of excitation on the part of adjacent muscle fibers. When the excitation is synchronous, muscle impulses may fuse together in their like phases, which results in increased amplitudes and decreased frequencies of oscillations. With desynchronization of excitations the amplitudes, on the contrary, diminish and the frequencies increase.

Thus, in analyzing summated electromyograms (especially in case of weak muscular contractions), one should not rely exclusively on the magnitudes of the amplitudes of recorded potentials, so that more stable quantitative indices of the electrical activity in muscles must be searched for. A number of investigators (E. Jacobson, V. Inman and coworkers, O. Lippold,

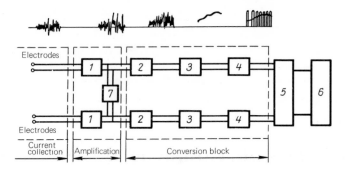

Fig. 42. Block diagram of the integrator of biopotentials: 1) linear amplifier; 2) full-wave rectifier; 3) integrating block; 4) thyratron reducer; 5) power amplification; 6) ink-writing oscillograph; 7) control oscilloscope.

G. A. Shminke, V. S. Gurfinkel') have noted the possibility of measuring the integrated strength of biopotentials, which can be represented planometrically as the area enclosed with the curve of oscillations of biopotentials. The electronic integrators used for this purpose record the summated electrical biocurrent activity and measure it in units of integrated potential, of current intensity, or simply in arbitrary units of electrical activity (in the latter case the integrated intensity of quiescent current is taken as the arbitrary unit of electrical activity).

For our electromyographic investigations of hidden articulation we made use of one such type of biopotential integrator, developed for an electronic hand prosthesis (M. G. Breido, V. S. Gurfinkel', A. E. Kobrinskii, A. Ya. Sysin, and others [35]. The block diagram of the integrator is shown in Fig. 42.

The integrator of biopotentials was hooked to an electromyograph which recorded frequencies from 1 to 1000 Hz. Owing to the presence in the integrator of additional amplifiers, the device designed proved to be sensitive enough to record very weak tonic muscle tensions which arise during ideomotor acts. That this is so is convincingly demonstrated by the adduced electromyograms. Fig. 43 shows a record of muscle potentials with integrator and pulse-counter markings* during actual and imaginary (ideomotor) clenching of a fist; Figs. 44 and 45 show records of muscle potentials of the lower lip during mental arithmetic.

The initial evaluation of electromyograms first of all involved determination of the indices of summated (integrated) electrical activity:

---

* In further experiments we limited ourselves to readings of the integrator of biopotentials alone.

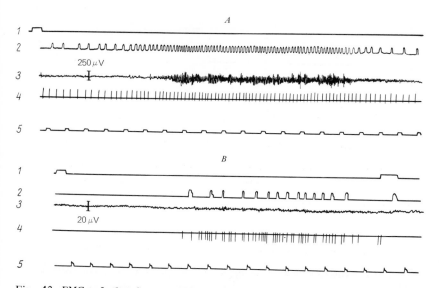

Fig. 43. EMG of the flexor of the right hand during actual (A) and imaginary (B) clenching of the fist: 1) signals marking the beginning and the end of the task; 2) integrator markings; 3) EMG of the right hand; 4) pulse counter markings (conversion coefficient is 1/16 for actual fist clenching and 1/4 for imaginary clenching); 5) time intervals, 1 sec. Recording was done with an ink-writing oscillograph.

1. Summated electrical activity, or total energy, of motor speech excitation, expressed in arbitrary units provided by integrator markings (for short, total energy will henceforth be designated by the symbol A);

2. time of motor speech excitation in seconds (t'');

3. power, or intensity, of motor speech excitation per sec (W).

The intensity was determined by dividing total energy by a time of motor speech excitation $(W = A/t)$ and was expressed as a percentage of the background (state of rest).

When muscular contractions were more or less intense, it was not too difficult to calculate the intensity and energy of motor speech excitation. All that was required here was to count the total number of integrator pulses and the overall solution time for a given problem and to express their ratio as a percentage with respect to background per second. As the background, we took a resting electromyogram of limited duration (5 or 10 sec) and determined mean background intensity* by counting the number of the

---

* With very quick solutions (lasting less than 10 sec), the duration of the background electromyogram was equalized with that of the solution.

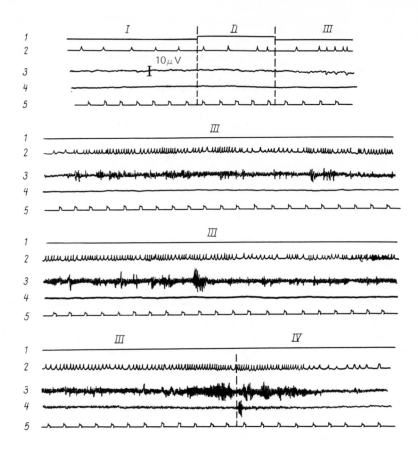

Fig. 44. EMG of the lower lip during mental arithmetic (23×13) ÷ 4. Subject K. (slow calculator). The motor speech reactions are very intense: 1) signals indicating presentation of the task and its execution; 2) integrator markings; 3) EMG of the lower lip; 4) EMG of the right hand; 5) time intervals, 1 sec. Roman numerals designate: I) moment of rest (background); II) moment of auditory perception of task; III) moment of mental solution; IV) signal indicating completion of the task and verbal report of the result.

integrator's background pulses. Subsequently, taking into account the background electrical activity, total energy was determined from the formula $A = W \cdot t''$, where W was expressed as a percentage with respect to background intensity. To make all these indices more reliable, we allowed for permissible deviation from the background within ± 10%.

Thus we obtained relative values, or indices, of electrical activity (in terms of both intensity and total energy) which enabled us to compare the motor speech reactions in different subjects, since the measuring scale was the same in all cases—a percentage ratio with respect to background electrical activity.

When muscular contractions were weak, the method of evaluating the electrical activity recorded became somewhat more complicated, for in such cases the integrator would start to "deliver" its signals with greater time intervals in between (each 1.5-2.0 sec). This being the case and the electromyograms being analyzed second-by-second, it is inevitable that instances occur where there are no integrator signals. However, these cannot be interpreted as signifying a complete absence of motor speech excitation at this moment. The electrical activity of muscles is most likely to be so small at this time (even with maximum amplification of muscle potentials) as to be unable to stand out against the background level. Taking this circumstance into account, a more laborious method must be resorted to in order to calculate the intensity of electrical activity, e.g., by measuring the time intervals between the integrator signals and then interpolating mean intensity per unit time (1 sec).

These calculations are based on the fact that the magnitude of the interval between two adjacent signals of the integrator may be regarded as the time of a signal's "accumulation"—an arbitrary unit of the electrical activity being recorded. It is evident, moreover, that the time of signal accumulation

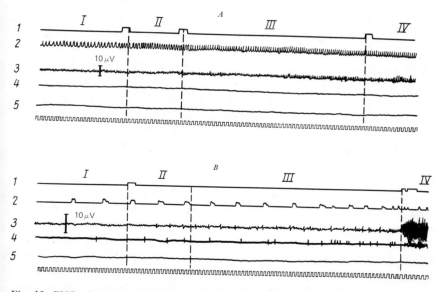

Fig. 45. EMG of the lower lip during mental arithmetic: A) while solving (44×17) ÷ 6; B) while solving (23×13) ÷ 4. Subject P., a student. The motor speech reactions are very faint. Time intervals, 0.25 sec. The rest of designations as in Fig. 44.

varies inversely with the magnitude of total electrical activity; that is, the less the time of signal accumulation the greater is the summated electrical activity. Hence it is not difficult to determine the fraction of a unit of total electrical activity for one second.

The quantitative data obtained were subjected to statistical test by calculating the following: 1) standard (root-mean-square) deviation (σ); 2) standard (quadratic) error (m); 3) coefficient of variability (C); 4) coefficient of rank-correlation $(R_r,$ after Spearman); 5) reliability of mean differences (according to Student-Fisher's t-criterion for small samples). A difference was considered significant if the probability (P) of chance did not exceed 0.05, which corresponds to a reliability of 95% or more [180; 76].

In some cases these statistical criteria were used to compare the results obtained on individual subjects, but for such all the estimates referred to the totality of experiments, which was always sufficient for the statistics of small samples.

2. MEASUREMENT OF INTEGRATED ELECTRICAL ACTIVITY OF THE SPEECH MUSCULATURE DURING MENTAL ARITHMETIC

Let us deal first with the quantitative analysis of the electromyograms taken from two subjects—university students with different aptitudes for mental arithmetical calculations. One of them—subject P.—solves all arithmetical problems three times faster than K., the other subject. Experimenting with these subjects enabled us to find out how a difference in the rates of arithmetical calculations as substantial as this would affect the electromyographic indices of the tonus of speech musculature when those calculations were in progress.

From the results presented in Table 16 it follows that, despite the great difference in the rates of their calculations, both subjects solved arithmetical problems with a great amount of attending motor speech excitation, although no statistically significant difference was found in the intensity of their motor speech excitation (MSE); but the difference in the time and total energy of motor speech excitation was reliable statistically.

The absence of a statistically reliable difference in the intensity of motor speech excitation in these subjects may be explained by its greater variability in subject K. than in subject P. The variability coefficient for the mean intensity of integrated action potentials was 25 for subject P. and 46 for subject K. Hence K., a slow calculator, is characterized by a greater irregularity of motor speech excitation than is the fast calculator, subject P. This is also confirmed by measurements of the maxima and minima of the intensity of motor speech excitation in both subjects. The results of these measurements are shown in Table 17.

TABLE 16. Mean Intensity (W), Time (t''), and Total Energy $(A = W \cdot t'')$ of MSE during Mental Solution of Arithmetical Problems by Subjects P. and K.

Number of problem	Subject P.			Subject K.			Difference		
	W	t''	A	W	t''	A	W	t''	A
1	200	22	4400	300	54	16,200	+100	+32	+11,800
2	188	11	2068	800	59	47,200	+612	+48	+45,132
3	313	7	2191	310	39	12,090	−3	+32	+ 9,899
4	178	7	1246	375	25	9,375	+197	+18	+ 8,129
5	214	28	5992	633	76	48,108	+419	+48	+42,116
M	219	15.0	3180	484	50.6	26,595	+266	+35.6	+23,415
σ	54	9.5	1959	223	18.5	18,793	247	12.7	18,527
C	25	63.4	62	46	35.0	69	13	35.7	79
m	24	4.3	879	100	8.3	8,427	110	5.7	8,271
Reliability of difference							92	>99	96

The table of the maxima and minima of motor speech excitation thus confirms the latter's very irregular character in the mental work (in this case, during mental arithmetic) of both subjects, but particularly of subject K. In view of this fact we deem it possible to distinguish among several different levels of motor speech excitation, basing this differentiation on a statistical criterion—the value of the standard (quadratic) deviation (σ).

TABLE 17. Maxima and Minima of MSE Intensity and Their Difference (d) during Mental Solution of Arithmetical Problems by Subjects P. and K.

Number of problem	Subject P.			Subject K.			Difference	
	max.	min.	d	max.	min.	d	max.	min.
1	269	115	154	625	125	500	+ 356	+10
2	417	119	298	2285	143	1242	+1868	+24
3	625	178	447	1000	100	900	+ 375	−78
4	209	156	53	1000	125	875	+ 791	−31
5	857	143	714	2500	167	2333	+1643	+24
M	475	142	333	1482	132	1350	+1007	−10
σ	267	37	260	849	25	828	707	37
Reliability of difference			96			96	96	40

On the basis of this criterion we can single out the following three levels of motor speech excitation: 1) the highest level, exceeding the sum of the arithmetic mean and the standard deviation of the intensity of motor speech excitation ($> M + \sigma$); 2) medium level, equal in magnitude to the arithmetic mean of motor speech excitation plus or minus the standard deviation ($= M \pm \sigma$); 3) lower level, falling below the difference between the arithmetic mean of the intensity of motor speech excitation and the standard deviation ($< M - \sigma$).

Table 18 gives the values of the power, time, and total energy of motor speech excitation, calculated according to the levels of its intensity for subjects P. and K. Table 19 shows the statistical reliability of the difference obtained for the levels of motor speech excitation in these subjects.

It follows from these tables that the medium level of motor speech excitation is the most stable one in terms of all indices of electrical activity.

TABLE 18.   The Intensity, Time, and Total Energy for the Various Levels of MSE in Subjects P. and K. during Mental Solution of Arithmetical Problems

Number of problem	MSE level	Subject P.			Subject K.		
		W	t''	A	W	t''	A
1	High	269	1	269	538	10	5,380
	Medium	212	17	3604	300	32	9,600
	Low	142	4	568	125	12	1,500
2	High	417	1	417	1600	10	16,000
	Medium	168	10	1680	757	37	28,009
	Low	0	0	0	257	12	3,084
3	High	625	1	625	510	10	5,100
	Medium	250	6	1500	320	29	9,280
	Low	0	0	0	0	0	0
4	High	206	3	618	688	6	4,128
	Medium	0	0	0	350	12	4,200
	Low	156	4	624	125	7	875
5	High	614	3	1842	1617	11	17,787
	Medium	171	25	4275	483	65	31,395
	Low	0	0	0	0	0	0
	High	426	1.8*	754*	991	9.4**	9,679**
	Medium	160*	11.8*	2212*	442**	35.0**	16,496**
	Low	59	1.6	238	101	6.2	1,092

Note: one asterisk designates the mean values of MSE in the first subject, which yield statistically significant differences with the corresponding values of MSE in the second subject (marked by two asterisks). The results of a statistical analysis of these differences are given in Table 19.

TABLE 19. Statistical Reliability of Mean Differences Given in Table 18.

Measurement parameters	MSE level	Difference	σ of difference	m of difference	Reliability of differences
W	High	+ 565	469	209	92
	Medium	+ 282*	214	96	96
	Low	+ 42	100	45	55
t	High	+ 7.6*	2.60	1.16	>99
	Medium	+ 232.2*	10.68	4.78	>99
	Low	+ 4.6	5.27	2.36	85
A	High	+ 8,925*	6,271	2812	96
	Medium	+14,284*	11,429	5125	96
	Low	+ 854	1,304	585	75

Note: asterisks mark statistically significant differences.

The major portion of the time and energy of motor speech excitation is expended at this level, but the level's magnitude varies from subject to subject. The indices characterizing the medium level of subject K. exceeded those of subject P. by the following amounts: intensity, by 272%; time, by 302%; total energy, by 746%. At the higher level, statistically significant are found to be the differences in terms of time and total energy; at the lower level the indices showed no significant differences.

From the point of view of the neurodynamics of thought processes, the singling out of the motor speech excitation levels listed above is of interest in that it allows one to relate them to the levels of difficulty in reasoning, and to regard them as objective physiological indicators of those difficulties (when these are great the level of electrical activity goes up; when difficulties are absent, the electrical activity goes down). Also, the above differences in the levels of electrical activity evidently are connected not only with peripheral but with central (cerebral) processes as well, and as such they may serve as indices of the neurodynamics of thought processes.

In connection with that presented above, it is of interest to examine a few charts of motor speech excitation recorded during the mental solution of arithmetical problems by our subjects.

Fig. 46 shows two graphs of motor speech excitation in subject K. while calculating mentally $(23 \times 13) \div 4$, and in subject P. while he was calculating the result of $(44 \times 17) \div 6$. The electromyograms with markings made by the integrator of recorded potentials, on the basis of which the graphs being analyzed have been plotted, are shown in Figs. 44 and 45.

At the moment of the auditory perception of the task subject K. displayed a marked inhibitory orienting reaction, replaced by a progressively

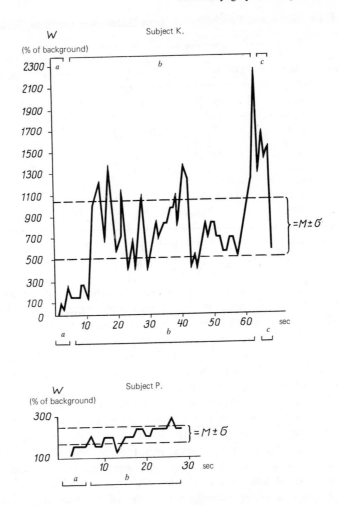

Fig. 46. Graphs indicating the intensity of the motor speech responses of subjects K. and P. during mental arithmetic [(23×13) ÷ 4 and (44×17) ÷ 6]. The graphs were plotted on the basis of the integrated EMGs shown in Figs. 45 and 46. Horizontal dotted lines indicate the intensity levels of motor speech responses. The medium level is marked by braces. Brackets along the absciassa designate the successive moments of solution: a) auditory perception of the problem; b) mental solution; c) articulation of the answer aloud or in a whisper.

increasing motor speech excitation which, however, turns out to be unstable and fluctuates all the time, now waxing, now waning, during the entire solution period of a given task.

Such intensity fluctuations of motor speech excitation represent a rather characteristic pattern of the neurodynamics of mental problem solving. This pattern may undergo considerable changes, depending on the complexity of the given task and the acquired habits of problem solving, but the main factor—the alternating waxing and waning of the level of motor speech excitation—is there whenever the task presented offers difficulties of any kind for the subject's reasoning capacity. And indeed, the graphs representing subject P.'s motor speech excitation, (his habits of mental problem solving are, as we know, more automatized), point to a much lesser intensity of motor speech excitation; yet the intensity of the latter are observed here too, although in a lesser degree than they are in subject K.

Among the arithmetical problems presented to subjects P. and K., three were of a more complex nature (1, 2 and 5) and two (3 and 4) were quite simple; the latter were solved more rapidly by both subjects and, using the most stable and statistically reliable mean level of motor speech excitation (see Table 18), with less motor speech excitation than the former. Thus, these random samples allow the conclusion that the intensity of motor speech excitation is a function of the complexity of the problems being solved: the more complex the problems (in this case, the greater the number of mental operations required for their solution), the greater is the intensity of motor speech excitation. Later on we shall present a number of other data confirming this conclusion.

In the next experiment, the intensity of motor speech excitation attending mental solution of the simplest arithmetical problems by second-grader D., who found them more or less difficult, was compared with the same factor in university student L., who solved the same problems without any difficulties, almost automatically. The problems were read by the experimenter, and the results were written down by the subjects themselves (silently).

The quantitative data presented in Table 20 refer to the interval of mental problem solving (prior to the writing down of the answers) by the subjects. The table makes it clear that during the solution of these problems the intensity of motor speech excitation exceeded the background level, on the average, by 87% in the second-grader and only by 12% in the university student. The maximum upswings of intensity reached 633% in the school pupil and 175% in the student, in relation to the base level; the minimum downswings of intensity were 100 and 90%, respectively. Taking into account our background-correction of ± 10%, the student solved 10 problems out of 15 without marked motor speech excitation, while the school pupil solved only three.

This difference in the degree of motor speech excitation displayed by the pupil and the student can have only one explanation: a difference in the degree to which their arithmetical operations are automatized. A definite indication of this is the considerably longer duration of the solution of each problem in the school pupil than in the university student (the mean duration

TABLE 20. Intensity of MSE Attending Mental Solution of the
Same Problems by Second-grader D. and Student L.

Problems	Pupil D.		Student L.		Difference	
	t''	W	t''	W	t''	W
3+2	5.25	200	1.25	100	+ 4.00	+100
5+3	3.75	633	2.25	124	+ 1.50	+509
11+5	10.00	160	2.50	94	+ 7.50	+ 66
4+3	6.50	137	1.50	103	+ 5.00	+ 34
14+5	10.00	300	2.25	125	+ 7.75	+175
8-2	5.00	200	2.00	97	+ 3.00	+103
17-5	11.00	100	2.75	90	+ 8.25	+ 10
16-3	16.25	100	1.75	93	+14.50	+ 7
18-7	11.00	107	2.00	140	+ 9.00	- 33
14-9	6.75	118	2.00	175	+ 4.75	- 57
20-13	6.25	112	2.75	132	+ 3.50	- 20
4x3	8.50	176	2.00	102	+ 6.50	+ 74
8x2	5.00	143	2.25	110	+ 2.75	+ 33
4x5	7.00	166	2.25	104	+ 4.75	+ 62
23x3	11.00	150	2.25	94	+ 8.75	+ 56
M, mean	8.22	187	2,12	112	+ 6.10	+ 75
σ of difference					3.31	125
m of difference					0.85	32
Reliability of difference					>99	96

of the solution of a single problem was 8.22 sec for the second-grader and
2.12 sec for the student). Thus, the level of motor speech excitation evidently
is in inverse proportion to the automatization of mental operations: the
greater the degree to which mental operations are automatized, the weaker is
motor speech excitation. The graph in Fig. 47 demonstrates this quite clearly.
From the psychophysiological point of view, the lowering of electrical activity
apparently is related to the concentration of the excitatory process in definite,
locally circumscribed points of the brain's speech structures, whereas an
increase in electrical activity is associated with a generalization of the
excitatory process and its spreading to a broader region of the cerebral end of
the motor speech analyzer.

According to the averaged data from analogous experiments conducted
with a group of first-graders (the group contained three boys and two girls 7
to 8 years old), the tension was greatest during the solution of the first five
arithmetical problems (at this time the electrical activity was more than 8
times as high as that at base level); then it dropped somewhat, but
subsequently it started again to rise. These data are presented in Table 21.

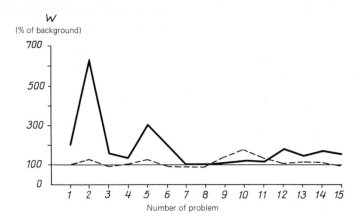

Fig. 47. Graphs of the intensity of motor speech responses during mental solution of the same arithmetical problems by school pupil D. (solid line) and university student L. (dotted line). Data from the processing of electromyograms of the lower lip.

Of interest are the results of the experiments during which motor speech excitation was recorded while subjects were performing maximally automatized mental operations, e.g., a mental sequential count. In these experiments the subjects were asked to count silently from 1 to 10, and then to pause slightly. The task was repeated several times in a row. The subjects were next asked to count-down silently (from 10 to 1); this too was repeated several times with intervening short pauses. Thereupon the subjects passed to a sequential count involving different numbers (e.g., from 42 to 53 and back

TABLE 21. Magnitude of the Integrated Electrical Activity of Tongue Muscles during Mental Solution of Arithmetical Problems by First-Graders*

Subject	Sequential numbers of arithmetical problems					
	1-5	6-10	11-15	16-20	21-25	26-30
1	1274	879	792	767	736	616
2	937	787	709	963	432	825
3	918	455	445	689	423	632
4	552	381	496	283	751	734
5	520	368	464	310	672	−
Mean	840	574	581	602	607	702

*In percent of background.

from 53 to 42), and so on. The EMG of the lower lip was recorded. Prior to the start of experiments the measuring apparatus was adjusted to zero level.

The zero adjustment was done only to make the values being compared more vivid, but since this was done at the expense of the apparatus' sensitivity, no absolute value can be assigned to zero readings here. The intensity of electrical activity was determined by counting the integrator's signals and dividing their total number by the time spent in performing a corresponding task.

The results of these experiments are given in graphs (Figs. 48 and 49). They are of interest not only because they demonstrate a rapid decrease (reduction) of motor speech excitation on repetition of the same mental operations, but also because transition to new operations, even though the latter be sufficiently automatized, at first produces a short-lived intensification of motor speech excitation, followed by its rapid decline. Such an increase in motor speech excitation during transition to new mental operations evidently may be explained by the fact that additional neurons of the motor speech analyzer become excited at this moment (or additional systems of neural connections between this analyzer and other analyzers of the brain), this closing or switching of nervous connections, in which other neurons become involved, being accompanied by a short-lived intensification of their electrical activity.

Since transition from mental operations of one kind to mental operations of another kind involves selection of adequate acts from a series of possibilities, the raised electrical activity observed in the speech musculature in such cases indicates that a switch to a mental operation of a different type

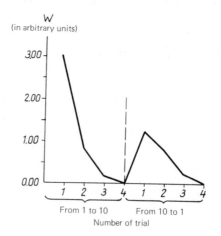

Fig. 48. Graph of the integrated electrical activity of the lower lip in Subject L. during mental count from 1 to 10 and from 10 to 1.

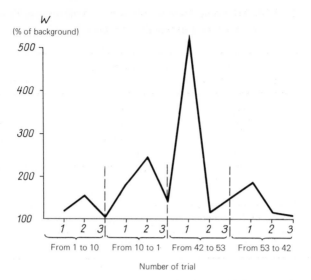

Fig. 49. Graph of the integrated electrical activity of the lower lip in subject D. (second-grader) during transition from one counting sequence to another.

remains under conscious control even when all subsequent operations are maximally automatized.

From these considerations it may be assumed that the more complex the task, i.e., the greater the number of operations and switchings to other operations required for solution, the greater the intensity of motor speech excitation. In general, this was confirmed by our first experiments on subjects P. and K. when they had to solve both simple and more complicated arithmetical problems.

In addition to these data we deemed it necessary to set up special experiments in which subjects had to solve two sets of arithmetical problems known to involve different numbers of operations. The results of one such experiment are described below.

Subject R., a university student, had to solve mentally two sets of arithmetical problems. The first set consisted of five problems involving one- and two-digit numbers; the second set, two- and three-digit numbers. The electromyogram of the tongue was recorded (the answer and course of solution were recorded by the subject himself).

The quantitative results of this experiment are presented in Table 22. They indicate that during the solution of the first set of problems the electrical activity of the speech musculature increased, on the average, by 138% and during the solution of the second (more complicated) set by 221%.

TABLE 22. MSE Attending Mental Solution of Arithmetical Problems
of Varying Complexity (Subject R.)

First set of problems	MSE (% of background)	Second set of problems	MSE (% of background)
44+8	150	895 ÷ 15	166
37−9	125	288 ÷ 12	250
42 : 6	120	658 ÷ 56	169
34×8	157	(96 ÷ 32) × 24	213
43×4	140	(378 + 534) ÷ 16	320
Mean (M)	138		221
Difference	σ of difference	m of difference	P
83	46.68	29.41	0.05−0.02

Thus, it is evident that both the degree to which mental operations are automatized and the degree of complexity of the operations being performed can be assessed with a high degree of probability on the basis of the intensity of hidden motor speech reactions. It should also be emphasized that even when the automatism of mental operations is at a maximum, motor speech excitation does not disappear completely: it remains, as it were, on guard for protection of automatism, manifesting itself whenever the latter is disturbed and whenever there is transition to novel mental operations.

The intensity of motor speech potentials during mental arithmetical problem solving is affected strongly by the manner of presentation of problems: for auditory presentation, the electrical activity level of the speech musculature was almost twice as high as it was for visual presentation (in the former case arithmetical problems were delivered over a microphone, in the latter the subject received them in written form). The results of these experiments are summarized in Table 23, and their explanation is quite evident: when arithmetical problems are presented acoustically, they have to be retained in memory by means of additional, silent enunciation; whereas with visual presentation this is necessary to a much lesser extent, with the result that the electrical activity of the speech musculature is lowered.

3. MEASUREMENT OF THE INTEGRATED ELECTRICAL ACTIVITY OF THE SPEECH MUSCULATURE DURING SILENT READING OF TEXTS

The ability to read to oneself is achieved as a result of rather long training, the initial stage consists of reading aloud, and is followed by reading

TABLE 23. Time of Solution (t'') and Intensity of Integrated Electrical Activity (W)* of the Speech Musculature with Visual and Auditory Presentation of Arithmetical Problems

Subject	Visual presentation		Auditory presentation	
	t''	W	t''	W
K.	30.9	107	31.0	310
O.	82.6	137	74.9	164
M.	45.8	160	18.2	306
L.	45.0	105	49.1	173
Mean	54.1	127	43.3	238
Reliability of difference, %	with respect to solution time		35	
	with respect to electrical activity		96.5	

*In percent of background.
Note: each series of these tests involved solution of 15 problems.

in a whisper. Reading to oneself emerges gradually later on and is characterized not only by its soundlessness but also by a very complex organization of all the processes of perception and thought, which enables one to grasp rapidly the individual graphical elements of letters, to synthesize them into whole words and phrases and to comprehend the meaning of the material read. As a matter of fact, the soundlessness of reading signifies automatization and curtailment (abbreviation) of verbal thought processes, and this is what makes it possible to translate almost instantaneously the visually-perceived graphemes into silently enunciated (inner) speech.

It is also known that the picture changes drastically when reading involves more difficult texts, such as texts in a foreign language insufficiently mastered, or texts containing obscure terminology and concepts: from the almost instantaneous act of perceiving and comprehending a text, reading turns into a quite detailed discursive process, not too different from mathematical problem solving. By varying texts in terms of difficulty, we obtain the means of studying the dynamics of hidden motor speech reactions with varying degrees of automatism of reading, and of determining quantitative indices of their electrical activity.

In these experiments, subjects (university students and scientific workers) were instructed to read silently texts in their native (Russian) and a foreign (English) language which they were studying. The subjects were warned that following the reading of each text they would have to relate its contents. The texts were usually broken down into phrases, and the integrated electrical activity was calculated for each phrase separately and for the text as a whole. In addition, estimations of time and magnitude of integrated electrical activity were made for each typographical unit, which enabled us to compare the results of experiments involving reading of texts differing in length. Since these experiments were conducted on new subjects, they could be presented with the same texts which had been used in the preliminary experiments described earlier. The principal Russian text used was an excerpt from I. S. Turgenev's short story "Bezhin Meadow." It consisted of seven sentences with a total of 797 typographical units. English excerpts were taken from American literature: an adapted excerpt from M. Dodge's novel *The Silver Skates,* consisting of seven sentences with 487 typographical units, and a rather complicated, in terms of grammatical structure and contents, excerpt from O'Henry's short story "Squaring the Circle," consisting of five sentences with 342 typographical units. These texts are presented below.

Russian text (excerpt from Turgenev's short story "Bezhin Meadow")

1. "It was a splendid day in July, one of those days which occur only during a long spell of fine weather."
2. "Since earliest morning the sky is clear; the dawn glow does not glow with fire; it diffuses itself like a gentle blush."
3. "The sun is not fiery, not incandescent as in time of stifling draught, not dull purple, as before a storm, but bright and affably radiant, rises peacefully from under a narrow and lengthy cloud, shines out freshly and then pledges into its lilac haze. The thin upper rim of the distended cloudlet flashes in little snakes of light; their gleam is like the gleam of wrought silver."
5. "But now the playful rays have again flashed forth—and majestically and with joy, as though winging upward, the mighty luminary rises."
6. "About noontime a host of round, high clouds usually appears, golden-grey, with soft white edges."
7. "Like islands scattered over a river in infinite flood that runs around them in deeply transparent channels of uniform blue, they scarcely stir."

Adapted English text (excerpt from M. Dodge's novel *The Silver Skates*)

1. "Hans and Gretel on the ice."
2. "On a cold December morning two poorly dressed children, Hans and Gretel, were standing on the bank of a frozen canal in Holland."
3. "It was still very early and almost all the people of the little Dutch town of Broek were asleep."
4. "Only some peasant women skated along the canal, with heavy baskets on their heads."
5. "The two children, who were brother and sister, wanted to skate a little before their mother called them home."
6. "They were so poor that they had only wooden skates."
7. "The children tied those wooden skates to their feet with strings and skated as well as they could."

Complicated English text (excerpt from O'Henry's short story "Squaring the Circle")

1. "Squaring the Circle."
2. "At the hazard of wearying you this tale of vehement emotions must be prefaced by a discourse on geometry."
3. "Nature moves in circles; art is straight lines."
4. "The natural is rounded; the artificial is made up of angles."

5. "A man lost in the snow wanders, in spite of himself, in perfect circles; the city man's feet, denaturalized by rectangular streets and floors, carry him ever away from himself."

As in the experiments with arithmetical problem solving, we encounter here great individual differences both with respect to the rate of silent reading and to the intensity of the attendant motor speech reactions. The overall dynamics of motor speech excitation are likewise preserved, said excitation being undoubtedly present during the silent reading of all the texts (including those in mother tongue), accompanied by changes in the intensity of the excitation dependent on the complexity of the text read.

Most illustrative in this respect are the data obtained in the experiments with subjects B. and M., university students with differing rates of silent reading in their mother tongue and with approximately the same (elementary) knowledge of English, a subject of their study. Table 24 gives these subjects' rates of silent reading in Russian and in English. It may be seen from the table that there is an appreciable difference in the reading rates in the Russian language and an absence of such for the English language, since the English texts were equally difficult to understand for both subjects (particularly the excerpt from O'Henry's short story).

Tables 25 and 26 summarize the results of detailed processing of the electromyograms obtained (the indices of the electrical activity in the tongue and lower-lip muscles were averaged to obtain greater accuracy) and present estimates of the statistical reliability of differences in the intensity of motor speech excitation during the silent reading of the above texts.

The data presented in the tables and the charts based upon them (Fig. 50) make it evident that silent reading of all the texts, including those in the mother tongue, was accompanied by intensified (relative to background) electrical activity of the speech musculature. This refers to all indices of hidden motor speech reactions—their intensity, time, and total energy.

Silent reading of English texts was accompanied by considerable increase in electrical activity. This was the case with both adapted and complicated

TABLE 24. Silent Reading Times (in seconds) for Subjects B. and M.

Text	Subject B.	Subject M.	Difference	Percent of reliability*
Russian	34.75	44.25	+ 9.50	96
English, adapted	69.00	83.50	+14.50	92
English, complicated	66.50	63.50	− 3.00	35

* Reliability of the difference in reading rates was calculated on the basis of the reading-time difference ratio for individual sentences of each text (see Table 25).

TABLE 25. Intensity, Time, and Total Energy of MSE during Silent Reading by Subjects B. and M.

Sentences	Number of typographical units	Subject B.				Subject M.			
		W	t'' of sentence	t'' of unit	A of unit	W	t'' of sentence	t'' of unit	A of unit

Sentences	Number of typographical units	W	t'' of sentence	t'' of unit	A of unit	W	t'' of sentence	t'' of unit	A of unit
Russian text (797 typographical units)									
1	98	125	3.50	0.036	4.57	142	6.75	0.069	9.78
2	85	138	4.00	0.047	6.49	217	4.75	0.056	12.13
3	196	127	7.25	0.037	4.70	208	10.75	0.055	12.24
4	93	145	4.50	0.048	7.02	200	5.00	0.054	10.75
5	89	121	4.50	0.051	6.12	291	3.50	0.039	11.44
6	101	170	4.25	0.042	7.15	291	5.50	0.055	15.85
7	135	167	6.75	0.050	8.36	228	8.00	0.059	13.51
Mean	114	142	4.96	0.044	6.34	225	6.32	0.055	12.24
English text, adapted (487 typographical units)									
1	22	310	3.50	0.159	49.32	433	3.75	0.170	73.81
2	106	270	11.50	0.108	29.29	633	14.25	0.134	85.09
3	78	281	10.75	0.138	38.73	708	14.25	0.183	129.34
4	69	279	7.75	0.112	31.34	758	14.75	0.214	162.04
5	90	170	14.75	0.164	27.86	958	17.00	0.189	180.95
6	42	253	7.50	0.179	45.18	984	8.00	0.190	184.43
7	80	238	13.25	0.166	39.42	858	11.50	0.144	123.34
Mean	70	257	9.86	0.147	37.31	762	11.93	0.175	134.14
English text, complicated (342 typographical units)									
1	18	279	4.00	0.222	62.00	152	6.00	0.333	50.67
2	88	204	14.00	0.159	32.45	302	16.00	0.170	54.90
3	39	210	7.50	0.192	40.38	291	8.00	0.205	59.69
4	50	200	11.00	0.220	44.00	439	9.50	0.190	83.41
5	147	153	30.00	0.204	31.22	559	24.00	0.163	91.27
Mean	68	209	13.30	0.199	42.01	349	12.70	0.212	67.99

texts and, strange as it may seem; particularly with adapted texts. This circumstance may be explained by the fact that nonadapted English texts turned out to be too difficult for our subjects, requiring recourse to a dictionary; without the latter all the subjects could do was to read the text cursorily and separate familiar words without comprehending the meaning of the excerpt as a whole.

If we now turn to a second-by-second analysis of the electrical activity of the motor speech reactions accompanying silent reading of various texts,

TABLE 26. Statistical Reliability of Mean Differences in MSE Indices for Subjects B. and M. during Silent Reading

Compared Texts	Subject	W		t″		A	
		Difference	Reliability of difference	Difference	Reliability of difference	Difference	Reliability of difference
Russian, adapted English	B.	+115	>99	+0.103	>99	+ 30.97	>99
	M.	+536	>99	+120	>99	+121.90	>99
Russian, complicated English	B.	+ 67	>99	+0.155	>99	+ 35.67	>99
	M.	+124	92	+0.157	>99	+ 55.75	>99
Complicated English and adapted English	B.	− 34	75	+0.052	>99	+ 4.70	55
	M.	−466	>99	+0.037	75	− 71.97	98

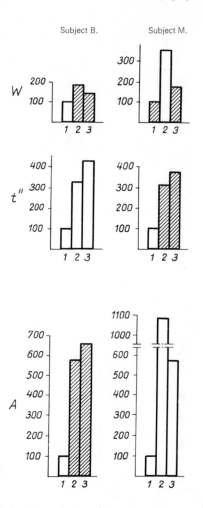

Fig. 50. Comparison of the electromyographic indices of motor speech excitation during silent reading of various texts: W, mean intensity; t'', time; A, total energy of motor speech excitation (W and A were calculated per typographical unit of each text). The electromyographic indices recorded during the reading of the Russian text were taken as 100%. 1) Russian text; 2) English text, adapted; 3) English text, complicated. Hatching indicates indices with statistically insignificant differences.

we shall obtain very characteristic data, indicating that in this case, also, fluctuations in the intensity of motor speech excitation and partial inhibition (that is, waxing and waning of the electrical activity of speech musculature) are as great here as those observed with arithmetical problem solving. Three graphs of this kind are shown in Figs. 51 and 52.

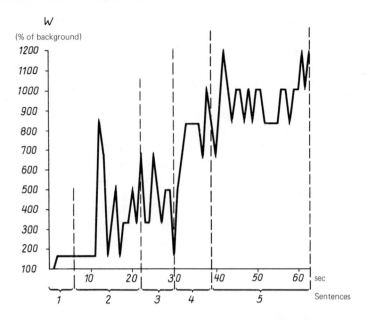

Fig. 51. Graph of the integrated electrical activity of the lower lip and tongue (averaged readings for both indices) during silent reading of a foreign (English) text. The moments of cessation of reading of each sentence are marked by vertical dotted lines. Not only the gradual increase in tonus of the speech musculature but its fluctuations during the reading of each sentence can be distinctly seen. Subject M., a student.

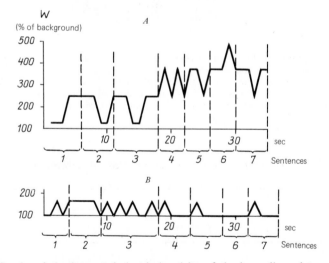

Fig. 52. Graphs of the integrated electrical activity of the lower lip and tongue during the first (A) and repeated (B) silent reading of a text in the native (Russian) language. Vertical dotted line marks off the reading time for each sentence. Subject L., a student.

The first graph (Fig. 51) refers to a complicated English text read silently by subject M. and reflects gradual intensification of motor speech excitation and fluctuations in its intensity during reading. To a lesser degree, but clear enough, a similar picture is also found in the second graph, which reflects the dynamics of motor speech excitation during the first reading of a Russian text by subject L. (Fig. 52A). When the same subject rereads the Russian text, the motor speech excitation is very weak (there even being moments when it disappears altogether) (Fig. 52B).

In contradistinction, repeated reading of the text with the instruction, "Reread it more attentively" or "Memorize it more accurately" results in an intensification of motor speech excitation as compared to the first reading of the text without instructions of this kind (Fig. 53).

Finally, let us note once more that in these experiments, too, the electrical activity of motor speech reactions was found to vary considerably from subject to subject; for example, in subject B. those reactions were less intense than in subject M. (see Table 27).

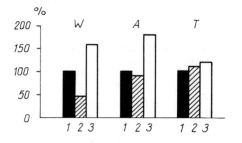

Fig. 53. Comparison of the electromyographic indices of motor speech excitation of subject L. during reading and rereading silently of the same text. The indices obtained during the first reading were taken as 100%. *W*, intensity; *A*, total energy; *T*, time of reading; 1) first reading of Russian text; 2) repeated reading of the same text without special instructions; 3) subsequent reading of the same text with the instruction, "Reread it more attentively."

TABLE 27. Differences in the Indices of MSE of Subjects B. and M.

Text	*W*		*A*	
	Difference	Reliability of difference, %	Difference	Reliability of difference, %
Russian	+ 83	>99	+ 5.98	>99
English, adapted	+505	>99	+96.83	>99
English, complicated	+140	92	+25.99	96

Despite the considerable difference in these subjects' motor speech reactions, however, the latter remain marked in both subjects, and this not only in the case of texts in an unfamiliar foreign language but also in the case of texts in the native language. It may be asserted, thcrefore, that silent reading is always accompanied by motor speech tensions of varying intensity, depending on the complexity of texts and on reading habits. There is no significant difference between mental arithmetical problem solving and reading to oneself in this respect. Both represent verbal mental operations, and these are impossible without a hidden articulation of words, if only in a very reduced form.

In the next chapter we are going to show to what extent these conclusions are valid for the concrete form of thinking.

Chapter VIII

Electrical Activity of the Speech Musculature in Concrete Thinking

1. ISSUES AND METHODS OF THE ELECTROMYOGRAPHICAL INVESTIGATION OF CONCRETE THINKING

Proceeding from Pavlov's theses concerning the unity and interconnection of the two signal systems—visual-concrete and speech [119: 476]—it may be assumed that they act jointly not only in the case of abstract, verbal thinking but also in the case of so-called objective, or concrete, thinking which operates directly with the material being perceived (usually of the visual, graphic type); the results of this type of thinking, too, can be expressed in a first signal, graphically perceived form.

Little light has been shed so far, however, on the interrelation between the visual and speech signal systems as far as concrete thinking is concerned. Neither the psychology nor the physiology of higher nervous activity have as yet at their disposal any fairly accurate experimental data pertaining to this issue. The principal explanation of this is that, in concrete thinking, vocalized speech is usually inhibited and replaced by inner speech, i.e., soundless verbal reactions which still represent an almost inaccessible region for investigation by objective methods.

Even in those few instances where attempts have been made in psychology and neurophysiology to study inner speech by objective electrophysiological methods, the object of investigation was for the most part reasoning acts of a verbal type, such as reading and enunciating to oneself individual words and phrases, solving arithmetical problems, etc. As for the problems of a graphic-pictorial type, i.e., problems whose basic data do not include any verbal designations or formulations (except the general instruction to find, point to, or do something) have remained almost untouched by investigation, apart from the isolated data contained in the first works by E. Jacobson and L. Max. And yet it is precisely these problems which pose many crucial questions to be tested experimentally.

First of all, is it really absolutely necessary to have recourse to verbal acts, such as naming, logical definition, and reasoning if the object of reasoning activity is being perceived directly at a given moment, the thought operations being restricted to visual analysis and synthesis of the object's parts, or is the participation of verbal (i.e., abstract and generalized) symbolization nevertheless required in cases like these? For instance, does the designer, the control panel operator, the driver, or the chess-player have to verbalize his acts, if only in a concealed, soundless form? If such verbalization is observed, is it always necessary? What function does it perform? These are questions to which psychology has as yet no well-substantiated answers, although their elucidation would be of great importance not only for a theoretical analysis of the complex and extremely intricate problem of the relationship between speech and thought but also for control over the mechanisms of our practical, operational thinking, where concrete perceptions and representations, speech and actions are interwoven in complex interactions.

Introspective psychology, which deals with analysis of the states of consciousness only, does not enable us to form very accurate judgments concerning the dynamics of interrelationships between the concrete and speech components of thinking activity, since during an intense external activity, especially motor activity, inner speech usually ceases to be noticed.

Nor is this shortcoming of the introspective analysis of inner speech compensated for sufficiently by the other method, very common in psychology—that of thinking aloud, where the subjects are required to verbalize all their mental acts for the purpose of being recorded by the experimenter. Since in this case verbalization acquires a compulsory character, it cannot be known whether it would have arisen in the absence of this factor. In addition, vocalized speech usually unfolds much more slowly than does inner, silent speech; hence, a substantial portion of the speech process, which precedes its external expression, again remains elusive.

Electromyographic methods offer much greater possibilities for objective study of speech. First among them is electromyographic recording of the tonus of the speech musculature (tongue, lips, and larynx), which, as we have seen, increases noticeably with silent enunciation of words and with mental solution of verbal problems. Would hidden motor speech reactions of this kind arise during the solution of concrete (nonverbal) problems whose basic premises can be presented directly, in a visual manner? If these reactions manifest themselves, at what particular moments do they arise and under what conditions? And, finally, is it possible to assess, on the basis of an analysis of electromyographic speech reactions, the neurodynamic interrelations between the two signal systems in the process of concrete thinking, and the role played by the speech system in this process?

To elucidate these questions, we used Raven's Progressive Matrices Test [261] as our experimental material. The matrices are made up of several series of problems of gradually increasing complexity, involving concrete thinking by analogy. Each matrix consists of two parts: a) a principal drawing (some meaningless figure or a combination of such figures) with a blank space in the right lower corner and b) a set of 6 to 8 pieces placed next to the drawing; one piece has to be elected so as to fit exactly into the blank space of the main pattern. Examples of matrix problems can be seen in Figs. 54 and 55.

The progressive matrices are divided into five series (A, B, C, D, and E), each containing 12 matrices (a total of 60 matrix problems). Series A and B are the simplest, the subsequent ones are of increasing complexity. The gradual increase in complexity is also present within each series: they all begin

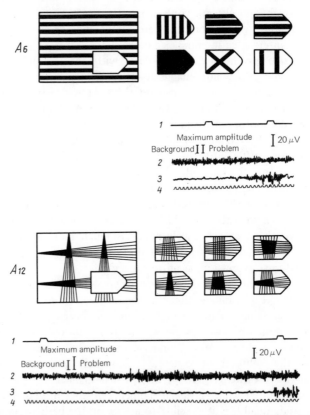

Fig. 54. Examples of Raven's matrix problems (A6 and A12) and EMG of the lower lip of subject K., recorded during the solution of these problems in preliminary experiments: 1) signal marking the beginning and termination of solution of a problem; 2) EMG of lower lip; 3) EMG of right hand (bursts of hand muscle potentials occurring at the end of solution are related to movements of the hand when the latter points with a pencil to the element selected to fill the blank in the principal pattern of the matrix); 4) time interval, 0.25 sec.

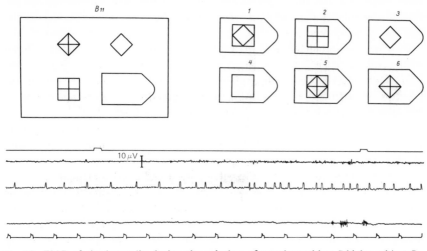

Fig. 55. EMG of the lower lip during the solution of matrix problem B11 by subject P. (from the main test series): 1) signals marking the beginning and the end of problem solving; 2) EMG of the lower lip; 3) integrator signals; 4) EMG of right hand (hand muscle potentials are recorded at the moment of pointing to the fragment selected); 5) time interval, 1 sec.

with simple and end with more complex matrices. This graduated structure of matrix problems makes it possible to investigate the various forms of concrete thinking, from the direct grasping of the identity and difference of the figures being compared to a discursive establishment of their relationships by means of somewhat detailed reasoning. It was precisely for this reason that we made use of Raven's progressive matrices as suitable experimental material for electromyographic study of inner speech in concrete problem solving, disregarding the testological value usually ascribed to these matrices. As in the preceding experiments, speech electromyograms were recorded with the aid of electrodes attached to the lower lip. The GSR and, in some of the experiments, occipitotemporal and Rolandic electroencephalograms were recorded simultaneously. The total magnitude of electrical activity was determined on the basis of the markings made by the biopotential integrator.

The subject was placed in a room with normal illumination, screened from external electrical interference. He would sit comfortably in a chair, to the arms of which was fixed a writing board with sheets of matrices, 18X24 cm in format. The matrices were supplied or removed by the experimenter's assistant present in the same room. The first matrix (A1) was presented first, and the subject was instructed in the following manner: "Look at this figure (the principal pattern of the matrix was pointed to). One piece in it is missing. Now take a look at the lower pieces. Among them there is one that fits precisely into the upper figure and can fill the blank space in it. You must state which one fits the upper figure and the reason why all the rest do not fit." If the subject pointed to a wrong piece, his error was explained to him and the question repeated.

When presented the next matrix (A2), the subject was reminded, "Point with your pencil only to that piece which fits exactly the upper figure." The EMG was recorded beginning with matrix A3. The subjects' reports on the progress of matrix problem solution were recorded by the experimenter or by the subjects themselves upon termination of an experiment.

Eight subjects—Moscow university students aged 20 to 25—took part in the experiments. As a result, 464 speech electromyograms were obtained with parallel recordings of galvanic skin and electroencephalographic responses.

The processing of electromyograms consisted in the main in counting the markings of the integrator made both during the entire period covering the solution of a given problem, and during discrete moments of that solution. On the basis of these data, the mean intensity of the potentials recorded was determined by dividing total energy by time; the intensity was expressed in arbitrary units—per cent of the background, the latter being represented by an electromyogram at rest, 5 or 10 seconds in duration.

The above calculations served as a basis for determining the difference in the intensity of muscle tonus during the solution of easy and difficult problems; also, rank correlation coefficients were determined for motor speech, galvanic skin, and electroencephalographic responses, as well as individual and typological differences in terms of these indices.

2. DYNAMICS OF THE INTEGRATED ELECTRICAL ACTIVITY OF THE SPEECH MUSCULATURE DURING THE SOLUTION OF RAVEN'S MATRIX PROBLEMS

In most general terms, the result of this investigation is as follows: with the exception of a few matrix problems belonging to the self-evident category (chiefly the initial numbers of A and B series), the remaining problems were solved with a more or less discernible tension of the speech musculature, the intensity of that tension increasing with the increasing complexity of matrices. In order to assess the significance of this general result and to draw from it more definite psychological and physiological conclusions, however, a more comprehensive, detailed analysis of the experimental material is required.

As pointed out earlier, the method of EMG analysis used enabled us to determine not only the mean values of the electrical activity recorded but also the dynamics of its successive (from second to second or in intervals measuring tenths of a second) changes during the solution of matrix problems of varying complexity. Changes of this kind indicated that the intensity and duration of muscle tensions tend to fluctuate within a very wide range in the

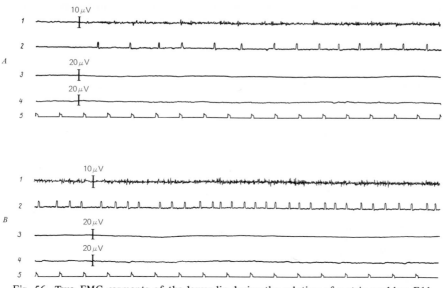

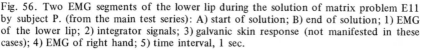

Fig. 56. Two EMG segments of the lower lip during the solution of matrix problem E11 by subject P. (from the main test series): A) start of solution; B) end of solution; 1) EMG of the lower lip; 2) integrator signals; 3) galvanic skin response (not manifested in these cases); 4) EMG of right hand; 5) time interval, 1 sec.

speech organs. At certain moments during attempted solution the tension increases by 200% or more with respect to the background level; at other moments it declines considerably, occasionally dropping to the base level. Fig. 55 shows one such electromyogram. The fluctuations in intensity of speech musculature tensions during matrix problem solving may be seen quite distinctly also in the electromyograms shown in Fig. 56.

Great significance is attached to measurements of the duration of the time intervals in which motor speech excitation is at a maximum, since the mean values of electrical activity determined for the entire period of problem solving may mask their actual value at discrete moments of problem solving. We deemed it necessary, therefore, to determine, along with the mean value of integrated electrical activity over the entire problem solving period, also the mean values of all the summated moments of motor speech excitation maxima and the mean values of all the summated moments of motor speech excitation minima, including in the latter all instances when the electrical activity of the speech musculature dropped to the base level or below it. These data are given in Table 28.

This table indicates that motor speech excitation manifests itself to a greater or lesser extent during the solution of matrix problems belonging to all series. Moreover, in the first three series (A, B, and C) the intensity of motor speech excitation increases gradually from series to series; in the last two

Electromyographic Study of Inner Speech

TABLE 28. Muscular Tension in the Lower Lip during the Solution of Ravens Matrix Problems

| Subject | Matrix series ||||| Mean |
	A	B	C	D	E	
P	$149\frac{219}{95}$	$275\frac{314}{91}$	$238\frac{330}{89}$	$183\frac{207}{95}$	$143\frac{180}{95}$	$198\frac{257}{91}$
K	$114\frac{155}{76}$	$158\frac{180}{79}$	$288\frac{322}{78}$	$135\frac{201}{76}$	$297\frac{313}{82}$	$198\frac{234}{78}$
A.	$146\frac{209}{67}$	$154\frac{191}{85}$	$160\frac{187}{74}$	$161\frac{210}{77}$	$146\frac{202}{73}$	$153\frac{200}{75}$
M.	$130\frac{193}{94}$	$156\frac{191}{79}$	$101\frac{153}{79}$	$116\frac{166}{79}$	$139\frac{199}{78}$	$128\frac{180}{80}$
L.	$124\frac{177}{74}$	$110\frac{159}{72}$	$126\frac{180}{69}$	$128\frac{198}{76}$	$127\frac{148}{77}$	$123\frac{172}{74}$
V.	$125\frac{145}{93}$	$109\frac{136}{85}$	$96\frac{141}{86}$	$104\frac{129}{81}$	$109\frac{146}{78}$	$109\frac{139}{85}$
I.	$98\frac{164}{73}$	$102\frac{153}{76}$	$107\frac{140}{69}$	$114\frac{191}{79}$	$118\frac{151}{81}$	$108\frac{160}{76}$
G.	$111\frac{131}{84}$	$106\frac{117}{91}$	$101\frac{116}{85}$	$112\frac{146}{76}$	$96\frac{142}{71}$	$105\frac{148}{81}$
Mean	$125\frac{174}{82}$	$146\frac{180}{82}$	$152\frac{196}{78}$	$131\frac{181}{86}$	$146\frac{185}{81}$	$140\frac{187}{80}$

Note: an integer denotes the mean value of electrical activity; a numerator designates the maximum, the denominator the minimum, of electrical activity.
*In percent of background activity.

series (D and E) it diminishes slightly with respect to the maximum recorded in series C. It is also typical that when the summated value of electrical activity approaches that of the background, the mean value of motor speech excitation nevertheless remains fairly high. For instance, for subject I. the summated mean electrical activity during the solution of problems from series A, B, and C comprises 98, 102, and 107% of the background, whereas the mean values of the maxima of motor speech excitation comprised respectively 164, 153, and 140% of the background, motor speech inhibition reaching a high level at individual moments of the process of problem solving.*

---

* The term "motor speech inhibition" here designates a lowering of the electrical activity level in the speech musculature, which, evidently, may arise by virtue of various neurodynamic processes. For instance, in some cases it may be elicited by negative induction due to the action of visual stimuli during an attentive examination of matrices; in other cases it may be due to the stereotyped nature of the acts being performed; in still other instances it may be caused by transmarginal inhibition arising during the solution of very difficult problems.

This table also shows very distinctly the individual differences of subjects with respect to the degree to which their motor speech responses are manifested. If we accept the group value of mean electrical activity, given in this table (140% of the background), with a correction amounting to $\pm$ 0.5σ (i.e., $\pm$ 19), the range of significant differences in the intensity of the motor speech reaction of individual subjects is easy to establish. Proceeding from these data, two of the subjects (P. and K.) evidently can be classified as belonging to the pronounced motor speech type, three subjects (A., M., and L.) as belonging to the medium type, and the remaining three (V., I., and G.), to the weak type. Since the problems presented were of the visual type, the last three subjects can be relegated to the visual type.

Thus, on the basis of these experiments, three types of subjects can be singled out: a verbal (or motor speech) type, characterized by maximal motor speech reactions; a visual type, characterized by minimal motor speech reactions; and the mixed type, characterized by medium values of electrical speech activity. Since some degree of motor speech activity is found in all the subjects during the solution of more complex problems, we may regard it as a necessary component of thought activity in general. Let us also note that the degree of motor speech activity is not related directly to the rate of problem solving: subject P. solved all matrix problems very rapidly, while his motor speech activity remained at the same level, whereas subject K. did it slowly (the mean time of matrix problem solving was 22 sec in P. and 94 sec in K., their mean motor speech electrical activity being the same: 198% of the background).

In analyzing the mean data given in Table 29 concerning the duration of matrix problem solving, with an indication of the duration of the maxima and minima of electrical activity, we find that the problems belonging to the first four series (A, B, C, and D) were solved with little variation in the times of the maxima and minima of electrical activity; whereas the problems belonging to the last, most difficult series (E) were solved with an obvious predominance of maxima times over the minima times of electrical activity, that is, with a much longer period of motor speech excitation than that shown for the problems belonging to all the preceding series.

Of interest also is an analysis of rank correlation coefficients pertaining to the successive matrix numbers of each series, the time of their solution, and the electrical activity of the speech musculature (Table 30). The rank correlation coefficients for the successive matrix numbers and the time for their solution are high (from + 0.80 to + 0.93); those for the successive matrix numbers and electrical motor speech activity being lower, however (from + 0.35 to + 0.73), while in the A series this coefficient is close to zero. The latter circumstance seems to be due to the fact that the first matrices of the A series present some difficulties despite their being, objectively speaking, the easiest, since the subjects encounter problems of this kind for the first

TABLE 29. Mean Time of Solution of Raven's Matrix Problems.

Subject	Matrix series					Mean
	A	B	C	D	E	
P.	$5\frac{3}{2}$	$9\frac{8}{1}$	$13\frac{9}{4}$	$32\frac{20}{12}$	$48\frac{29}{19}$	$22\frac{14}{8}$
K.	$61\frac{24}{37}$	$32\frac{26}{6}$	$92\frac{77}{15}$	$68\frac{49}{19}$	$216\frac{192}{23}$	$94\frac{74}{20}$
A.	$4\frac{2}{2}$	$5\frac{3}{2}$	$13\frac{8}{5}$	$24\frac{14}{10}$	$28\frac{13}{15}$	$25\frac{8}{7}$
M.	$14\frac{5}{9}$	$16\frac{11}{5}$	$36\frac{12}{24}$	$43\frac{16}{27}$	$195\frac{110}{85}$	$61\frac{31}{30}$
L.	$15\frac{11}{4}$	$24\frac{7}{17}$	$75\frac{38}{37}$	$78\frac{31}{47}$	$144\frac{111}{33}$	$67\frac{39}{28}$
V.	$8\frac{4}{4}$	$15\frac{10}{5}$	$27\frac{5}{22}$	$40\frac{17}{23}$	$172\frac{69}{103}$	$52\frac{21}{31}$
I.	$25\frac{7}{18}$	$44\frac{14}{30}$	$67\frac{34}{33}$	$56\frac{24}{32}$	$81\frac{41}{40}$	$55\frac{24}{31}$
G.	$3\frac{2}{1}$	$8\frac{4}{4}$	$44\frac{27}{17}$	$44\frac{18}{26}$	$52\frac{16}{36}$	$30\frac{13}{17}$
Mean	$17\frac{77}{10}$	$19\frac{10}{9}$	$46\frac{26}{20}$	$48\frac{24}{24}$	$117\frac{73}{44}$	$49\frac{28}{21}$

Note: numerator denotes duration of maximum, denominator, duration of minimum.

TABLE 30. Rank Correlation Coefficients (R_r) for Successive Matrix Numbers (NN), Time (t'') of Their Solution, and Electrical Speech Activity (W)

Matrix series	R_r between NN and t''	R_r between NN and W
A.	0.85	0.13
B.	0.93	0.73
C.	0.83	0.59
D.	0.80	0.35
E.	0.92	0.72
Mean	0.86	0.50

time—hence the absence of correlation between the gradually increasing complexity of the problems and the electrical speech activity in this test series. At the same time, the extreme points of the correlation diagrams point, in almost all cases, to a correlation between matrix numbers, their solution time, and the magnitude of motor speech tension (Fig. 57).

The second factor that masks the consecutive increase in electrical speech activity in transition from one series to another, is the greater complexity of some of the problems belonging to series D and E. Matrix problems such as E11 and E12 require long and detailed analysis of figures before some verbal idea occurs with respect to their structure. Problems of this kind are rarely solved on first trial, requiring repeated trials which are accompanied by a long-lived decrease in electrical activity. Aside from the E11 and E12 matrices, matrices E9, E10, and D12 turned out to be very difficult and frequently were incorrectly solved. During the solution of these matrix problems the electrical activity of the speech musculature frequently dropped to the background level and below it, not exceeding, on the average, 117% of the base level.

As the second half of each matrix series is more difficult than the first, and some of the problems are superdifficult, depending on the complexity of

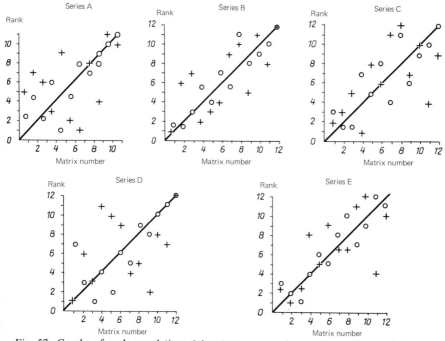

Fig. 57. Graphs of rank correlation: (+) between successive matrix numbers and time of their solution; (o), between successive matrix numbers and the electrical activity of the lower lip during the solution of these matrices.

the problems solved, we deemed it necessary to carry out additional calculations of the distribution of electrical speech activity taking as a starting point not the grouping of matrices according to Raven's series, but according to a criterion which, for our purposes, is of a more definite nature, namely, the mean time of solution of problems and the standard (quadratic) deviation from it. On the basis of these statistical data, we classify as easy those matrices whose solution time was less than the arithmetical mean minus the quadratic deviation ($< M$ - σ); the medium group included those whose time of solution was equal to the arithmetical mean plus or minus the quadratic deviation ($= M \pm \sigma$); the difficult group included those whose solution time exceeded the arithmetical mean plus the quadratic deviation ($> M + \sigma$); the superdifficult group embraced those whose solution time exceeded the arithmetical mean plus triple the quadratic deviation ($> M + 3\sigma$), as well as those which were found to be unresolved after three trials.

Table 31 gives the main results of these calculations. They show that, if the last group of the superdifficult matrices containing 7 solutions out of the total number of 464 solutions is excluded, a definite relationship is obtained: the intensity of motor speech activity increases with the degree of matrix complexity. As for the attempts to solve the superdifficult matrices, they were inevitably accompanied (in the cases mentioned) by long-lasting diminution in electrical activity, which was the factor responsible for the deviation from the principal regular pattern observed during the solution of these matrices.

This regularity manifests itself even more clearly and is statistically more significant when all the matrices are divided into but two groups: an easy one, consisting of the first six matrices of all series (Nos. 1-6), and the difficult one, consisting of the matrices comprising the second half of all the series (Nos. 7-12). The results of this comparison are presented in Table 32, according to which the reliability of the mean difference between the indices of these groups in terms of the t-criterion for electrical activity is 96.5% ($P = 0.035$), and in terms of time of solution, over 99% ($P < 0.01$).

Of great interest also is the analysis of the electromyograms of motor speech tensions recorded during the repeated solutions of matrix problems in those cases when the first solution turned out to be wrong. There were 85 solutions of this type in our experiments. Their comparison with the initial solutions discloses a number of interesting dependencies on the dynamics of motor speech excitation and inhibition during the initial solution of these matrices.

1. If during the first trial, found to be unsuccessful, a given matrix was solved with a low motor speech tension, the repeat trial is accompanied by a considerable increase in motor speech tension (there were 29 such solutions, with the mean increase of motor speech tension from 110% during the first trial to 167% during the second trial). If this problem was not solved on the second trial either, on the third trial the motor speech activity was, on the

TABLE 31. Distribution of the Electrical Activity of the Speech Musculature according to the Statistical Ranks of Matrix Problem Solution Duration.

Ranks of complexity	Time of solution, sec.	Number of solutions	Motor speech EMG, % of background	MSE time, % of total time of solution
Easy ($<M - \sigma$)	8	263	$127\frac{169}{87}$	56
Medium (= $M \pm \sigma$)	41	125	$134\frac{187}{73}$	51
Difficult ($>M + \sigma$)	199	69	$174\frac{203}{80}$	55
Super difficult ($>M + 3\sigma$)	309	7	$117\frac{167}{75}$	37

contrary, reduced (there were 25 such solutions, the mean indices of electrical speech activity being 147% on the first trial, 160% on second, and 148% on third trial, in per cent of background). The graphs illustrating one such solution (subject K., matrix A12) are shown in Fig. 58.

TABLE 32. Electrical Activity of the Speech Musculature and Time of Solution of Easy and Difficult Matrices

Subjects	EMG of solution, % of background			Time of solution, sec.		
	Easy	Difficult	Difference	Easy	Difficult	Difference
P.	151	231	+80	7	32	+25
K.	179	222	+43	45	141	+96
A.	142	162	+20	8	23	+15
M.	126	131	+ 5	17	103	+86
L.	113	132	+19	22	111	+89
V.	102	116	+14	29	75	+46
I.	105	113	+ 8	20	88	+68
G.	104	106	+ 2	10	48	+38
M	127.75	151.62	+23.87	19.75	77.62	+57.87
σ of difference			26.01			31.10
m " """			9.3			11.0
t " " "			2.580			5.273
p " """"			0.035			< 0.01
Reliability of difference			96.5			>99

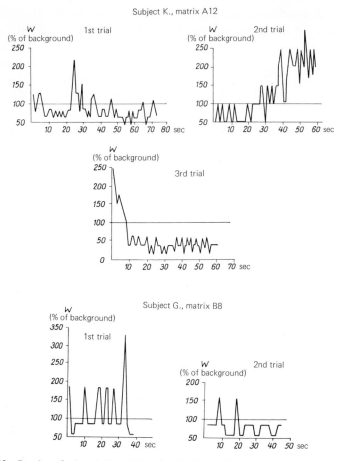

Fig. 58. Graphs of electrical activity in the lower lip during consecutive attempts at solving the same matrices (the first trials were unsuccessful; the last trial resulted in a correct solution). Subject K., matrix A12 (1st, 2nd, and 3rd trials). Subject G., matrix B8 (1st and 2nd trials).

2. If during the first trial motor speech excitation was relatively high, during the second trial it diminished sharply (there were 28 such cases in our experiments, the mean reduction in motor speech activity being from 204% to 107% of background). This case is exemplified by the graphs of the solution of matrix B8 by subject G. in the same figure.

3. Repeated solution usually takes a much more rapid course than the initial one, so that the subjects sometimes have the impression that it occurs "suddenly and unexpectedly" and "without words." The suddenness of this kind of solution is only seeming, however, since it had been preceded by a prolonged first trial accompanied by intense motor speech excitation.

Of interest in this respect is the solution of matrix E5 by subject K. The first trial with this matrix lasted 140 sec and was accompanied by a very high motor speech tension which reached up to 750% of background. The second trial, which resulted in a correct solution, lasted for a much shorter period of time (only 27 sec) and was attended by a long-lasting reduction in electrical activity, with weak bursts of motor speech excitation of short duration. In other similar cases, the solution time is reduced to an even greater degree: 8- to 10-fold in comparison with the first trial.

The consistent alteration of the maxima and minima of electrical activity observed in the speech musculature seems to be related to the switching of thought activity—in some cases, from visual analysis to verbal; in other cases, on the contrary, from verbal analysis to visual. At the moment of attentive visual analysis the motor speech tension is reduced by virtue of the negative induction generated by the visual activity which is predominant at the given moment and which inhibits the motor speech analyzer. If visual analysis encounters difficulties, the speech analyzer is activated, and this is precisely what is manifested electromyographically as an increase in motor speech tension.

It should be emphasized also that if the visual analysis is not complicated, the intervals between the visual grasping of the figures' characteristics and the motor speech reactions become increasingly shorter, becoming almost synchronous when the visual and verbal connections are firm enough, in a manner similar to that occurring with well-established reading habits, when visually-perceived elements (graphemes) are translated into sound units (phonemes and syllables) within microintervals of time (hundredths of a second). On the contrary, when reading involves difficulties in carrying out graphic analysis of letters, the intervals between the visual perception of graphemes and their utterance become longer. In this respect, the solution of the majority of matrix problems may be regarded as a *sui generis* variation of reading a text which is graphically difficult to read.

3. INSTANCES OF SOLUTION OF MATRIX PROBLEMS WITHOUT DISCERNIBLE MOTOR SPEECH EXCITATION

All that remains for us to do now is to analyze those cases of matrix problem solving which occurred without any noticeable motor speech excitation, i.e., not recorded by our apparatus. There were 41 such solutions out of 464, comprising 8.8% of the total number of solution; and they all belonged to the easy, or self-evident, category of matrices, chiefly of the A and B series; a few belonged to the first (again, very easy) numbers of the remaining series. The solution time of these matrices varied between 2 and 24 sec, in the majority of cases not exceeding 5 sec. The distribution of solutions according to individual matrix series is given in Table 33.

TABLE 33. Distribution of Matrix Problems Solved without Marked MSE
(estimated per single subject)

Indices under consideration	Matrix series					Total
	A*	B	C	D	E	
Quantity of matrices	1.62	1.75	0.75	0.75	0.25	5.12
Percent of total number of solutions	16.25	14.58	6.25	6.25	2.08	8.84
Mean time of solution	3.6	3.7	6.0	10.6	14.0	6.3

* With the exception of matrices A1 and A2 which had been demonstrated at the beginning of experiments as examples of solution.

Solutions without motor speech excitation were observed most frequently in subjects with weak motor speech reactions, who, as stated above, may be classified as the visual type; on the average, each of these subjects accumulated seven such solutions. The subjects whom we classified as the verbal type had many fewer such solutions of only 2 per person; and the subjects of the mixed type had five solutions per person. The difference was particularly marked in this respect between subject K. (verbalist), who did not have a single solution without motor speech excitation, and subject V. (visualist) who had 11.

It is also of interest to note that despite the facility and simplicity of these problems the solutions achieved at first glance had not always been correct, so that with repeated trials motor speech excitation would easily be detected in such cases. This points once again to the importance of interrelationships between the visual-image and speech components of mental activity, and the solution of matrix problems, if they indeed are reasoning problems—that is, represent a challenge for the subject—is subject to this general rule. In other words, in time of difficulties both the visual and the speech analyzers act jointly, complementing and controlling each other.

4. RELATIONSHIP BETWEEN SPEECH MUSCULATURE TENSION AND OTHER PHYSIOLOGICAL INDICES (GSR AND EEG)

One of the most complex problems of study is to ascertain the speech specificity of the muscle tensions recorded and to differentiate them from the emotional and over-all motor tensions, usually seen to accompany orientation in a problem situation. In order to reduce the over-all motor tension, the subjects underwent preliminary training in successive relaxation of the various muscle groups of the face, hands, feet, and trunk, as has been done in Jacobson's experiments [245]. Subsequently, in the course of experiments, hand muscle tension was subjected to continuous electromyographic monitoring, and the experiments were discontinued as soon as this tension arose. In addition, there was monitoring of the state of the GSR and the EEG reaction of alpha-rhythm depression—recognized physiological indices of the autonomic component of the emotional and orienting responses.

In our experiments, the palm GSR was recorded (one electrode was placed on the external, another on the inner surface of the palm of the left hand). The magnitude of the GSR was determined planimetrically in square millimeters of the area, contained between the base line (at the moment of rest) and the characteristic GSR curve which bends around the latter. The GSR was always recorded with the same amplification. The latent period of the GSR (1.5-2.0 sec) was also taken into account.

Table 34 gives mean GSR values per sec of solving easy and difficult matrices according to the data of random samples totalling 177 solutions of

TABLE 34. Mean GSR Intensity per Second of Solution of Easy and Difficult Matrix Problems and Rank Correlation Coefficients for GSR and Electrical Activity of Speech Musculature.

| Subjects | Matrix series | GSR intensity | | | Rank correlation coefficient for GSR and speech EMG as a whole |
		Easy matrices	Difficult matrices	Difference	
	A	0.35	0.58	+0.23	+0.60
	B	0.36	0.29	+0.07	+0.28
P.	C	0.45	0.19	−0.26	−0.17
	E	0.56	0.12	−0.44	+0.60
	C	0.38	0.17	−0.21	−0.65
K.	D	0.29	0.20	−0.09	+0.10
	E	0.13	0.15	+0.02	−0.10
	A	1.21	0.88	−0.33	−0.16
	C	0.21	0.13	−0.08	+0.39
V.	D	0.97	0.21	−0.76	−0.32
	E	0.56	0.12	−0.44	+0.34
I.	C	0.45	0.19	−0.26	−0.19
	A	1.54	0.58	−0.96	−0.46
G.	B	0.77	0.20	−0.57	−0.12
	C	0.46	0.52	+0.07	+0.37
M		0.58	0.30	−0.28	+0.03
σ of mean difference				0.32	
m " " "				0.08	
t " " "				3.50	
P " " "				<0.01	
Reliability of difference, %				>99	

matrix problems from different series and by different subjects. The data summarized in this table make it clear that the intensity of the GSR is greatest during the solution of the first matrices which are the easiest; the subsequent matrices, which gradually increase in complexity and are accompanied by increasing electrical activity, were solved with progressively decreasing GSR. There is therefore no direct relationship between the magnitude of the GSR and speech muscle tonus: the GSR is associated with the novelty of the stimulus, whereas the speech EMG is related to the complexity of the problems solved.

This is also attested to by the rank correlation data related to the GSR and the electrical activity of the speech musculature: in the overwhelming majority of cases, as may be seen from the rank correlation coefficients presented in the same table, they are close to zero. However, in those few cases when the rank correlation coefficients are significant to some degree or other, they may be either positive or negative. In many instances no GSR at all was observed at the time of solution, manifesting itself only during the anticipation of matrices and after their solution. Such a failure to coincide on the part of these reactions has also been noted in a recent investigation carried out at the Pavlov Institute of Physiology in Leningrad (K. A. Smirnov, V. L. Asafov, and O. V. Osipova [146]).

The electroencephalographic reaction of alpha-rhythm depression displays just as little specificity with respect to thinking activity. According to the occipital and occipitotemporal brain potential measurements, their level is markedly reduced, more frequently and to a slightly greater extent during the solution of difficult matrices than it is during the solution of easy ones. Analogous alpha-rhythm depression and the appearance of beta rhythm (with a frequency of 18 to 25 Hz) are also observed, however, during the action of all more or less strong and unexpected stimuli (mere opening of the eyes is known to produce marked alpha-rhythm depression); this reaction is therefore similar to that of the GSR in not being to any significant extent a specific index of thought activity. This is due to the fact that the alpha-rhythm depression reaction is produced not by "the afferent impulses as such but by the functional significance of a given stimulus for the individual" (W. Penfield and H. Jasper [125: 153]). This is a general reaction to the situation, evoking alertness and related directly to the activating activity of the brain reticular formation.

A seeming exception to these observations is the frontotemporal EEG recording which at the moment of solution of matrix problems, shows strong irregular discharges. These, we believe, have no direct bearing on the electrical activity of the cerebral cortex, arising rather as a result of the spreading of corneoretinal potentials from eye movements to the frontotemporal area during the examination of matrices; with the eyes at rest, these discharges disappear. It would seem that the so-called "kappa waves," or "thought rhythms," observed by Kennedy and coworkers [250], which they observed in the tempral region of some of their subjects, might also be attributed to this kind of interference.

A more specific index of verbal thought activity might be the depression reaction of the so-called Rolandic rhythm which has the same frequency as that of the alpha rhythm but, in contradistinction to the latter, is depressed only in the case of motor reactions [229]. In our experiments, however, Rolandic rhythm depression was not too pronounced, apparently because of the weak intensity of the motor speech reactions attending inner speech. In those cases when it was manifested, however, there was no certainty as to whether it had been produced by motor speech reactions or movements of some other kind (e.g., by eye movements during the examination of matrices).

The electroencephalographic reactions mentioned above do not yet suffice in themselves to be used as indices of verbal thought activity, there being much more reason to turn, for this purpose, to indices of the electrical activity of the speech musculature.

5. ANALYSIS OF THE SUBJECTS' VERBAL REPORTS AND GENERAL DISCUSSION OF THE PROBLEM OF CONCRETE THINKING

In the course of psychological investigations into concrete thinking, of indubitable interest is a comparison between the subjects' verbal reports concerning the course of their solution of matrix problems and the results of electromyographic records. Analysis of these reports enables us to elucidate when and under what circumstances the necessity arose for verbal definitions and reasoning, what it was, precisely, that was verbalized mentally, and what was not in the course of solving these problems.

Following the solution of the first matrices of series A and B, belonging to the easy category, we usually received the following responses from our subjects: "I solved it in a purely visual way. I simply saw a correspondence or noncorrespondence between figures" (subject I., matrix B2). Or: "I didn't have to think. The similarity of figures was striking, and when I found the figure, I told myself, This figure has to be completed to make a circle" (subject V., matrix B4).

It follows from these reports that in solving matrix problems of this type (very simple), with the attributes of the part sought being clearly defined, the process of solution consists in visual grasping (rapid differentiation) of these attributes, without any marked verbal reasoning, not only in external but in inner speech as well. This is indicated by those speech EMGs which in such cases display no increase in the electrical activity of the speech musculature, pointing, moreover, to its marked drop below the background level. Even if the subjects did make use of words in solving matrices of this kind, it was solely for the purpose of expressing the result in words ("This one," "Here we are," and so on).

But as soon as the matrices start to increase somewhat in complexity, the subjects begin to use their inner speech, this time in the process of solution itself, to designate the characteristic features of the figures sought. "I see a field with a great number of points and *I say to myself,* There are many points ... There are many points, and according to this attribute I locate the suitable figure among the lower samples" (subject P., matrix A4). When solving a more complicated matrix problem (All), the same subject would say: "At this point I *asked myself:* How should the lines interweave in this place? Then I visualized this interweaving and went on to locate the appropriate piece." In solving other matrices he pointed out that "his *choice was determined verbally."* For instance, in solving matrix B7, he reported having defined the attribute of the piece sought in the following words, "As in the upper row, but with hatching;" and in the case of matrix C6, "The vertical stripe shrinks down to the size of the horizontal one."

Looking for the correct piece for matrix C1, subject G. reported: "First I counted the number of circles in the bottom row of the main pattern. Then I started looking for a circle with the same number of smaller circles." In another instance she remarked: "I look for a regularity in the main pattern. I notice that one petal is added in each row. Therefore, the seventh piece is the one that fits" (matrix C5).

Thus, even small complications in the structure of matrix problems call for verbal definitions and inferences, so that concrete thinking becomes verbal-concrete thinking. Of particular interest in this respect was the solution of the first six matrices of series E, whose structure is based on the principle of "adding" or "subtracting" one figure from another. During the solution of such matrices visual analysis is accompanied by weak motor speech reactions which, according to the subjects' verbal reports, approximately involve the following line of reasoning: "This one (the upper figure is being fixated visually); that one remains (the figure in the middle is being fixed visually). Therefore, this one minus that one, and the blank square remains" (subject P., matrix E4).

The last example may be regarded as typical for concrete-verbal reasoning: three rows of figures are given here visually as the basic premises for inferences; their comparison implies that the unknown (absent) figure is formed by "subtracting" one figure from another (Fig. 59), and this general principle of matrix structure, discovered by the subject, is formulated by him verbally in the abbreviated form: *"This one minus that one..."* Obviously, such reduction of verbal expression in inner speech is produced here by the visual obviousness of the situation and not by the automatization of speech operations, as during the solution of verbal (e.g., arithmetical) problems.

At the same time, this replacement of the elements of verbal deductions

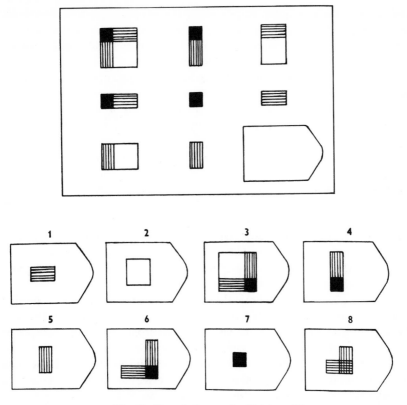

Fig. 59. Raven's Progressive Matrices, E4.

by visual objectiveness indicates that everything which we perceive visually at any given moment is far from being reflected in the second signal system. Massive "recoding" of visual objectiveness into verbal form has never been observed in our experiments. Even in those cases when we specifically asked our subjects, while reconstructing the course of solution, to verbalize all their thoughts and actions, there was very little for them to verbalize; and this is not because the subjects failed to find appropriate words to designate some characteristic or other of the matrix figures or his mental actions (all of our subjects were sufficiently educated and experienced no difficulties with verbal formulations of this kind) but because there was no need for it. The need for more detailed verbal designations and reasoning arose only in those cases where the visual characteristics of figures were singled out not at once but as a result of visual searches of varying durations.

The obvious conclusion is that in concrete thinking (in this case, with visual search for similar figures) the situation is for the most part perceived in the form of images; and it is only when the situation has to be analyzed in greater detail that mechanisms of the second signal system become activated, whereby 1) there takes place verbal fixation of the characteristic features of the figures perceived and, by the same token, translation of visual objectiveness into a system of verbal signs; 2) deductions required by the problem (in this case, first of all, differentiation and inferences by analogy) are realized in the form of logical enthymemes, that is, with omission of the basic premises, since the latter are usually represented graphically.

Thus, despite the abbreviated nature of these verbal operations, they perform the important role of a symbol connecting the individual visually perceived elements of figures in some cases, and of a differentiating symbol in other cases. When the relationships between the figures being compared are of a simple nature, the similarities and differences between the figures become self-evident to such an extent that problems of this type can be solved automatically following the pattern of first signal conditioned reflexes or, which seems to be the same, of Helmholtz' "unconscious inferences" (as is known, Pavlov [117: 101] himself recognized the possibility of a rapprochement between the latter and conditioned reflexes).

It is of interest to note that Sechenov, who made a very profound analysis of the acts of recognition and differentiation of objects in the course of objective, or concrete, thinking, proceeded from an analogy between this type of thought and a three-membered grammatical sentence consisting of a subject, a predicate, and a copula: in concrete thinking the subject, according to Sechenov, is "the separateness of two objects"; the predicate, "comparison of objects"; and the copula, "the motor reaction of the trained sense organ, entering as a component into the act of perception" [144: 376-381]. Owing to the fact that the eyes have repeatedly exercised such comparisons, the process of concrete thinking acquires an automatic, unconscious character. But, in analyzing the subsequent development of thought, Sechenov arrives at the conclusion that "automatic-sensory thinking" of this type is "a transient phase," followed, as soon as the child begins to master speech, by the appearance of verbal-concrete (or mixed) and then of abstract (symbolic) thinking. In *The Elements of Thought* [143] he says: "Owing to education, our thoughts are expressed in words even in childhood; and little by little man learns to think in three different ways: 1) by more or less disconnected and abbreviated reproductions of what we actually feel, without translating the language of sensory elements into the language of conventional symbols; 2) by the same abbreviated reproductions expressed in words; 3) by words alone.

The stronger the sensory elements in a given impression, the greater are the chances for the reproduction of this impression in the first form. The more symbolic, on the contrary, the sensory elements of the moment, the greater are the chances for their expression in the habitual symbolic (abbreviated) form. For the overwhelming majority of people, this habitual form is the spoken word" [143: 496-497].

In this particular case we are interested especially in the verbal and motor speech reactions attending concrete thinking, almost invariably found in our experiments to some extent or other (except in the case of very simple matrices), as determined by objective electromyographic investigation and from subjects' verbal reports. This justifies us in regarding man's concrete thinking as verbal-concrete, or mixed, thinking.

It should be noted that the existence of such verbal-concrete, or mixed, forms of thinking (comparisons, assessments, conclusions), where the verbal element is represented in the form of inner speech, still remains a largely unexplored region of psychology and is often simply ignored by researchers. Thus, according to M. Wertheimer [280], thinking is the segregation of structural relationships predominantly in a visual way, without verbalization. To characterize concrete thinking, N. N. Volkov introduced the concept of "visual judgment," or "judgment of the eye" (the latter term had been used by Leonardo da Vinci), noting that such judgments are often accompanied directly by speech [39: 45-48]. But if this is so, the term "visual judgment" evidently should be regarded as nothing but a metaphor which requires scientific interpretation, without which its use in psychology is quite unfounded. Even when judgment is derived directly from the situation perceived at a given moment, it still retains its verbal basis, although the latter is usually expressed here in the form of inner speech.

In matrix problem solving the verbal-concrete comparisons are, as we have seen, a fact constantly observed. The person solving matrix problems fixes in his mind the problem which had been verbally formulated by the experimenter: to fill the blank in a given matrix by selecting a figure that would fit it precisely, and this task directs the entire course of the solution, controlling and accelerating visual search. Even when the matrix problems are solved "at first glance"—as it seems to the subjects—the latter very often find it necessary to check their solutions verbally: "I examine the main pattern slowly; I become aware of a regularity at once, but do not yet see what it is—it has to be determined . . ." and determination of the regularity turns into concealed verbal reasoning: "The entire figure . . . upper part, lower part . . . It's the same. This means, I need a blank square" (subject G., matrix E4).

Proceeding from the above verbal reports of the subjects and correlating them with the speech electromyograms, we can now with some measure of probability answer the question as to what is and what is not verbalized in inner speech during matrix problem solving. The identifying or meaningful features of the given figures (their general shape and distinguishing details, the number of details, etc.) are the first to be verbalized if the latter offer no contrast on perception (that is, are not discerned immediately among other features). Also verbalized are the intermediate results of visual search (individual visual comparisons) and the final conclusion based on all those comparisons, usually expressed in a very reduced verbal form ("Yes," "No," "This one," "That's it," "Eureka," and so on). Nor are very complex (superdifficult) combinations of figures verbalized. As noted earlier, verbal reasoning becomes difficult during the solution of very complicated matrix problems; it is often interrupted and occasionally ceases altogether. At moments like these the EMGs displayed a sharp drop in electrical activity. In such cases the subjects state that they have "reached a deadlock" and "do not know what to do next."

Thus, in the process of matrix problem solving it was predominantly the weak (hard to discern) components of the perceived complex that are verbalized, while the strong, or contrasting, components could be singled out with verbal designation. This circumstance constitutes an essential distinction between the ordinary (non-goal-directed) perception and concrete thinking: with ordinary perception, the weak components of a concrete stimulus go unnoticed and are therefore not transmitted to the second signal system, whereas concrete thinking is based on the necessity of converting the weak components from unnoticed to noticeable ones, which is exactly what is achieved by their verbal designation.

The fact that weak components go unnoticed in the process of perception has been demonstrated well in the experiments of S. I. Kotlyarevskii [83] and V. K. Fadeeva [181], where children aged 8 to 12 were motor conditioned (pressing a rubber balloon with the hand) to a complex stimulus consisting of strong and weak components.* Despite the fact that the motor reaction elaborated was repeated many times (10 to 15 times) during both the action of the complex as a whole and during that of its individual components, the children noticed a connection between their motor reaction and the strong component only, without noticing any connection with the weak component of the complex. The authors attributed these facts to manifestation of negative induction from the strong component of the complex stimulus, influencing the weak component and resulting in a dissociation (disconnection) in the operation of the signal systems. The weak component was therefore not transmitted to the second signal system. It was assumed, furthermore, that negative induction could take place both within the first signal system and along the paths of excitation transmission to the second signal system.

---

* In Kotlyarevskii's experiments, the strong component was represented by brief illumination of a green square and the weak component, by a slight increase in the total illumination of the experimental room. In Faddeeva's experiments, the strong component of a complex stimulus was a flash of bright red light and the weak component, the sound of an electric buzzer.

In connection with what has been stated above, of interest is the interpretation of the problem of translation, or recoding, of the first signal data into verbal data, presented in N. I. Zhinkin's book *The Mechanisms of Speech* [284]. In principle, language possesses all the necessary means for translating any first signal datum into a recorded verbal system. In reality, however, there is found to exist a very extensive region of the so-called imperceptible phenomena which are recorded into verbal form. This includes an infinite multitude of elements making up the objects perceived. The perceived objects are singled out in their entirety, and this entirety is assigned a normative designation. And yet any element of an object can be designated as a whole and assigned a name" [64: 27; 284: 46].

The "possibility in principle" of a verbal recoding of all first signal stimuli, emphasized by Zhinkin, and the actual absence of it in the perception of many elements of things evidently should be regarded only as an eventual possibility of such recoding in a situation involving a difficult visual search related to detailed examination of objects, their comparison, establishment of their common and specific features and verbal designation of some of them (but, as we have seen, not by any means of all of them) in inner speech.

It is precisely this reduced nature of verbal expressions that represents one of the characteristic features of concrete thinking. In a concrete-thinking situation there is no need to verbalize everything that is perceived. In such a situation, inner speech is extremely abbreviated and highly selective; all it does is to direct the processes of visual analysis and synthesis, introducing corrections in accordance with the available visual experience (visual representations) and its verbal generalization; however, it performs these tasks by constantly referring to the visual perception of the objects present in front of one's eyes. In such conditions, verbalization of everything that is perceived would not only be superfluous, but it also would delay and make extremely difficult the intellectual activity by "translating" into the second signal system that which is clearly perceived and retained in the form of visual images without those "translations." The potential possibility of such a translation of first signal stimuli into verbal designations is nevertheless preserved here and actually realized, as, for instance, when the essential or significant (from the standpoint of the problem to be solved) elements of the concrete situation being analyzed have to be separated from the non-essential or insignificant elements, or when they have to be reproduced more accurately later on.

As applied to matrix problem solving, this means that the subject is guided constantly by a verbally-formulated purpose of action (to select figures fitting the given sample), so that this purpose determines the direction of all of the subject's visual search; where this search is made difficult by the complexity of the matrices being presented, it becomes necessary to assign verbal designations to the characteristic features of matrices and to construct, on the basis of this verbal foundation, a concrete visual image of the missing part through reasoning by analogy. The increase in the electrical activity of the speech musculature during matrix problem solving is an objective index of action on the part of the speech mechanisms of thought at this moment: the coupling of nervous connections within the second signal system or via the second signal system, instrumental in the implementation of the higher (i.e., voluntarily controlled) conscious orientation in the situation.

This activation of speech to participate in the processes of visual analysis and synthesis converts those processes from being an automatic sensory act of unconscious inferences to a consciously directed and controlled process of concrete or, more precisely, verbal-concrete thinking which, in terms of its inner mechanisms, is none other than a goal-directed processing of sensory data with the aid of logic and language and, in terms of its functional significance, a basis for the development of abstract and generalized thought. Therefore, neither in educational work nor in any other kind of activity should the priority be given to the word or the visual methods alone; instead, there should be a dynamic interaction, mutual complementation, and mutual control.

This conclusion is valid not only for the processes of perception and thought but for the process of memory as well. As demonstrated by the investigations of A. A. Smirnov and his coworkers, memorization is at its best in the case of interaction between words and graphic images. Furthermore, the role of verbal designation of objects or their individual characteristics increases progressively with increasing age, owing to which memory becomes increasingly generalized and intelligent [145: 378-397]. At the same time, it has been established that under the influence of verbalization, memory images may become similar to the general concepts related to words. This is found in the reproduction of both visual (I. M. Solov'ev [162]) and, particularly, of kinesthetic images (T. V. Rozanova [138]).

In summing up, we now may single out the following most characteristic features of verbal-concrete thinking, as manifested during solution of Raven's matrix problems:

1. The presence of a verbally-formulated instruction concerning the purpose of visual search ("To select an appropriate figure to fill the blank in a given matrix");

2. The singling out, in the process of visual analysis, of details previously "unnoticed," of relationships between the figures being compared, and their verbal designation in inner speech (translation into the second signal system), which is expressed objectively by an increase of the electrical activity level in the speech musculature;

3. The operating, in inner speech, with reduced forms of judgments and inferences after the pattern of logical enthymemes; the logical elements omitted in the process (individual premises or inferences) are replaced by

visual perceptions and representations of the real objects and their spatial relationships, being juxtaposed at the given moment;

4. Mutual control and complementation on the part of visual and verbal logical operations.

6. PRINCIPAL CONCLUSIONS FROM THE PHYSIOLOGICAL EXPERIMENTS WITH MATRIX PROBLEMS

The results of electromyographic study of the solution of Raven's matrix problems indicate that individual moments of the solving process are attended by weak motor speech impulses which increase as the matrices become more complicated. There are, moreover, strong fluctuations in the level of motor speech excitation in the form of rises and drops—occasionally down to the base level (state of rest)—when the motor speech impulses become insignificant. As for the unsuccessful attempts at solving very difficult (superdifficult) problems, they eventually resulted in transmarginal inhibition and in refusals to continue trying.

The experiments disclosed considerable individual differences in the degree to which motor speech reactions were present in different subjects. Analysis of these differences permits us to classify the subjects into three types: 1) verbal type (verbalists), characterized by a high level of electrical activity in the speech musculature; 2) visual type (visualists), characterized by a low level of electrical activity; 3) mixed type, which occupies an intermediate position. Since, however, motor speech activity is in some measure or other found in all the subjects, regardless of type, it must be regarded as a necessary component of thought activity in every subject during the solution of verbal or visual problems.

Those cases, where matrix problems were solved without an increase in the tonus of speech musculature—occasionally observed in the experiments—involved easy matrices (chiefly, from among the first items in series A and B), which for adult subjects presented no intellectual difficulties whatever. These matrices were solved in as automatic a manner as any act of perceiving familiar objects and were not accompanied by any reasoning. Solutions of this type were observed most frequently in subjects belonging to the visual type.

The experiments established no direct connection between the magnitude of the galvanic skin response (GSR) and the tonus of the speech musculature during the solution of these problems. Alpha-rhythm depression was observed during the solution of all the problems, being somewhat greater in the case of difficult matrices than in the case of the easier ones. Neither the GSR nor the EEG, however, are differential indices of concealed speech activity. In this respect the priority belongs, as before, to the EMG of the speech musculature.

The data cited permit us to characterize concrete thinking as verbal-concrete, or mixed, thinking, where the verbal component is represented as inner speech in a very reduced form. Concealed verbalization for the most part referred to the weak (noncontrasting) components of the complex being perceived; the strong (contrasting) components were for the most part singled out visually, without verbalization. This permits one to distinguish perception, as an act of immediate reflection of real objects and phenomena, from concrete thinking. The latter always presupposes the presence in the situation perceived of a definite task (to find something or to determine or do something in a given situation), whose accomplishment is only possible through a more or less prolonged analysis of the situation; and in a person with a mastery of speech this is always related not only to visual (or graphic-pictorial in general) but also to verbal processes.

Hence it may be concluded that the actual thought process is always—whether the solution of verbal or concrete problems is involved— associated with language, although at individual moments or phases of this process verbal actions may be absent (inhibited). We have no ground whatever, however, to separate one phase of thought from another and to infer the existence of thought without language. Such an inference would be a completely unjustified assumption, since the thought process as a whole cannot be replaced by one of its phases. For the same reason thought should not be identified with speech, for thinking contains not only a verbal but also a nonverbal (concrete or object-operational) phase of action, usually accompanied by a certain inhibition of speech processes.

According to the findings of the experiments described, the phase of speech inhibition is related to the need for detailed visual analysis; and though in the solution of concrete problems it may be of more or less extended duration, it is inevitably followed by a phase of verbal acts, which either terminates the thought process or directs it along a different route; it is only both phases combined, by alternating with each other, that comprise the unified and indissoluble process of human thought.

Chapter IX

Motor Speech Afferentation and the Cerebral Mechanisms of Thought

1. DYNAMIC LOCALIZATION OF SPEECH FUNCTIONS

On the basis of clinical studies of various forms of aphasia—motor and sensory disturbances of speech—the neurologists of the 19th century developed a doctrine on the presence in the cerebral cortex of speech areas, or centers, narrowly localized and independent of each other: 1) the motor speech center, or Broca's area, localized in the third frontal gyrus of the left hemisphere; 2) auditory center of speech, or Wernicke's area, localized in the first temporal gyrus of the same hemisphere; 3) center of verbal designation, or nomination, located, according to Mills, in the lower portion of the temporal gyrus; 4) writing center, located, according to Wernicke and Exner, in the second frontal gyrus of the left hemisphere; 5) reading center, located, according to Dejerine, at the junction between the occipital and parietal lobes in the same hemisphere. Fig. 60 gives a summary of the basic clinical data on the localization of various speech disturbances, on the basis of which the above map of brain speech centers had been constructed.

Detailed studies of aphasia and the results of neurosurgical operations made it increasingly clear, however, that the concept of narrow localization and independent speech centers did not conform to the actual operation of the brain. First, it was ascertained that extensive damage to any portion of the left hemisphere produced marked speech disturbances (Jackson [241]); second, asphasic patients often experienced restitution of speech despite considerable injuries to or even extirpation of individual speech areas if other speech areas remained intact, which was direct indication of a possible replacement of some speech areas by other speech areas, and this was completely out of tune with the principle of their narrow localization and autonomy. This resulted in the principle of static localization of functions being replaced by the principle of their dynamic localization, which presupposes an interaction among all the speech areas of the brain and their functional replacement by each other.

239

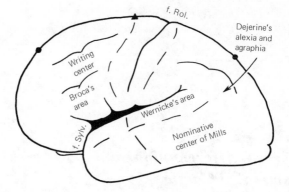

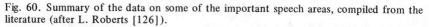

Fig. 60. Summary of the data on some of the important speech areas, compiled from the literature (after L. Roberts [126]).

The principle of dynamic localization of functions was described in a general form by Pavlov. He regarded the cerebral cortex as a complex system of numerous analyzers, each consisting of a nucleus and peripheral part, as well as of individual nerve cells ("diffused elements") scattered over a certain territory and equipped for analysis and synthesis of specific stimuli. In conditioning, temporary nervous connections are established between the nerve cells of the various analyzers. Moreover, the greatest activity is displayed, according to Pavlov, by cells of the cerebral motor cortex, where both efferent (kinetic) and afferent (kinesthetic) cells are represented. In accordance with histological and physiological data, Pavlov believed the afferent motor cells to lie in the upper layers of the cortex and the efferent motor cells, in the lower layers.

In the adult human, the nerve cells of all analyzers are connected with the efferent motor cells, with the result that any afferent stimulus can produce a corresponding movement. Pavlov attached particular importance to connections between the afferent motor cells and the efferent cells, believing these connections to be the most energetic, since they are constantly functioning whatever our activity may be. "He who talks or walks is constantly using these cells, other cells acting haphazardly: now one, now another, now we are stimulated by some picture, now by a sound; but when I am alive, I am always on the move. There is no doubt whatever, this is a most precise and indubitable fact that the efferent cell enters into connection with all other cells more frequently and readily than those other cells among themselves" [123: 483]. It is this conditioned-reflex connection between afferent motor cells and efferent cells, elaborated in early childhood, that Pavlov used to explain the initiation of "voluntary movements" and the possibility of transition from a mental image of movement to actual movement [118].

The existence of bilateral connections between various afferent nerve cells demolished the previous concept of the autonomy of nervous centers, impelling one to acknowledge the possibility of the formation of most diversified combinations of cerebral ganglionic structures among themselves in accordance with the afferent and efferent structure of the acts being performed. A. A. Ukhtomskii called this type of functional unification of various brain structures *"constellations of ganglionic regions working in unison,* mutually exciting each other" [175: 102]. Analyzing speech activity from this standpoint, Ukhtomskii wrote: "If in the case of speech the apparatus necessary for its processing at a higher level and for its correlation with the current visual-phonetic signals arriving from the environment resides in the cerebral cortex, namely, the auditory, visual, and kinesthetic (proprioceptive and tactile) areas of the cortex, the central mechanisms just as necessary for normal speech (the setting up of the musculature of larynx, head, neck, shoulders) must be operating in the cerebellum and in the medulla (respiratory musculature). And these cortical, cerebellar, medullary relay stations . . . must be correlated by signals passing back and forth during the entire period over which the process of speech is being implemented." Further, according to Ukhtomskii, there must be a certain correspondence in time between the "train of thought" and the "rate at which thoughts become fitted into the framework of speech," i.e., bringing the stream of cortical associations into agreement with the stream of verbal phonation, which presupposes a connection between the speech centers and the parietal, temporal, and frontal associative centers of the cortex, as well as with the temporopontocerebellar and frontopontocerebellar tracts. Subsequently, the concept of "cerebral functional systems" found wide theoretical and experimental support in numerous neurophysiological (P. K. Anokhin [9]; N. A. Bernshtein [26]; I. N. Filimonov [183]), clinical (A. R. Luria [102]), and psychological (A. N. Leont'ev [98]) studies, where the localization of all more or less complex psychic functions is interpreted as a systemic organization of various cerebral structures, activated simultaneously or in succession for implementation of a given function. According to this conception, the only relatively stable elements are the points of "entrance" of afferent impulses into the projection (primary) cortical zones and the points of "exit" of efferent impulses onto the common terminal pathways of the motor periphery. As for the processing of the incoming impulses with allowance for past experience and the results of return (proprioceptive) afferentation, it takes place in the so-called secondary and tertiary areas of the cortex, which are much more complex in structure than are the primary projection zones. Thus, in the secondary cortical zones, located on the periphery of cortical analyzers, association neurons with short processes are greatly developed; they are instrumental in transmitting excitation to the deeper cortical layers. Too, fibers are present here which connect these areas with the ganglia of the optic thalamus. It is also assumed that in the closed circuits of the association neurons there takes place a circulation of excitation, which ensures its containment over long periods of time and provides for a possible convergence here of various sensory impulses. Still more complex in structure are the tertiary cortical areas, where there is "overlap" of the cortical terminals of various analyzers (visual, auditory, cutaneokinesthetic, etc.). The system of connections between the primary, secondary, and tertiary cortical areas is shown in Fig. 61 (after G. I. Polyakov [133]).

According to the results of Luria's clinical investigations, speech activity presupposes a rather complex functional organization on the part of a whole series of primary, secondary, and tertiary areas of the cerebral cortex. For

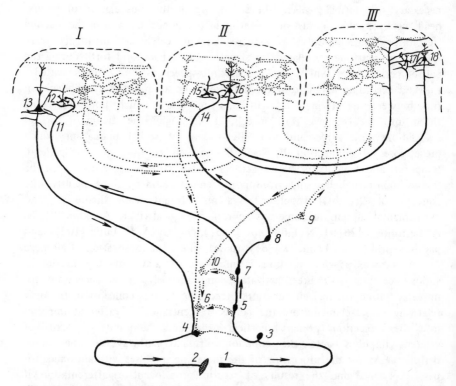

Fig. 61. System of connections in the primary, secondary, and tertiary areas of the cortex (after G. I. Polyakov [133]). I) primary (central) areas; II) secondary (peripheral) areas; III) tertiary areas (zone of overlap of analyzers). Heavy lines indicate: I) projection system of cortical-subcortical connections; II) projection-association system of cortical connections; III) association system of cortical connections. 1) Receptor; 2) effector; 3) sensory ganglion neuron; 4) motor neuron; 5-6) interneurons of spinal cord and brain stem; 7-10) interneurons of subcortical structures; 11, 14) afferent fiber from subcortex; 13, 16, 18) pyramidal cells of cortex; 12, 15, 17) cortical stellate cells.

instance, in order to implement the writing process, joint activity of at least five areas of the cortex is necessary: 1) primary and, in particular, secondary segments of the auditory cortex in the left temporal region, where auditory analysis and synthesis of speech impulses take place; 2) lower segments of the postcentral and premotor cortex of the left hemisphere, where kinesthetic and kinetic impulses are initiated, which are necessary for the articulation of words during writing; 3) the visual-kinesthetic segment of the left parieto-occipital cortex, which does the recording of sounds into graphemes; 4) the lower segments of the left premotor cortical area, which carry out the recoding of graphic schemes into smooth "kinesthetic melodies" of the motor act of writing; 5) frontal area which exercises control over the overall program of the writing process and ensures the inhibition of side associations [102: 64].

Subsequently, as the process of writing becomes increasingly automatic, a number of changes take place in its neurological structure, since there is no longer need for a detailed analysis of word sounds and the center of gravity is shifted to the process of word recording itself, implemented by the appropriate areas of the premotor cortex. According to Luria, there are also considerable differences in the neurological structures of writing from language to language. For example, in terms of the constellations of neuronal connections, writing in Russian or in German should differ appreciably from the logographic Chinese writing or even from the French writing, since in the latter, along with the phonetic elements, there are also significant conventional elements [102: 64-65].

2. PENFIELD'S CONCEPT OF THE FUNCTIONAL ANATOMY OF SPEECH AND ITS SHORTCOMINGS

The above-mentioned dynamic localization of brain structures during speech activity is supported by the numerous investigations carried out by the Canadian neurosurgeon W. Penfield and H. Jasper [125] and W. Penfield and L. Roberts [126]. In the course of surgical operations on the brain (the surgery was performed on epileptic patients with the purpose of removing the epileptogenic focus) they stimulated various areas of the brain with weak electric currents of 2-3 V, delivered by means of stimulating electrodes. Simultaneously, an electrogram was recorded with the aid of recording electrodes, permitting one to follow the electrical activity in individual areas of the cerebral cortex. Since the operations were performed under local anesthesia, the patients retained consciousness and were able to talk to the surgeon.

The effect of electrical stimulation was twofold: in some cases it was positive in that it evoked activity in some of the areas; in other cases it was, on the contrary, negative in that it produced temporary blocking of these areas. Thus, on stimulation of the primary visual cortex, a segment of the visual field was blocked, and, according to the patients' statements, was filled by flashes of light; on stimulation of the primary auditory cortex there was reported the hearing of some kinds of noise. Stimulation of the "interpretive" cortical area in both temporal lobes (i.e., an area which apparently should be classified among the secondary or even tertiary areas of the cortex, since it is adjacent to other cortical areas) produced "flashbacks of past experience" in the form of vivid visual, auditory and other images connected with the patients' past. The patients seemed to be looking at a film which recreated single episodes of their lives. Penfield concludes on the basis of these reports that the memory of past experience is localized in the "interpretive" zone of the temporal cortex.

The main purpose of the neurosurgeons in these experiments was, however, to study the cerebral mechanisms of speech. Stimulation of a number of zones in the left hemisphere was found to produce arrest, repetitions and distortions of speech or to render impossible voluntary naming of the objects shown (or their images), and to make reading, writing, and counting difficult. Penfield arrived at the conclusion that in the cortex of the left hemisphere there are three interconnected speech areas which act as a unified speech mechanism (Fig. 62). The principal speech area (Penfield calls it the "main citadel of the cortical speech mechanism") lies in the posterior temporal region which for brevity's sake Penfield calls Wernicke's area but

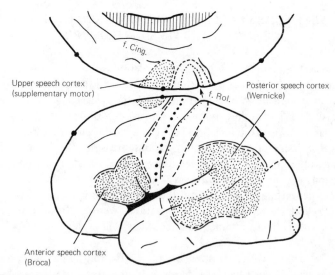

Fig. 62. Speech mechanisms in the dominant hemisphere (after Penfield).

which is actually much larger than the latter. The other two speech areas lie in the motor cortex of the left hemisphere: one of them in Broca's area—in the immediate vicinity of the lower portion of the central (Rolandic) fissure, the other, previously unknown, in the supplementary motor area of the left hemisphere. Furthermore, according to Penfield, the left hemisphere is always the dominant one, whether the patient is right- or left-handed, with the exception of very few cases, involving injury to the left hemisphere in very early childhood.

Penfield believes the main function of all the three speech areas to be identical despite their spatial separation. The principle of "redundancy" seems to be involved in the organization of cerebral speech mechanisms, which makes it possible for an area to be replaced by another in case of malfunctioning. They are, nevertheless, different as far as their significance is concerned. This is confirmed by data on extirpation of individual speech areas, great amounts of which were obtained by Penfield and his collaborators. Speech functions were found to be restored most readily in cases of extirpation of the upper speech area (in the supplementary motor field); aphasic speech disturbances are more persistent on removal of Broca's area, but even in this case speech can be restored. The most drastic speech disturbances—often irreversible—arise when the posterior speech area (Wernicke's area and adjacent regions) is affected, especially if the lesion is massive and involves the subcortical nuclei of the posterior thalamus.

In general, Penfield assigns a major role in cerebral speech mechanisms to the activity of the thalamus and of other subcortical structures, where he believes the "centrencephalic system" to be located. He holds that the above cortical speech areas are connected and interact with each other only in the "vertical" direction—via the thalamus. In his opinion, the thalamus is the main integrating center for all speech impulses and where their coding and modelling takes place in the form of sound units of words during listening to speech, in the form of word units during the utterance of speech, in the form of visual units during reading, and in the form of motor units during writing. The speech impulses formed here proceed next to the implementing apparatus of both hemispheres, which supervise the vocalization of speech and the hand movements in writing.

Passing from neurology to psychology, Penfield develops a dualistic conception of thought and speech. He separates words from concepts and relegates them to different neuronal mechanisms, localizing words in the "ideational" mechanisms of speech connected with the three above-mentioned speech areas of the left hemisphere. Concepts are linked to the activity of both hemispheres, yet are localized not in the cortex but, supposedly, somewhere in the depth of the subcortex with which, according to him, human consciousness is associated. For belittling the role of the cortex in thought activity, this part of Penfield's hypothesis is being increasingly criticized by neurologists who point to the presence in the cortex of an extensive network of associative fibers interconnecting all cortical zones with each other. In addition, an appreciable portion of the cortex (approximately 43% of its total area) is occupied by the zones of overlap between individual analyzers [102:26]. Taking this into account, it may be assumed that Penfield's excisions of the cortical areas lying between the speech zones, left speech activity unaffected not because the speech zones are interconnected via the thalamus only, but because with excisions of this type the regions of overlap of the speech zones remain intact and, therefore, the cortical ("horizontal") connections between them remain relatively intact, too.

Penfield himself notes the presence of overlap of this kind between various cortical areas, noting, for instance, the considerable overlap between the "interpretive" cortex of the left temporal region and Wernicke's area, and the difficulty involved in spearating Broca's area from the facial field in the lower portion of the central fissure. In addition, microelectrode studies conducted in recent years indicate that the merging of impulses of different sensory modalities takes place not only at the level of the reticular formation of the brain stem and thalamus, as assumed previously (H. Magoun [110], H. Gastaut [48], etc), but also directly in the cerebral motor cortex, where agglomerations of polysensory nerve cells have been found to respond to not only cutaneokinesthetic but visual and auditory stimuli as well (A. Fessard [182]; P. Buser and M. Imbert [37]; V. Mountcastle [106]). These findings permit one to regard, in a certain measure, Penfield's cortical speech areas, too, as polysensory regions integrating impulses from various analyzers, including speech impulses of different modalities (auditory, visual, and kinesthetic).

The centrencephalic conception of speech integration is being opposed by neurocyberneticists as well. Thus, analyzing Penfield's work and emphasizing the significance of the corticothalamic connections in speech activity described by Penfield, Wooldridge comments: "The intellectual activities involved in speech must be fantastically complex. If ever an organ of elaboration and refinement, such as we assume the cortex to be, was called for, it would be here" [42:231].

Lastly, let us point out that the role of the cortical motor centers involved in the vocalization of speech and in hand movements during writing is, also interpreted in a very restricted way. Penfield regards these centers as strictly implementive organs receiving speech impulses from the "ideational" organs of speech and acting according to their program. It is, of course, true that the speech code is stored not in the speech musculature of the larynx, tongue, or lips, and not in the musculature of the hand engaged in writing, but in the speech mechanisms of the brain; the speech musculature does participate, however, in the setting up of any speech code (auditory, visual, kinesthetic) in all cases. Suffice to say, that mastery of any language presupposes very precise differentiation of all the elements of the speech heard, uttered, or read (phonemes, articulemes, and graphemes), and this analysis is inevitably bound up with a motor speech enunciation of words aloud, in a whisper, or to oneself. When one learns to write, there is added the necessity of distinct graphic representation of all speech elements. Subsequently, after these different-modality codes have been formed, the need for the detailed enunciation of words no longer exists, but even in this case the controlling function of the motor speech mechanism remains in force, manifesting itself as hidden impulses of inner speech (concealed articulation).

This, evidently, implies that the motor link of the speech chain, besides being an implementing mechanism, also plays a role in the establishment of a verbal code by means of return (proprioceptive and tactile) afferentation to all cortical and subcortical speech structures, including the brain stem reticular formation and the thalamus. Due to the great importance of this issue we shall dwell on it in greater detail.

3. THE NEUROPHYSIOLOGICAL MECHANISMS OF MOTOR SPEECH AFFERENTATION

On the basis of current neurophysiological data we may visualize the action of return kinesthetic speech afferentation within the framework of the overall mechanism of speech activity as follows:

1. Excitation of cortical speech areas by afferent impulses of various kinds evokes reciprocal speech impulses transmitted via the efferent motor speech pathways of the pyramidal and extrapyramidal systems to the musculature of speech organs and carrying out the phonation and articulation of speech. The degree of contraction on the part of speech musculature is controlled by the cerebral cortex via the reticular formation of the brain stem and the thalamus and, further, by means of the gamma-efferent mechanism which, also, is connected with the brain stem reticular formation. When the excitation of the speech musculature is low, phonation is absent, functioning in this case as concealed (soundless) articulation, or inner speech. When the excitation of the speech musculature is stronger, this corresponds to speech in a whisper or loud speech. As a result of overt or covert articulation, the proprioceptors of the speech musculature* as well as those of related postural musculature of the head, neck, shoulders, and chest region generate feedback and proprioceptive afferentation along the afferent motor pathways toward the spinal cord and the medulla and further toward the cerebellum and various subcortical and cortical structures of the brain.

---

* The histological structure of the tongue proprioceptors in man has recently been described by S. Cooper [215].

2. The intensity of proprioceptive impulses depends on the gamma-efferent mechanism mentioned above. According to the electrophysiological studies of R. Granit and other workers [61: Chapters VI and VII], this mechanism consists of gamma motor neurons and the fine motor fibers associated with them which innervate the intrafusal fibers of proprioceptors (muscle spindles), producing in them slight contraction and, correspondingly, proprioceptive impulses even prior to the contraction of the extrafusal fibers in the skeletal musculature. A diagram of the action of the gamma-efferent mechanism is shown in Fig. 63. This mechanism is assumed to be well adapted for the regulation of muscle tone (slow, long-lived muscle tensions), being less suitable for the regulation of rapid phasic contractions which, to a greater extent, depend on the pathways proceeding directly from the alpha motor neurons which innervate skeletal musculature. A more comprehensive investigation has led Granit and others to conclude that the alpha motor neurons also are affected by the reticular formation, in part directly and in part

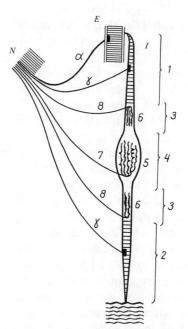

Fig. 63. Schematic structure and innervation of a single intrafusal muscle fiber from a muscle spindle: I) intrafusal muscle fiber;   E) extrafusal muscle fiber (sectioned); N) nerve to muscle; 1) proximal end of intrafusal fiber, attached to an extrafusal fiber; 2) distal end of intrafusal fiber, attached to fascia; 3) myotube region; 4) nuclear bag region; 5) primary sensory terminal; 6) secondary sensory terminal; 7) and 8) afferent fibers from primary and secondary sensory terminals; a) alpha motor fiber to an extrafusal muscle fiber; γ) gamma motor fibers to contractible portions of intrafusal fiber (a simplified variant of Barker's diagram, after Shelikhov [196]).

via gamma activity (J. Rossi and A. Zanchetti [139: 88-93]). Recent studies have established that proprioception is one of the most powerful stimulants of the brain stem reticular formation and, via the latter, of the cerebral cortex. According to these findings, painful and proprioceptive stimuli are most effective in evoking an electrographic arousal response, auditory and visual stimuli being less so (experiments of Gellhorn and Rasmussen, cited in [139: 132]).

3. The transmission of proprioceptive impulses to the various brain segments takes place over both specific (lemniscus) and nonspecific fibers of the brain stem reticular formation. The lemniscus pathway runs from muscle receptors to interneurons in the nuclei of posterior columns of the spinal cord or medulla, whence the fibers pass toward the cells of the ventrobasal nuclear complex in the thalamus, and then to the cells in the postcentral gyrus of the cortex. A nonspecific pathway is formed by collaterals of lemniscus fibers to the brain stem reticular formation. Some of the collaterals proceed toward the cerebellum and basal ganglia. Excitation of the brain stem reticular formation produces generalized (diffused) activation of the cortex. In addition, there is a more specific activation of the cortex on the part of the thalamus, which exerts a selective tonic effect on various cortical areas.

4. The central representation of kinesthetic sensitivity lies in the postcentral gyrus of the cortex, which has connections with the precentral gyrus. Furthermore, according to N. I. Krasnogorskii [87] and Penfield [125: 65-75], the cortical representation of kinesthetic sensitivity is distinctly differentiated from cutaneous sensitivity. Krasnogorskii demonstrated this by conditioned-reflex methods in conjunction with extirpation of certain cortical areas in dogs,* and Penfield did it by electrical stimulation of various areas of the exposed cortex in man. The presence of cortical representation of proprioceptive sensitivity is also attested by the appearance, at the moment of proprioceptive stimulation (clenching one's fist), of a specific electroencephalographic reaction—Rolandic rhythm depression (H. Gastaut [229]).

Experiments involving recording of reaction potentials turned out to be less conclusive, however, in this respect. Thus, according to the data obtained by Mountcastle, Covian, and Harrison [257], only the finest fibers of muscle spindles are represented in the cerebrum, the fibers originating at the nuclear bag terminals of muscle spindles going no further than the cerebellum. Similar data are also presented by McIntyre [255] but, according to Snider [268], some of the cerebellar fibers may also proceed to the posterolateral thalamic nucleus, which is connected with the postcentral gyrus, while the majority of

---

* Upon removal of the cortical part of the motor analyzer, conditioned responses to paw flexion disappeared, but those to cutaneous stimulation were retained. Upon removal of the cortical part of the cutaneous analyzer, conditioned motor reflexes, on the contrary, were retained while the cutaneous disappeared. However, Krasnogorskii notes the presence in the motor analyzer of certain elements of cutaneous sensitivity [85: 184, 203].

other cerebellar fibers course to the anterolateral thalamic nucleus, which is connected with the anterior central gyrus. This contraindication in electrophysiological data on the cortical representation of kinesthetic sensitivity persists in the later studies as well. Rose and Mountcastle believe kinesthetic sensations to be related not to muscle but to joint receptors [264]. Mountcastle also points to the distinct separation between the central stations of the lemniscus systems of cutaneous and kinesthetic sensitivity [106]. According to Swett and coworkers [274], afferent discharges from muscle spindles and Golgi's end organs do not affect the EEG of cats either with passive or active movements, whereas stimulation of cutaneous receptors is readily detected in the EEG.

Recently, Ya. M. Kots and V. L. Naidin [86] arrived, on the basis of their clinical observations, at the conclusion that muscle spindles may play the role of receptors for certain muscular sensations of a more general nature (such as the "sensation of resistance to movement"), arising with active (voluntary) muscle contraction. This involves activation of the gamma-efferent mechanism, which antecedes the activation of spinal neurons.

5. No matter how contradictory the neurophysiological data concerning the central representation of kinesthesis, the existence of kinesthetic sensitivity is unquestionable. This is undoubtedly true of speech kinesthesis as well. The proprioceptive impulses arising during overt or covert (soundless) articulation of words, proceeding from the speech musculature to the cerebral cortex and reinforced by the activity of the reticular formation of the brain stem and thalamus, are capable of initiating both a generalized (nonspecific) and a local (specific) speech activation in the cortex. As a result, motor speech "dominants" (Ukhtomskii) or "foci of heightened excitation" (Pavlov) may arise in the cortical and subcortical structures which attract excitation from other cortical areas, thus regulating the stream of cortical associations (temporary nervous connections) in the process of intellectual activity. Motor speech "dominants" of this kind must be relatively stable since they are produced by proprioceptive impulses which, as already noted, possess a greater stimulatory efficiency compared to visual and auditory stimuli. Evidently, this should be true also of the comparative effectiveness of verbal stimuli belonging to different modalities (auditory for listening, visual for reading, and proprioceptive for either overt or concealed articulation of words). Let us note that the predominant importance of speech proprioception in this respect is stressed also in Pavlov's characterization of it as "the basal component of the second signal system."

4. TONIC AND PHASIC ELECTRICAL ACTIVITY OF THE SPEECH MUSCULATURE IN THE PROCESS OF INTELLECTUAL ACTIVITY

As indicated by our electromyographic investigations, the degree of tension found in the speech musculature in the process of intellectual activity is far from stable. Motor speech impulses can be intensified or reduced depending on numerous factors, e.g., a) difficulty and novelty of the mental tasks being performed; b) degree of automatization of intellectual operations carried out during the implementation of those tasks; c) inclusion of graphic images (visual perceptions and representations) in intellectual activity; d) individual disposition toward some particular types of images or memory. Motor speech impulses increase in intensity when the problems to be solved are difficult and decrease in intensity when the problems are easy. Reduced intensity is also observed when the problems are very difficult (or superdifficult) and, after many unsuccessful trials, the subjects refuse to continue their attempts.

The discrete, quantum, character of motor speech impulses is a very important factor in their dynamics. During ongoing intellectual activity there are, in many cases, "bursts," or "volleys," of motor speech impulses separated from each other by intervals of considerable length. However, there is also a gradual increase in muscle tonus and, moreover, not only in the speech musculature but in the nonspeech musculature as well (for example, in forehead and hand muscles).

The onset of bursts of muscle impulses against the background of a steadily increasing overall tonus of the speech muscles permits us to speak of the presence in speech electromyograms of two different, but interelated, components: the tonic, without a concomitant motor effect and the phasic, accompanied by speech movements, if only minimal ones. On this basis, the tonic component may be regarded as relatively generalized "tuning" of the speech mechanisms, while the phasic component is most likely related to local ("specific") speech activity—soundless articulation of words. In addition, more detailed analysis reveals the presence of intermediate forms of electrical activity in the speech musculature—gradually increasing discharges of muscle potentials which elicit micromovements of the speech organs, and which are followed by vocalized speech, as, for instance, during transition from mental problem solving to oral reporting of the results.

These forms of the electrical activity of the speech musculature are, to some degree or other, all present in every kind of mental activity, but in the process of perception and concrete thinking, the predominant form is, nevertheless, the tonic electrical activity, while in the case of mental reasoning, bursts or volleys related to micromovements of the speech organs are a more frequent occurrence. For example, while listening to other people speak, although not repeating every word uttered by the speaker—just some of them—the overall tonus of the speech musculature is nevertheless raised to a high level, single bursts of electrical activity being visible against its background (Fig. 64). During arithmetical problem solving it is, on the contrary, the phasic impulses which are most pronounced; they are related to

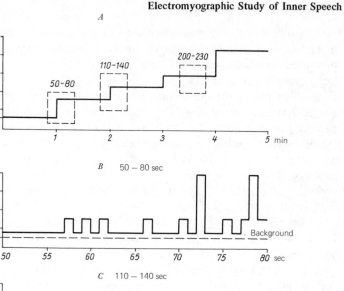

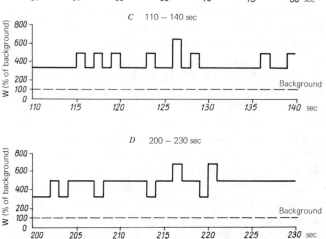

Fig. 64. Graphs of tonic and phasic electrical activity of lower-lip muscle during attentive listening to a text being read to the subject. To determine slow (tonic) electrical activity, mean values were calculated from minute-by-minute integration of potentials (graph A); to determine fast (phasic) electrical activity, the same was done with the values yielded by second-by-second integration (graphs B, C, and D). Second-by-second integration periods are marked in graph A by rectangles.

the silent enunciation of individual words (Fig. 65). There are identical differences in the degree to which the tonic and phasic components are pronounced when the electrical activity of the speech musculature is correlated with automatized and nonautomatized writing (Fig. 66).

Since the tonic electrical activity of the speech musculature is characterized by a slow and gradual increase of muscle potentials, it may be assumed to be related, to a considerable degree, to the generalized activating

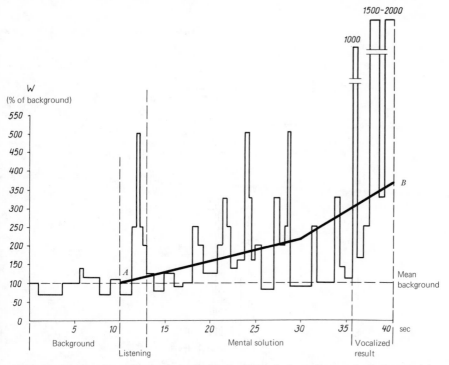

Fig. 65. Graphs of tonic and phasic electrical activity in lower-lip muscle during mental multiplication 34 X 8. Subject K. (slow calculator). The magnitude of electrical activity (heavy line AB) was determined from the results of integration of recorded potentials over a 10-sec period. The magnitude of phasic oscillations was determined by second-by-second integration. Horizontal dotted line designates electrical background activity and its subsequent changes occurring at individual moments of problem solving; vertical dotted lines indicate separate moments of solution. Along the ordinate, integrated electrical activity in % of background; along the abscissa, time in seconds.

influence of the brain stem reticular formation, as is common with all orienting reactions; in this respect the tonic electrical activity of the speech musculature may be regarded as the speech component of the orienting reaction. As for the volley-type phasic electrical activity, it is, for the most part, a result of a local, or "specific," excitation of motor speech neurons whose selective activity is intensified by the reticular formation of the thalamus which is more specific in its function.

In other words, the tonic electrical activity of the speech musculature arises as a result of an overall sensitization of the motor speech analyzer and of the system of other analyzers related to it, whereas the phasic activity is related to the process of speech proper, i.e., it results from the operation of certain second signal system connections selected from the sum total of all the rest of the brain's functional systems tonically excited.

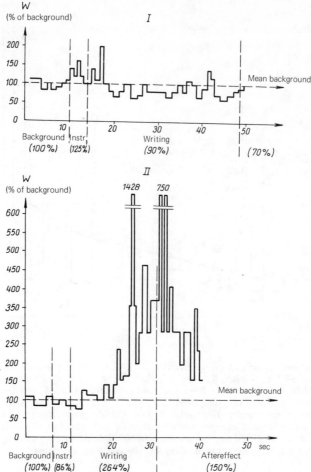

Fig. 66. Graphs of the integrated electrical activity of the lower-lip muscle during automatized (I) and nonautomatized (II),writing. Subject B., a laboratory technician. In the case of automatized writing (writing down one's first name, patronymic, and last name), the electrical activity increased but slightly, whereas when an unfamiliar word had to be written down ("equipotentiality"), it underwent a sharp increase. The rest of designations as in Fig. 65.

The interrelation of the tonic and phasic electrical activities of the speech musculature is attested to primarily by the fact that the onset of phasic impulses is preceded by an increase in the overall tonus of the speech musculature. Moreover, the higher the tonic electrical activity, the greater the increase in phasic electrical activity. Phasic bursts of motor speech impulses result, in turn, in further increase of the overall tonus of the speech musculature, and with prolonged mental tension the tonus of nonspeech musculature, too, may rise. This is confirmed by second-by-second measurement of the integrated electrical activity of the speech musculature, which makes it possible to single out in the electromyogram both components of that activity (tonic and phasic) and to trace their dynamics in the process of solving mental problems of various kinds.

On the other hand, correlation of electromyographic speech reactions with the GSR and alpha-rhythm depression permits rather precise differentiation between general tonic and specific speech components in the EMG. According to the studies of many neurophysiologists, the reaction of alpha-rhythm depression is, like the galvanic skin response, an indicator of the general activation of the cortex by the autonomic nervous system and the brain stem reticular formation (H. Magoun, Moruzzi, Penfield, Gastaut, Sokolov, and Voronin). However, when speech electromyograms, alpha-rhythm depression reaction, and GSR are recorded concurrently, it is often found that they are not by any means synchronized. The bursts of motor speech impulses coincide with the GSR and alpha-rhythm depression most frequently only in the initial, or orienting, stage of problem solving (Fig. 67). But in the

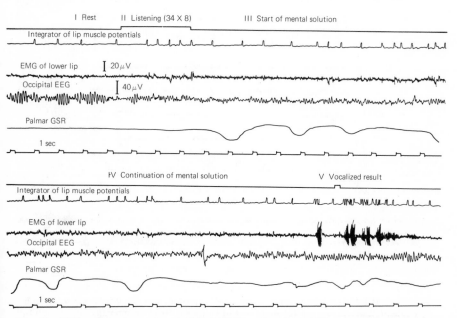

Fig. 67. EMG of the lower lip, occipital EEG, and palmar GSR, recorded during the mental multiplication 34×8. Subject K., a university student (slow calculator). The solving process is accompanied by prolonged alpha-rhythm depression and an intense GSR. The integrated electrical activity of the lower-lip muscle increases, on the average, up to 170% at the moment of solution and up to 500% at individual moments, with respect to background level (state of rest).

foliowing stages, when the "action program" becomes operational, the synchrony between motor speech activity, GSR, and alpha-rhythm depression becomes less and less frequent, and their overall correlation approaches zero (Figs. 68 and 69).

The interrelation noted between the tonic and phasic motor speech reactions seems to be in fairly good agreement with the data of E. I. Boiko and coworkers on the second signal mechanisms of human voluntary activity. According to Boiko [31], the presence of tonic and phasic excitation in the cerebral cortex is a necessary prerequisite for any voluntary activity implemented according to verbal instruction or self-instruction. He demonstrated the validity of this proposition by means of a very simple experiment. Four signal lamps with a fixation point in the middle were placed before a subject whose right hand rested on the reaction key. The subject was instructed to look at the fixation point and, without shifting his gaze to the lamps (which had to remain all the time within the subject's peripheral field of vision), depress the key as quickly as possible whenever any of the four lamps was extinguished. The experiments showed that when the subject had

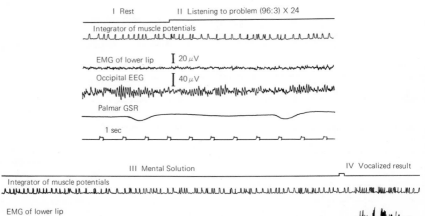

Fig. 68. EMG of the lower lip, occipital EEG, and palmar GSR during the solution of a subsequent problem by subject K., who had to divide 96 by 3, mentally, and to multiply the result obtained, by 24. The initial orienting reflex recorded in the preceding experiment (Fig. 67) has been considerably reduced and, judging by the GSR and alpha-rhythm depression, is manifested now only at the start and end of solution, while the electrical activity of the lower-lip muscle is heightened during the entire period of problem solving (on the average, up to 150% of background, and at individual moments, up to 200%).

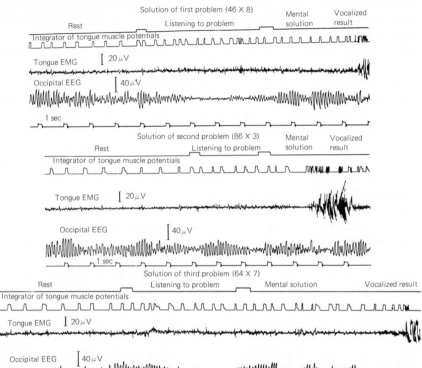

Fig. 69. EMG of the tongue and EEG of the occipital area during listening to the problem statement and mental arithmetic. Subject P. (fast calculator). Alpha-rhythm depression is found only during listening to conditions of the first problem and is absent at the moment of solution. It is also absent during the solution of the next two problems. The tongue electromyograms display, however, in all cases an increase in integrated electrical activity by 150-180% with respect to background.

been warned in advance as to the place where a lamp would flash, the latent period of motor response (pressing on the key) was in all cases considerably shorter (by approximately 100 msec) compared to a similar response when no such warning had been received, i.e., when the lamp flash was unexpected, the latent period, lengthened. These experiments make it evident that verbal instruction produced, even prior to the triggering signal (lamp flashes) a local increase in the excitability of certain visuomotor pathways in the first case and their tonic or urgent (phasic) inhibition in the second. These findings were confirmed by the work of N. I. Chuprikova [188] and T. N. Ushakova [176].

The experiments also make quite obvious the fact of selective tonic sensibilization of the conducting first signal pathways and associated brain structures by verbal (second-signal) impulses arriving from the speech areas of the cerebral cortex; they justify the conclusion that second signal impulses are the mechanism governing voluntary acts and thinking in man. The tonic (positive and inhibitory) influence of verbal stimuli on the first signal stimuli, results in constant interaction between the two kinds of stimuli. This, in turn, leads to a situation where "under normal conditions all direct stimuli in general are invested with some sort of verbal qualification which may be more or less abstract and abbreviated, but which *always* provides an impetus toward reproduction of verbal associations. On the other hand, first signal elements *always* participate, overtly or covertly, in the various representations whenever abstract objects of thought are compared" [30: 51] (italics added—Au.).

By virtue of the connection between motor speech impulses and other impulses of various modalities, speech proprioception acquires a certain concrete significance, becoming its abstract signal, or code. It is precisely in this synthesizing signal function of speech proprioception that its principal significance for intellectual activity seems to lie. *The crux of the matter here is not in the speech kinesthesis per se and not in the mere enunciation of words aloud, in a whisper, or to oneself, but in the formation of generalized interanalyzer connections on the basis of speech kinesthesis.* The enunciation of words in any form, but without the formation of such connections between analyzers, cannot serve as an activating stimulus either for thought or for understanding or for any sensible memorization.

Such interpretation of the function of speech kinesthesis in the thought process requires that both phasic and tonic electrical activity of the speech musculature be taken into account. It has to be emphasized therefore once more that an absence of phasic motor speech activity in the form of bursts or volleys of speech muscle potentials does not quite mean a total reduction of motor speech activity since slow tonic activity of the motor speech musculature is retained (or even increased) here. For the same reason it would be ill-advised to infer the possibility of "wordless" thinking from the reduction of phasic impulses observed during automatization of mental operations and formation of dynamic stereotypes, as is assumed by some psychologists.

In reality, the picture is quite different, according to electromyographic experiments. Motor speech impulses are detected in all subjects even those solving graphic visual tasks, e.g., Raven's progressive matrices. The impulse intensity may fluctuate considerably, exceeding the base level by 200-300% at moments of maxima (resting state) or falling to the base level or slightly below it at moments of minima. This last seems to have been due to negative induction arising as a result of attention being focused on visual objects, whereupon the motor speech impulses again increased in intensity.

Taking into account the presence of phasic and tonic electrical activity of speech musculature and their ratio in the process of intellectual activity, two different forms of inner speech may be postulated—a relatively unfolded form, characterized by frequent bursts of motor speech impulses, and a relatively condensed, or reduced, form, characterized chiefly by tonic motor speech impulses with infrequent phasic outbursts. Given this kind of interaction between tonic and phasic electrical activity, the reduction of inner speech is associated with the phasic component only, while the tonic component is a constantly-acting factor which removes the foundation from under the theories of "pure" thought, or thinking in "pure categories," which, from this point of view, are nothing but a delusion of introspection.

CONCLUSION

1. Our experimental investigation of inner speech and its role in the processes of intellectual activity demonstrates that to some degree inner speech manifests itself not only in verbal-conceptual but also in concrete thinking, as well as in the processes of perception, memorization, and reproduction of verbal and graphic-pictorial material. This was revealed by motor speech interference experiments, where inner speech was temporarily blocked by interference, and by the electromyographic studies of concealed motor speech reactions recorded when subjects were engaged in solving intellectual problems of various types.

2. The results of speech interference experiments varied, depending on whether the interference was restricted to a mechanical retardation of articulation (e.g., clamping the subject's tongue between his teeth) or were extended to the central (cerebral) part of the motor speech analyzer as well. In the former case normal, adult subjects solved all intellectual problems presented to them without any difficulties, whereas children and aphasics (according to Luria's findings) encountered great difficulties in solving them (committing various kinds of errors in writing, arithmetical calculations, sentence comprehension, etc.).

In experiments involving central speech interferences, where they affected not only the peripheral but also the cerebral part of the motor speech analyzer (in our experiments this was achieved by means of compulsory vocalization of extraneous verbal material with concurrent mental problem solving), intellectual activity underwent drastic inhibition. In such cases there took place something akin to "sensory aphasia" in the stage where only individual words are comprehended, while the meaning of a sentence as a whole remains obscure. Futhermore, memorization of verbal and, in part, concrete material was also impaired. On this evidence it may be assumed that concealed verbalization is related directly to the semantic processing of sensory information and its fixation in memory, and since in these experiments concealed verbalization was interfered with, intellectual activity experienced the difficulties described above.

3. Another fact that attracts attention in the speech interference experiments is that negative induction is equally strong for both motor speech and auditory speech interference, which is a definite indication of the existence of an interaction between the motor speech and auditory speech analyzers not only in the process of external speech but also in internal speech. To some degree, activity on the part of the auditory components of inner speech may also explain the adaptation to motor speech interference observed in our experiments with progressive automatization in enunciating extraneous words and, correspondingly, the progressively diminishing need for an auditory control over them, with the result that fragmentary listening to somebody else's speech and its subsequent reproduction became possible. However, the principal role in the mechanism of this adaptation was played by the micropauses in speech interferences, which allowed for abbreviated articulation of certain generalizing key words, especially if these words were supplemented with visual images (representations) in the role of operational mnemonic signs. Subsequently, the subjects were able to reproduce the speech with their aid and to perform numerous mental operations of other types.

4. The speech interference experiments enabled us also to elucidate some of the structural peculiarities of inner speech during various stages (or phases) of its functioning. If the subjects were able to utilize the micropauses in speech interferences, this evidently must mean that concealed verbalization was very fast and abbreviated in this case. It is also evident that during the subsequent oral or written reproduction of the speech under these conditions, the subjects had to translate (or recode) the fragments of words and sentences into whole words and sentences, i.e., they had to make a transition from mental speech structured according to the principle that statements be kept strictly to a *minimum,* to external speech (vocalized or written) which requires a great *redundancy* of communicated information (linguists have calculated that this redundancy amounts to 60-70% [19: 134]). This explains, on the one hand, the rapid ("almost instantaneous") operation of inner speech in the thought process and, on the other hand, the many difficulties involved in the transition from inner speech to external speech, usually described as the "throes of expression" (i.e., the search for words that would express one's thoughts [objective and verbal associations] most accurately).

5. Electromyographic studies showed that two types of motor speech reactions—tonic and phasic—are found in the process of performance of mental operations (both verbal-conceptual and concrete). Tonic reactions are characterized by slow, low-amplitude action potentials of the speech musculature and seem to be related to the overall activation of the motor speech analyzer by the reticular formation of the brain. Phasic reactions represent fast, high-amplitude potential oscillations in the form of bursts, or volleys, of local motor speech impulses arising during concealed articulation of words. Their time distribution is very uneven (discrete) since they act as

quanta of thought. The specifically verbal character of these potentials is indicated, in particular, by the fact that often they do not coincide with the galvanic skin response and the reaction of alpha-rhythm depression. These reactions are synchronous with the motor speech reactions only at the initial stage of problem solving, but on the whole their rank correlation coefficient is insignificant.

6. According to electromyographic data, the intensity and duration of motor speech reactions are quite variable: they may increase or decrease depending on a number of factors, such as the difficulty and novelty of the problems solved, the degree of automatization of the mental operations performed, inclusion in intellectual activity of concrete images (visual perceptions and representations), and individual disposition toward a certain type of memory. Motor speech impulses become intensified when the problems to be solved are difficult, and are reduced in the case of easy problems. A reduction of motor speech impulses is also found when the problems are very difficult (or superdifficult) i.e., when the subjects are unable to solve them. The magnitude of the electrical activity of the speech musculature is also strongly affected by the manner in which problems are presented: it is reduced with visual presentation and increases with auditory presentation. The electrical activity of the speech musculature during mental implementation of various tasks is considerably higher in children (elementary school pupils) than in adults.

7. Taking into account that all forms of intellectual activity which require some measure of reasoning in unfolded form, are always accompanied by an increase in motor speech impulses, whereas repetition of the same (or similar) mental operations involves a reduction of these impulses, an increase in the electrical activity of the speech musculature may be regarded as an objective index of intellectual difficulties, and a reduction in the level of that activity—as an index of already-established appropriate mental operations, their automatization.

This proposition is qualified, however, by two circumstances: the individual differences displayed by people in the degree of their motor excitability (in people belonging to the motor type the electrical activity of the speech musculature is always slightly higher than that in people of lower motor excitability); the variations in the emotional attitude toward, or interest in, the activity being carried out (if the subject lacks interest, the electrical activity of the speech musculature is lowered, as is known, for example, to take place during prolonged unsuccessful attempts at solving very difficult problems).

8. Since motor speech impulses are found not only in verbal-conceptual but also in concrete thinking (in our experiments the latter was represented by the solution of Raven's matrix problems) and, moreover, in every subject regardless of his memory type, it may be assumed that in each and every case

thinking is associated with language, although at individual moments, or phases, of solution (especially in concrete problem solving) motor speech impulses may be inhibited. This does not mean, however, that the last instance involves "speechless" thinking. Such an inference would be an unjustified assumption since it would be based on a segregation of one phase of thought from another, which is essentially impossible. The data presented also indicate that it is equally impossible to identify thinking with speech, since thinking contains, not only a verbal phase, but also a nonverbal phase of action, associated with the accumulation of sensory information. Therefore, we are dealing here with a constant interaction between objective and verbal information, described by Pavlov as the interaction between the first (objective) and second (speech) signal systems.

9. The facts concerning the dynamics of motor speech impulses during the performance of mental operations, discussed above, permit us also to form a more confident judgment concerning the physiological role of speech kinesthesis as a basal component of the second signal system. Their principal physiological function evidently consists in the motor speech (proprioceptive and tactile) activation of cerebral speech mechanisms on the part of the speech periphery (according to the feedback principle) and in establishing in the brain's speech areas motor speech dominants which integrate afferent impulses of various modalities and maintain the working tonus of the cerebral cortex.

From these considerations it follows that efferent motor speech impulses, too, may by regarded not only as a result of a passive ideomotor act, where a thought about movement involuntarily evokes that movement, but also—and this is more important—as a mechanism of active, voluntary control over intellectual processes by means of inner speech kinesthesis. This is the more probable since both the problem itself in its capacity as the determining (set-producing) factor of thought, and the plan elaborated for its solution, are fixed and reproduced in human memory with the aid of concealed verbalization which thus regulates the entire neurodynamics of thought processes associated with them.

It seems to us that the above propositions conform to Pavlov's conceptions of the integrating role of the cerebral cortex. They are also confirmed by numerous clinical observations and electrophysiological studies conducted in recent years. According to these, the motor cortex is a polysensory region which receives and integrates nervous impulses of different modalities.

10. If we take into account the integrating role of the motor cortex of the brain, it will also make clear the great significance of motor speech afferentation in the process of formation of mental acts (learning concepts and operating with them). The initial stages of the learning of abstract material by children are known to be associated with the need for its intensive

verbalization (enunciation aloud, then in a whisper, and, finally, to oneself). Supported by a number of special studies (P. Ya. Gal'perin and others), the educational effect of this stage-by-stage verbalization is based on the fact that the auditory and motor speech stimuli (speech kinesthesis) attending this process maintain excitation in the cerebral cortex, setting up in it appropriate motor speech dominants which direct and keep track of all the mental processes of analysis and synthesis. As learning takes root and mental operations become increasingly automatized, however, the need for external verbalization (enunciation aloud) arises no longer, and it is replaced by reduced, abbreviated verbalization-inner speech which underlies the so-called interiorization of mental actions, or their implementation on an internal (mental) plane, *the motor speech reactions being maximally reduced but not totally eliminated.*

The remaining concealed motor speech reactions manifest themselves at the time of mental difficulties or of transition to new mental acts, continuing to perform their function as the speech mechanism of thought.

11. In our electromyographic experiments this activating function of motor speech afferentation was brought out with particular clarity by the comparison of the indices of integrated electrical activity of the speech musculature during the solution of arithmetical and other problems of varying complexity and during the reading of texts in his native language or in a foreign language being studied by the subject. The text-reading experiments were of interest, also, because they pointed to a direct dependency of the understanding of speech on its active mastery. Since in the process of understanding the speech read and heard there arise reduced motor speech reactions (for the most part tonic but occasionally also phasic), the distinction between the understanding and active mastery of speech acquires a very relative character, consisting chiefly in the fact that the understanding of speech may be limited to an auditory or visual recognition of words, attended by incomplete articulatory reproduction of some (the most significant, or key words) of them, whereas an active mastery of language is only possible with their complete articulatory reproduction. This is what also determines the extreme importance which the fixation and reproduction of words and their grammatical connections within sentences by means of articulation has for the study of foreign languages. The student has to learn to understand oral and written speech quickly and accurately, with a *minimal* participation of articulatory movements (the only factor capable of ensuring a rapid rate in understanding utterances or a text being read). But the student can only achieve this by means of a *maximally* unfolded articulatory fixation of speech in the course of preceding practical experience in the spoken language. This may seem contradictory, yet there is no other solution for this problem.

12. The material presented permits us to regard inner speech and the concealed articulation associated with it, as the principal mechanism of

thought, with the aid of which there takes place goal-directed selection, generalization, and storage of sensory information (data provided by sensations and perceptions). Hence the enormous significance of inner speech not only in verbal-conceptual but also in concrete thinking, as well as in the formation and functioning of all voluntary acts of man. If this is true, then it is logical to assert that inner speech is a very important factor in human consciousness, verbal in its genesis, structure, and functioning. Further studies should work out these problems in greater detail, especially with respect to the physiological effect of motor speech afferentation and its relationships with all the rest of afferent stimuli.

Bibliography

1. K. Marx and F. Engels, *German Ideology*. [Russian translation], *Works*, Vol. 3, 2nd edition (1955).
2. K. Marx, Preparatory studies for "Die heilige Familie," K. Marx and F. Engels, *Works* [Russian translation], Vol. 3, 1st edition (1929).
3. F. Engels, *Anti-Dühring*, K. Marx and F. Engels, *Works*, Vol. 20, 2nd edition (1961).
4. F. Engels, *The Dialectics of Nature* [Russian translation], K. Marx and F. Engels, *Works*, Vol. 20, 2nd edition (1961).
5. *Archives of Marx and Engels*, Vol. 4 (1935).
6. V. I. Lenin, *Philosophical Notebooks. Collected Works,* Vol. 29, 5th ed.
7. B. G. Anan'ev, On the theory of inner speech in psychology, in: *The Psychology of Sensory Cognition,* Acad. Pedagog. Sci. RSFSR Press, Moscow (1960).
8. B. G. Anan'ev, Clinical-psychological analysis of the reinstatement of speech functions in motor aphasia, *ibid.*
9. P. K. Anokhin, The problem of localization from the standpoint of systemic concepts of nervous functions, *Nevropatologiya i Psikhiatriya,* No. 6 (1940).
10. P. K. Anokhin, Characteristic features of the afferent mechanism of the conditioned reflex and their significance for psychology, *Voprosy Psikhologii,* No. 6 (1955).
11. Aristotle, *Prior Analytics and Posterior Analytics* [Russian translation], Gospolitizdat, Moscow (1952).
12. Aristotle, *Categories* [Russian translation by A. V. Kubitskii], Sotsékgiz, Moscow (1934).
13. Aristotle, *Metaphysics* [Russian translation by A. V. Kubitskii], Sotsékgiz, Moscow (1934).
14. Aristotle, *De interpretatione* [Russian translation by É. L. Radlov] (1891).
15. Aristotle, *Historia animalium* [Russian translation by V. P. Karpov], Acad. Sci. USSR Press, Moscow-Leningrad (1940).
16. Aristotle, *De anima.* [Russian translation by P. S. Popov], Sotsékgiz (1937).
17. V. F. Asmus, *Logic*, Gospolitizdat (1947).
18. M. I. Astvatsaturov, Clinical and experimental-psychological studies of the speech function. Dissertation. Material from Academician V. M. Bekhterev's Clinic for Mental and Nervous Disorders, St. Petersburg (1908).
19. O. S. Akhmanova, N. A. Mel'chuk, E. V. Paducheva, and R. M. Frumkina, *Precise Methods of Language Studies.* Moscow State University Press, Moscow (1961), [Eng. trans.].
20. B. F. Baev, On certain peculiarities of inner speech in mental problem solving of various types, *Dokl. APN RSFSR,* No. 3 (1957).
21. B. F. Baev, Communication and inner speech, *18th International Psychological Conference, Abstracts,* Vol. 2, Moscow (1966).
22. F. B. Bassin and É. S. Bein, On the use of electromyographic methods in speech studies, in: *Materials of a Conference on Psychology, July 1-6, 1955,* Acad. Pedagog. Sci. RSFSR Press, Moscow (1957).

23. É. S. Bein, Reinstatement of speech processes in sensory aphasia, *Uch. zap. Moskovsk. Gos. Univ.*, No. 3 (1947).

24. É. S. Bein, *Aphasia and How to Overcome It*, Meditsina Press, Leningrad (1964).

25. G. Berkeley, *Treatise Concerning the Principles of Human Knowledge* [Russian translation], St. Petersburg (1905).

26. N. A. Bernshtein, *The Structure of Movements*, Medgiz, Moscow (1947).

27. L. V. Blagonadezhina, "Psychological analysis of the auditory representation of melody." *Uch. zap. Gos. Nauchno-issledovat. Inst. Psikhologii*, Vol. 1, Moscow (1940).

28. S. M. Blinkov, "Impairment of writing in temporal lesions," *Izvestiva APN, RSFSR*, No. 5 (1948).

29. P. P. Blonskii, "Memory and thought," in: *Selected Works on Psychology*, Prosveshchenie Press, Moscow (1964).

30. E. I. Boiko, "Interaction of conditioned-reflex processes in complex systemic reactions," in: *Problems in the Study of Higher Neurodynamics in Connection with Psychological Problems*, Acad. Pedagog. Sci. RSFSR Press, Moscow (1957).

31. E. I. Boiko, "Key problems in higher neurodynamics," in: *Boundary Problems in Psychology and Physiology*. Acad. Pedagog. Sci. RSFSR, Moscow (1961).

32. N. Bohr, *Atomic Physics and Human Knowledge* [Russian translation], Foreign Literature Press, Moscow (1961).

33. L. Borovoi, "New words," *Krasnava Nov'*, No. 1 (1940).

34. V. M. Borovskii, "Muscle tensions and the thought process" (an essay on Jacobson's work), in: *Reflexes, Instincts, and Habits*, Sotsékgiz, Moscow (1936).

35. M. G. Breido, V. S. Gurfinkel', A. E. Kobrinskii, A. Ya. Sysin, M. L. Tseitlin, and Ya. S. Yakobson, "On the bioelectrical system of control," *Problemy kibernetiki*, No. 2, Fizmatgiz, Moscow (1959).

36. F. Bacon, *Novum organum* [Russian translation], Sotsékgiz, Leningrad (1935).

37. P. Buser and M. Imbert, "Sensory projections in the motor cortex of the cat," in: *Theory of Communication in Sensory Systems*, Mir, Moscow (1964).

38. E. Weigl, "An experimental method of mechanical exclusion of specific speech movements in persons with normal and impaired speech," *Voprosy Psikhologii*, No. 4 (1962).

39. N. N. Volkov, *Perception of Objects and Pictures*, Acad. Pedagog. Sci. RSFSR Press, Moscow (1950).

40. V. D. Volkova, "Certain characteristics of formation of conditioned reflexes to verbal stimuli in children," *Fiziologicheskii Zh. SSSR*, Vol. 39, No. 5 (1953).

41. L. G. Voronin and E. N. Sokolov, "Cortical mechanisms of the orienting reflex. Relation between orienting and conditioned reflexes," in: *Electroencephalographic Study of Higher Nervous Activity*, Acad. Pedagog. Sci. RSFSR Press, Moscow (1962).

42. D. Wooldridge, *The Machinery of the Brain* [Russian translation], Mir, Moscow (1965).

43. L. S. Vygotskii, "Thought and Language," in: *Selected Psychological Investigations*, Acad. Pedagog. Sci. RSFSR Press, Moscow (1956).

44. P. Ya. Gal'perin, "Objective study of the formation of mental acts," in: *Proceedings of a Conference on Problems in Psychology*, Moscow (1954).

45. P. Ya. Gal'perin, "On the problem of inner speech," *Dokl. APN RSFSR*, No. 4 (1957).

46. P. Ya. Gal'perin, "Development of investigations into the formation of mental acts," in: *Psychological Science in the USSR*, Vol. 1, Acad. Pedagog. Sci. RSFSR, Moscow (1959).

47. P. Ya. Gal'perin and N. F. Talyzina, "Formation of elementary geometrical concepts on the basis of organized activity of students," *Voprosy Psikhologii*, No. 1 (1957).

48. H. Gastaut and J. Roger, "Participation of the principal functional brain structures in the mechanism of higher nervous activity," in: *Electroencephalographic Study of Higher Nervous Activity*, Acad. Sci. USSR Press, Moscow (1962).

49. G. Hegel, *Encyclopedia of Philosophical Sciences.* Part 1, *Logic; Works,* Vol. 1 [Russian translation], Gosizdat, Moscow–Leningrad (1929).
50. G. Hegel, *Encyclopedia of Philosophical Sciences.* Part 3, Philosophy of Spirit [Russian translation], Gospolitizdat, Moscow (1956).
51. G. Hegel, *Introduction to Philosophy.* (Philosophical Propaedeutic), [Russian translation], Timiryazev Scientific-Research Institute Press, Moscow (1927).
52. A. I. Herzen (Gertsen), Dilettantism in Science. *Works,* Vol. 2, Goslitizdat, Moscow (1955).
53. A. I. Herzen (Gertsen), Talks with Young People. *Works,* Vol. 7, Goslitizdat, Moscow (1958).
54. A. I. Herzen (Gertsen), Diary 1842-1845. *Works,* Vol. 9, Goslitizdat, Moscow (1958).
55. Yu. B. Gippenreiter, "Analysis of the systemic structure of perception Communication II. Experimental analysis of the motor basis of pitch perception," *Dokl. APN RSFSR,* No. 1 (1958).
56. T. Hobbes, *De corpore* [Russian translation], *Selected Works,* Vol. 1, Mysl', Moscow (1964).
57. G. Hopfert, "Regulation and control in the central nervous system," in: *Processes of Regulation in Biology* [Russian translation], Foreign Literature Press, Moscow (1960).
58. D. O. Gorbov, "On the operator's resistance to interference," in: *Engineering Psychology* (A. N. Leont'ev, V. P. Zinchenko, and D. Yu. Panova, eds.), Moscow State University Press, Moscow (1964).
59. A. G. Gornfel'd, "Throes of Creation," *Articles on Belles-Lettres,* Gosizdat, Moscow–Leningrad (1927).
60. D. P. Gorskii and P. V. Tavanets, eds., *Logic,* Gospolitizdat, Moscow (1956).
61. R. Granit, *Electrophysiological Study of Reception* [Russian translation], Foreign Literature Press, Moscow (1959).
62. R. Descartes, *Principia philosophiae* [Russian translation], Selected Works, Gospolitizdat, Moscow (1950).
63. N. I. Zhinkin, "Development of written speech in students," *Izv. APN RSFSR,* Moscow (1958).
64. N. I. Zhinkin, *The Mechanisms of Speech,* Izd. APN RSFSR (1958).
65. N. I. Zhinkin, "Investigation of inner speech by the method of central speech interference," *Izv. APN RSFSR,* No. 113, Moscow (1960).
66. N. I. Zhinkin, "On recoding in inner speech," *Voprosy yazykoznaniya,* No. 6 (1964).
67. A. V. Zaporozhets, *Development of Voluntary Movements,* Acad. Pedagog. Sci. RSFSR Press, Moscow (1960).
68. P. I. Zinchenko, *Involuntary Memorization,* Acad. Pedagog. Sci. RSFSR Press, Moscow (1961).
69. A. G. Ivanov-Smolenskii, "An experimental investigation into the interaction of direct and symbolic projections of the cerebral cortex in man," *Arkhiv biologicheskikh nauk,* 38:1 (1935).
70. A. G. Ivanov-Smolenskii, "An investigation into the co-operation and interaction of the first and second signal systems in relation to medical problems," *Zh. Vyssh. Nervnoi Deyatel'nosti,* Vol. 3, No. 4 (1953).
71. N. K. Indik, "The role of speech kinesthesis in the memorization of images and verbal material," in: *Problems in the Psychology of Memory,* Acad. Pedagog. Sci. RSFSR Press, Moscow (1958).
72. N. K. Indik, Intellectual Processes during Formation of New Actions (Candidate's dissertation), Moscow (1951).
73. Z. M. Istomina, "Concerning the relation between perception and color naming in preschool children," *Izv. APN RSFSR,* No. 113 (1960).
74. Z. M. Istomina, "Perception and color naming in early childhood," *Izv. APN RSFSR,* No. 113, Moscow (1960).
75. *History of Philosophy,* Vol. 1. Philosophy of Antique and Feudal Society, Politizdat, Moscow (1940).

76. L. N. Kadochkin, "The role of speech kinesthesis in formation of certain spelling habits," *Voprosy Psikhologii*, No. 3 (1955).
77. L. S. Kaminskii, *Processing of Clinical and Laboratory Data*, Medgiz., Leningrad (1959).
78. I. Kant, "Anthropology from a pragmatic viewpoint" [Russian translation], *Works*, Vol. 6, Mysl', Moscow (1966).
79. O. P. Kapustnik, "Relationships between direct conditioned stimuli and their verbal symbols," *Transactions of the Laboratory for the Physiology and Pathophysiology of Higher Nervous Activity in Children and Juveniles*, Vol. 2 (1930).
80. V. P. Karpov, *Commentaries on Aristotle's Treatise Historia animalium* (see No. 15 in the present list).
81. O. P. Kaufman, "Restitution of the speech process in motor aphasia," *Uch. Zap. Moskovsk. Gos. Univ.*, Iss. III (1947).
82. A. N. Kolmogorov, "Automata and life," in: *The Possible and Impossible in Cybernetics*, Acad. Sci. USSR Press, Moscow (1963).
83. L. I. Kotlyarevskii, "The reflection of direct conditioned connections in symbolic cortical projection," *Transactions of the Laboratory for the Physiology and Pathophysiology of Higher Nervous Activity in Children and Juveniles*, Vol. 4 (1934).
84. L. I. Kotlyarevskii, "Formation of pupillary conditioned reflexes differentiation of direct and verbal stimuli," *Arkhiv Biologicheskikh Nauk*, Vol. 39, No. 2 (1935).
85. L. I. Kotlyarevskii, "Cardiovascular conditioned reflexes to direct and verbal stimuli," *Fiziologicheskii Zh. SSSR*, Vol. 20, No. 2 (1936).
86. Ya. M. Kots and V. L. Naidin, "On the role of kinesthetic sense in voluntary movements control," *Voprosy Psikhologii*, No. 5 (1966).
87. N. I. Krasnogorskii, "On the process of inhibition and localization of the cutaneous and motor analyzers in the cerebral cortex of the dog" [Doctoral dissertation (1911)], in: N. I. Krasnogorskii. *Studies of the Higher Nervous Activity in Man and Animals*, Vol. 1, Medgiz, Moscow (1954).
88. N. I. Krasnogorskii, "The physiological activity of the brain in children as a new object of pediatric study," *ibid.*
89. N. I. Krasnogorskii, "On the physiology of formation of speech in children," *Zh. Vysshei Nervnoi Deyatel'nosti*, Vol. 2, No. 4 (1952).
90. N. I. Krasnogorskii, "On the physiology of formation of speech in children," *Proceedings of a Conference on Psychology*, Acad. Pedagog. Sci. RSFSR, Moscow (1955).
91. N. I. Krasnogorskii, "New findings on the physiology of speech activity," *Zh. Vys. Nervnoi Deyatel'nosti*, Vol. 6, No. 4 (1956).
92. Yu. G. Kratin, "On the method of recording oscillations of electrical potentials in the speech musculature," *Zh. Vys. Nervnoi Deyatel'nosti*, Vol. 5, No. 4 (1955).
93. V. Ya. Kryazhev, *Higher Nervous Activity in Animal Communication*, Medgiz, Moscow (1955).
94. O. Külpe, "Modern psychology of thinking" [Russian translation], in: *New Ideas in Philosophy*, Col. No. 16 (1914).
95. N. N. Lange, *Psychological Investigations*, Odessa (1893).
96. M. S. Lebedinskii, *Aphasia, Agnosia, and Apraxia*, Ukr. Psychoneurological Inst. Press, Kharkov (1941).
97. G. W. Leibnitz, *New Essays Concerning Human Understanding* [Russian translation], Sotsékgiz, Moscow-Leningrad (1936).
98. A. N. Leont'ev, *Problems in Psychic Development*, Acad. Pedagog. Sci. RSFSR Press, Moscow (1959).
99. A. N. Leont'ev and O. V. Ovchinnikova, "Analysis of the systemic structure of perception." Communication V: "On the mechanism of the high-frequency analysis of auditory stimuli," *Dokl. APN RSFSR*, No. 3 (1958).
100. J. Locke, An Essay Concerning Human Understanding [Russian translation], *Selected Philosophical Works, Vol. 1*, Sotsékgiz, Moscow (1960).
101. A. R. Luria, *Essays on the Psychophysiology of Writing*, Acad. Pedagog. Sci. RSFSR Press, Moscow (1950).

102. A. R. Luria, *Higher Cortical Functions and Their Disturbances in Local Brain Lesions in Man,* Moscow State University Press, Moscow (1962).
103. A. R. Luria, *The Human Brain and Psychic Processes.* Acad. Pedagog. Sci. RSFSR Press, Moscow (1963).
104. M. A. Dynnik (ed.), *Materialists of Ancient Greece. A Collection of Writings by Heraclitus, Democritus, and Epicurus,* Gospolitizdat, Moscow (1955).
105. M. V. Matyukhina, "Formation of a photochemical conditioned reflex to complex direct and verbal stimuli in man," *Izv. APN RSFSR,* No. 81 (1956).
106. V. Mountcastle, "Certain functional properties of the somatic afferent system," in: *Theory of Communication in Sensory Systems,* Mir, Moscow (1964).
107. E. Meumann, *Lectures on Experimental Teaching,* Part 3 [Russian translation], (1917).
108. J. S. Mill, *System of Logic, Ratiocinative and Inductive* [Russian translation], Moscow (1899).
109. J. S. Mill, *The Examination of Sir William Hamilton's Philosophy* [Russian translation], St. Petersburg (1869).
110. H. Magoun, *The Waking Brain* [Russian translation], Foreign Literature Press, Moscow (1960).
111. M. Müller, *The Science of Thought* [Russian translation], St. Petersburg (1892).
112. L. K. Nazarova, "On the role of speech kinesthesis in writing," *Sovetskaya Pedagogika,* No. 6 (1952).
113. L. A. Novikova, "An electrophysiological study of speech kinesthesis," *Voprosy Psikhologii,* No. 5 (1955).
114. D. N. Ovsyaniko-Kulikovskii, *The Psychology of Thought and Emotion. Creative Writing. Collected Works, Vol. 6* (1909).
115. O. V. Ovchinnikova, "Analysis of the systemic structure of perception. Communication III: On the effect of the vocal cord load on the estimation of pitch in sound discrimination," *Dokl. APN RSFSR,* No. 1 (1958).
116. O. V. Ovchinnikova, "Analysis of the systemic structure of perception. Communication IX: Experimental replacement of the motor link in the system of pitch hearing," *Dokl. APN RSFSR,* No. 3 (1960).
117. I. P. Pavlov, Natural Science and the Brain. *Collected Works, Vol. 3,* Acad. Pedagog. Sci. USSR Press, Moscow-Leningrad (1949).
118. I. P. Pavlov, The Physiological Mechanism of So-Called Voluntary Movements, *ibid.*
119. I. P. Pavlov, An Attempt to Understand the Symptoms of Hysteria Physiologically, *ibid.*
120. I. P. Pavlov, The Physiology of Higher Nervous Activity, *ibid.*
121. I. P. Pavlov, Types of the Higher Nervous Activity, Their Interdependence with Neuroses and Psychoses, and the Physiological Mechanism of Neurotic and Psychotic Symptoms, *ibid.*
122. I. P. Pavlov, Lectures on the Function of the Cerebral Hemispheres, *Collected Works, Vol. 4,* Acad. Sci. USSR Press, Moscow-Leningrad (1947).
123. Pavlovian Wednesdays. *Protocols and Stenographic Records of Talks on Physiology, Vol. 2,* Acad. Sci. USSR Press, Moscow-Leningrad (1949).
124. Pavlovian Wednesdays. *Protocols and Stenographic Records of Talks on Physiology, Vol. 3,* Acad. Sci. USSR Press, Moscow-Leningrad (1949).
125. W. Penfield and H. Jasper, *Epilepsy and the Functional Anatomy of the Human Brain* [Russian translation], Foreign Literature Press, Moscow (1958).
126. W. Penfield and L. Roberts, *Speech and Brain Mechanisms* [Russian translation], Meditsina Press, Leningrad (1964).
127. J. Piaget, *Speech and Thought in the Child.* [Russian translation], (1932).
128. J. Piaget, "Problems in genetic psychology," *Voprosy Psikhologii,* No. 3 (1956).
129. Plato, *Theaetetus* [Russian translation by V. Serezhnikov] (1936).
130. A. L. Pogodin, "Language as Creative Art," in: *Problems in the Theory and Psychology of Creative Art, Vol. 4* (1913).
131. L. I. Podol'skii, "On the mutual influence of inner and external speech," *Uch. Zap. LGPI im. A. I. Gertsena, 53* (1946).

132. G. Polya, *How to Solve It* [Russian translation], Uchpedgiz, Moscow (1959).
133. G. I. Polyakov, "Current data on the structural organization of the cerebral cortex," in: *Higher Cortical Functions in Man*, (A. R. Luriya, ed.), Moscow State University Press, Moscow (1962).
134. D. G. Pomerantseva, The Psychology of Errors in the Oral Speech of Junior School Children (Author's abstract of Candidate's dissertation), Moscow (1953).
135. A. A. Potebnya, Thought and Language, *Collected Works, Vol. 1*, Ukr. State Press (1926).
136. V. V. Pravdich-Neminskii (1925), "Electromyogram of voluntary muscle contraction in man," in: *Electrocerebrography, Electromyography, and the Significance of Ammonia Ions in the Organism's Vital Processes*, Medgiz, Leningrad (1958).
137. T. Ribot, *The Evolution of General Ideas* [Russian translation], Moscow (1898).
138. T. V. Rozanova, "The development of motor memory in deaf and normal children," in: *The Mental Development of Deaf and Normal Children* (I. M. Solov'ev, ed.), Acad. Pedagog. Sci. RSFSR Press, Moscow (1962).
139. J. Rossi and A. Zanchetti, *The Brain Stem Reticular System. Anatomy and Physiology.* [Russian translation], Foreign Literature Press, Moscow (1960).
140. S. L. Rubinshtein, *The Principles and Avenues of Development in Psychology*, Acad. Sci. USSR Press, Moscow (1959).
141. I. M. Sechenov, *The Reflexes of the Brain. Selected Philosophical and Psychological Works*, Gospolitizdat, Moscow (1947).
142. I. M. Sechenov, On the Brain Mechanisms Inhibiting the Spinal Cord Reflexes in the Frog, *ibid.*
143. I. M. Sechenov, The Elements of Thought, *ibid.*
144. I. M. Sechenov, Concrete Thinking from the Standpoint of Physiology, *ibid.*
145. A. A. Smirnov, *Problems in the Psychology of Memory*, Prosveshchenie Press, Moscow (1966) [Eng. translation, Plenum Press, N.Y. (in preparation)].
146. K. M. Smirnov, V. L. Asafov, and O. V. Osipova, "On the electrical activity of the speech musculature during respiratory and motor reactions," *Fiziologicheskii Zh. SSSR*, Vol. 18, No. 11 (1962).
147. É. P. Smolenskaya, "On the verbal symbols of conditional and differentiation stimuli," *Transactions of the Laboratory for the Physiology and Pathophysiology of Higher Nervous Activity in Children and Juveniles*, Vol. 4 (1934).
148. A. N. Sokolov, "Inner speech and understanding," *Uch. Zap. Gos. Nauchno-Issledovat. Inst. Psikhologii*, Vol. 2 (1941).
149. A. N. Sokolov, "Psychological analysis of the understanding of a text in a foreign language," *Izv. APN RSFSR*, No. 7 (1947).
150. A. N. Sokolov, "Thought processes in physical problem solving by students," *Izv. AN RSFSR*, No. 54 (1954).
151. A. N. Sokolov, "On the problem of the speech mechanisms in mental activity," *Proceedings of a Conference on Psychology* (July 1-6, 1955), Acad. Pedagog. Sci. RSFSR Press, Moscow (1957).
152. A. N. Sokolov, "On the speech mechanisms of mental activity," *Izv. APN RSFSR*, No. 81 (1956).
153. A. N. Sokolov, "An electrophysiological study of the speech mechanisms of mental activity," *Dokl. APN RSFSR*, No. 1 (1957).
154. A. N. Sokolov, "Electromyographic studies of concealed articulation in thought processes," in: *Problems in Speech Pathology*, Vol. 30 (81), Ukr. Psychoneurological Scientific-Research Institute Press, Kharkov (1959).
155. A. N. Sokolov, "Studies on the problem of the speech mechanisms of thought," in: *Psychological Science in the USSR, Vol. 1*, Acad. Pedagog. Sci. RSFSR Press, Moscow (1959).
156. A. N. Sokolov, "The dynamics and function of inner speech (concealed articulation)," *Izv. APN RSFSR*, No. 113, Moscow (1960).
157. A. N. Sokolov, "Inner Speech in the study of foreign languages," *Voprosy Psikhologii*, No. 5 (1960).

158. A. N. Sokolov, "Graphic comparison of the logically assumed and actual course of problem solving," *Voprosy Psikhologii*, No. 6 (1961).
159. A. N. Sokolov, "Electromyographic analysis of inner speech and the problem of the neurodynamics of thought," in: *Thought and Speech*. Acad. Pedagog. Sci. RSFSR Press, Moscow (1963).
160. A. N. Sokolov, "Inner speech as a mechanism of thought," *18th International Conference on Psychology, Abstracts*, Vol. 2, Moscow (1966).
161. E. N. Sokolov, *Perception and Conditioned Reflex*, Moscow State University Press (1958).
162. I. M. Solov'ev, "Conceptual changes as a function of similarities and differences of objects," *Uch. Zap. Gos. Nauchno-Issledovat. Inst. Psikhologii*, Vol. 1 (1940).
163. B. Spinoza, *Ethics, Selected Works, Vol. 1*, Politizdat, Moscow (1957).
164. I. V. Strakhov, "Internal monologues in L. M. Tolstoy's works as a source for studying emotional-volitional processes," *Sovetskaya Pedagogika*, No. 3 (1946).
165. I. V. Strakhov, "Problems in the psychology of inner speech," *Uch. Zap. Saratovsk. Pedinstituta*, No. 12 (1948).
166. G. V. Strokina, "An experimental study of the interaction between the first and second signal systems in neurotic children," *Zh. Vyssh. Nervnoi Deyatel'nosti*, Vol. 1, No. 5 (1951).
167. B. M. Teplov, "Representations," in: *Psychology (2nd Ed.)*, K. N. Kornilov, B. M. Teplov, and L. M. Shvarts, eds.), Uchpedgiz, Moscow (1949), Chapter VII.
168. B. M. Teplov, *The Psychology of Musical Abilities*, Acad. Pedagog. Sci. RSFSR Press, Moscow (1947).
169. B. M. Teplov, "Hertsen's psychological views," *Filosofskie Zap. AN SSSR*, Vol. 5, Moscow (1950).
170. E. B. Titchener, *Text Book of Psychology*, [Russian translation], Part 2, Moscow (1914).
171. G. Thomson, *Ancient Philosophers. Historical Studies on Ancient Greek Society* [Russian translation], Vol. 2, Foreign Literature Press, Moscow (1959).
172. N. N. Traugott, "Interrelations of direct and symbolic projections during formation of conditioned inhibition," *Transactions of the Laboratory for the Physiology and Pathophysiology of Higher Nervous Activity in Children and Juveniles*, Vol. 4 (1934).
173. J. Watson, *Psychology as a Science of Behavior*. [Russian translation], Gosizdat, Moscow (1926).
174. A. A. Ukhtomskii, The Dominant as the Working Principle of Nervous Centers, *Collected Works, Vol. 1*, Moscow State University Press (1950).
175. A. A. Ukhtomskii, An Essay on the Physiology of the Nervous System, *Collected Works, Vol. 4*, Moscow State University Press (1945).
176. T. N. Ushakova, "Interaction between the first and second signal systems in the acts of inferential concrete thinking," in: *Boundary Problems in Psychology and Physiology*, (E. I. Boiko, ed.), Acad. Pedagog. Sci. RSFSR Press, Moscow (1961).
177. K. D. Ushinskii, Man as an Object of Education. Experience in Educational Anthropology, Vol. 1, *Collected Works, Vol. 8*, Acad. Pedagog. Sci. RSFSR Press, Moscow (1950).
178. K. D. Ushinskii, Man as an Object of Education. Experience in Educational Anthropology, Vol. 2, *Collected Works, Vol. 9*, Acad. of Pedagog. Sci. RSFSR Press, Moscow (1950).
179. K. D. Ushinskii, On the Elementary Teaching of the Russian Language, *Collected Works, Vol. 5*, Acad. Pedagog. Sci. RSFSR Press, Moscow (1949).
180. K. D. Ushinskii, Native Speech. A Book for Students. *Collected Works, Vol. 6*, Acad. Pedagog. Sci. Press, Moscow (1949).
181. V. K. Fadeeva, "Characteristics of the interaction between the first and second signal systems during formation of responses to complex stimuli in children," *Zh. Vyssh. Nervnoi Deyatel'nosti*, Vol. 1, No. 3 (1951).

182. A. Fessard, "The role of cerebral neuronal networks in the transmission of sensory information," in: *Theory of Communication in Sensory Systems*, Mir, Moscow (1961).

183. I. N. Filimonov, "The localization of functions in the cerebral cortex in relation to the Pavlovian theory of higher nervous activity," *Klinicheskaya Meditsina*, Vol. 29, No. 6 (1961).

184. R. A. Fisher, *Statistical Methods for Research Workers.* [Russian translation], Gosstatizdat, Moscow (1958).

185. A. M. Fonarev, "A device for electrical recording of micromovements of the tongue in concealed articulation," *Izv. APN RSFSR*, No. 81 (1956).

186. L. A. Chistovich, V. V. Alyakrinskii, and V. A. Abul'yan, "Temporary delays during the repetition of the speech heard," *Voprosy Psikhologii*, No. 1 (1960).

187. L. A. Chistovich, Yu. 'A. Klaas, and R. O. Alekin, "On the significance of imitation in the recognition of sound sequences," *Voprosy Psikhologii*, No. 5 (1961).

188. N. I. Chuprikova, "On the local changes in the excitability of the optic analyzer under the influence of verbal stimuli," in: *Boundary Problems in Psychology and Physiology* (E. I. Boiko, ed.), Acad. Pedagog. Sci. RSFSR Press, Moscow (1961).

189. N. R. Shastin, "On the physiology of verbal stimuli," *Fiziologicheskii Zh. SSSR*, Vol. 15, No. 3 (1932).

190. L. A. Shvarts, "The word as conditioned stimulus," *Byulleten' Éksperimental'noi Biologii i Meditsiny*, Vol. 25, No. 4 (1948).

191. L. A. Shvarts, "The acoustic word image and its significance as a conditioned stimulus," *Byulleten' Éksperimental'noi Biologii i Meditsiny*, Vol. 27, No. 6 (1949).

192. L. A. Shvarts, "On the problem of the word as conditioned stimulus," *Byulleten' Éksperimental'noi Biologii i Meditsiny*, Vol. 38, No. 12 (1954).

193. N. Kh. Shvachkin, "An experimental study of early generalizations in children," *Izv. APN RSFSR*, No. 54 (1954).

194. P. A. Shevarev, "On the problem of the nature of algebraic skills," *Uch. Zap. Gos. Nauchno-Issledovat. Inst. Psikhologii*, Vol. 2 (1941).

195. P. A. Shevarev, *Generalized Associations in the School Work of Pupils*, Acad. Pedagog. Sci. RSFSR Press, Moscow (1959).

196. E. Shelikhov, "Proprioceptors," in: *Large Medical Encyclopedia*, 2nd Ed., Vol. 26 (1961).

197. F. N. Shemyakin, "On the problem of verbal and sensory generalizations," *Izv. APN RSFSR*, No. 113 (1960).

198. A. Schopenhauer, Minor Philosophical Works, *Collected Works, Vol. 3*, Moscow (1903).

199. W. Stern, *The Psychology of Early Childhood.* [Russian translation] (1922).

200. A. Einstein, Autobiographical Notes [Russian translation], in: *Physics and Reality*, Nauka, Moscow (1965).

201. Yu. S. Yusevich, "Clinical electromyography in the study of speech pathology," *Zh. Nevropatologii i Psikhiatrii*, Vol. 54, No. 12 (1954).

202. Yu. S. Yusevich, *Electromyography and the Clinical Aspect of Nervous Disorders*, Medgiz, Moscow (1958).

203. Yu. S. Yusevich, *Electromyography of the Tonus of Human Skeletal Musculature Under Normal and Pathological Conditions*, Medgiz, Moscow (1963).

204. E. Aserinsky and N. Kleitman, "Regularly occurring periods of eye motility, and concomitant phenomena during sleep," *Science*, Vol. 118 (1953).

205. G. Ballet, *Le Langage Intérieur*, Ancienne Librairie Germer Bailliere et Cie, Paris (1886).

206. A. K. Bartoshuk, "Electromyographic gradients as indicants of motivation," *Canadian Journal of Psychology*, Vol. 9 (4) (1955).

207. A. K. Bartoshuk, "EMG gradients and EEG amplitude during motivated listening," *Canadian J. of Psychology*, Vol. 10 (3) (1956).

208. R. Bärwald, *Zur Psychologie der Vorstellungstypen*, Leipzig (1916).

209. F. Bernheim, "L'évolution du problème des aphasies," *L'Année psychologique*, Schleicher, Paris (1907).

210. A. Binet, *L'Etude Expérimentale de l'Intelligence,* Paris (1903).
211. E. Buyssens, "Speaking and thinking from the linguistic standpoint," *Acta psychologica,* Vol. 10, No. 1-2 (1954).
212. K. Bühler, "Tatsachen und Problemen zu einer Psychologie der Denkvorgänge," *Archiv für die gesamte Psychologie,* Vol. 9 (1907), Vol. 12 (1908).
213. R. S. Clark, "An experimental study of silent thinking," *Archives of Psychology,* Vol. 48 (1922).
214. J. Cohen, "Thought and language," *Acta psychologica,* Vol. 10, No. 1-2 (1954).
215. S. Cooper, "Muscle spindles in the intrinsic muscles of the human tongue," *J. of Physiology,* Vol. 122 (1953).
216. H. C. Courten, "Involuntary movements of the tongue," *Yale Psychological Studies,* Vol. 10 (1922).
217. H. S. Curtis, "Automatic movements of the larynx," *Amer. J. Psychology,* Vol. 11 (1900).
218. R. S. Davis, "The relation of muscle action potentials to difficulty and frustration," *J. of Exper. Psychology,* Vol. 23 (1938).
219. R. Dodge, Die motorischen Wortvorstellungen. Abhandlungen zur Philosophie und ihrer Geschichte. VIII. Halle a. S. (1896).
220. A. W. Edfeldt, *Silent Speech and Silent Reading,* Almqvist & Wiksell, Stockholm (1959).
221. V. Egger, *La Parole Interieure,* Libraire Germer Bailliere et Cie, Paris (1881).
222. A. Einstein, "The Common Language of Science," (Broadcast recording for Science Conference. London, September 28, 1941), in: *A. Einstein, Ideas and Opinions,* Crown Publishers, Inc., New York (1954).
223. E. Eldred, R. Granit, and P. Merton, "Supraspinal control of the muscle spindles and its significance," *J. Physiology,* Vol. 122 (1953).
224. E. Eldred and K. E. Hagbarth, "Facilitation and inhibition of gamma efferents by stimulation of certain skin areas," *J. of Neurophysiology,* Vol. 17 (1954).
225. W. G. Eliasberg, "Speaking and Thinking," *Acta psychologica,* Vol. 10, No. 1-2 (1954).
226. K. Faaborg-Andersen, "Electromyographic investigation of intrinsic laryngeal muscles in humans," *Acta physiologica scandinavica,* Vol. 41, Suppl. 140 (1957).
227. K. Faaborg-Andersen and A. W. Edfeldt, "Electromyography of intrinsic and extrinsic laryngeal muscles during silent speech: correlation with reading activity," *Acta oto-laryngologica,* Vol. 49 (1958).
228. H. F. Friedlander, "The recalling of thoughts," *Brit. J. of Psychology,* Vol. 37 (1947).
229. H. Gastaut, "Etude électrocorticographique de la réactivité des rythmes rolandiques," *Revue Neurol.,* Vol. 87 (1952).
230. K. Goldstein, "Einige Bemerkungen über Aphasie," *Archiv für Psychiatrie und Nervenkrankheiten,* 45 (1908).
231. K. Goldstein, "Bemerkungen zum Problem 'Sprechen und Denken' auf Grund Hirnpathologischen Erfahrungen," *Acta psychologica,* Vol. 10, No. 1-2 (1954).
232. M. A. Goldstein, "Speech without a tongue," *J. Speech Disorders,* Vol. 5 (1940).
233. H. Göpfert, "Der reflektorische Tonus der Gesichtsmuskulatur unter dem Einfluss von Schmerzreizen und von psychischen Erregungen," in: *XX Congrès international de Physiologie,* Bruxelles (1956).
234. H. Göpfert, A. Bernsmeier und B. Stufler, "Über die Steigerung des Energiestoffwechsels und der Muskelinnervation bei geistiger Arbeit." *Archiv. für die gesamte Physiologie,* Vol. 256, No. 4 (1953).
235. L. N. Gould, "Verbal hallucinations and activity of vocal musculature. An electromyographic study," *Amer. J. Psychiatry,* Vol. 105, No. 5 (1948).
236. L. N. Gould, "Auditory hallucination and subvocal speech. Objective study in a case of schizophrenia," *Journal of Nervous and Mental Disease,* Vol. 109, No. 5 (1949).
237. H. Gruble, "Sprechen und Denken." *Acta psychologica,* Vol. 10, No. 1-2 (1954).
238. J. Hadamard, *An Essay on the Psychology of Invention in the Mathematical Field,* Princeton University Press, Princeton (1945).

239. D. Hartley, *Observations on Man, His Frame, His Duty and His Expectations*, London (1791).
240. V. Inman, P. Ralston, I. Saunders, A. Feinstein, and J. Wright, "Relation of human electromyogram to muscular tension," *Electroencephalography and Clinical Neurophysiology*, Vol. 4, No. 2 (1952).
241. J. Hughlings Jackson, *Selected Writings of John Hughlings Jackson*, Vol. 2 (J. Taylor, ed.), Hodder & Stoughton, London (1931).
242. E. Jacobson, "On meaning and understanding," *Amer. J. Psychology*, Vol. 22 (1911).
243. E. Jacobson, Electrical measurements of neuromuscular states during mental activities. VII. Imagination, recollection, and abstract thinking involving the speech musculature," *Amer. J. Physiology*, Vol. 97, No. 1 (1931).
244. E. Jacobson, "Electrophysiology of mental activities," *American Journal of Psychology*, Vol. 44 (1932).
245. E. Jacobson, *Progressive Relaxation*, 9th Edition, Univ. Chicago Press (1961).
246. E. Jacobson and F. L. Kraft, "Contraction potentials (right quadriceps femoris) in man during reading," *Amer. J. Physiology*, Vol. 137, No. 1 (1942).
247. P. W. Jessen, "Über das Verhältnis des Denkens zum Sprechen," *Archiv für pathologische Anatomie und Physiologie und für klinische Medizin*, Vol. 35, No. 1 (1866).
248. J. Jorgensen, "Some remarks concerning thinking and talking," *Acta psychologica*, Vol. 10, No. 1-2 (1954).
249. F. Kainz, "Vorformen des Denkens," *Acta psychologica*, Vol. 10, No. 1-2 (1954).
250. J. L. Kennedy, R. M. Gottsdanker, J. C. Armington, and F. S. Gray, "A new electroencephalogram associated with thinking," *Science*, Vol. 108 (1948).
251. S. W. Kuffler, C. C. Hunt, and J. P. Quilliam, "Function of medullated small-nerve fibers in mammalian ventral roots: efferent muscle spindle innervation," *J. of Neurophysiology*, Vol. 14 (1951).
252. E. Kurka, "Zur Beeinflussung der Stimme durch inneres Sprechen bei maschineller Schreibarbeit," *Z. Universität Halle, Ges. Sprachw*, Vol. 8, No. 6 (1959).
253. E. Kurka, Inneres Sprechen und Stimme, in: *Proceedings of the Fourth International Congress of Phonetic Science*, Helsinki (1961).
254. O. Lippold, "The relation between integrated action potentials in a human muscle and its isometric tension," *J. Physiology*, Vol. 117, No. 4 (1952).
255. McIntyre, A. K., "Cortical projections of afferent impulses in muscle nerves," *Proceedings of the University of Otago Medical School*, Vol. 31 (1953).
256. L. W. Max, "An experimental study of the motor theory of consciousness. I. Critique of earlier studies," *J. of General Psychology*, Vol. 2 (1934); III. Action current responses in deaf-mutes during sleep, sensory stimulation and dreams," *J. of Comp. Psychology*, Vol. 19 (1935);" IV. Action current responses of deaf during awakening, kinesthetic imagery, and abstract thinking," *J. Comp. Psychol.*, Vol. 24 (1937).
257. V. B. Mountcastle, M. R. Covian, and C. R. Harrison, "The central representation of some forms of deep sensibility," *Research Publications, Association for Research in Nervous and Mental Disease*, Vol. 30 (1952).
258. R. B. Onians, *The Origin of European Thought*, Cambridge Univ. Press, London (1951).
259. J. Piaget, "Le langage et la pensée du point de génétique," *Acta psychologica*, Vol. 10, No. 1-2 (1954).
260. R. Pintner, "Inner speech during silent reading," *Psychol. Review*, Vol. 20 (1913).
261. J. C. Raven, *Guide to Using Progressive Matrices* (Revised order), H. K. Lewis & Co., printed by Wm. Grieve & Sons, Dumfries, London (1956).
262. N. B. Reed, "The existence and function of inner speech in thought processes," *J. Exper. Psychol.*, Vol. 1 (1916).
263. G. Révész, "Denken und Sprechen," *Acta psychologica*, Vol. 10, No. 1-2 (1954).
264. J. E. Rose and V. B. Mountcastle, "Touch and kinesthesis," in: *Handbook of Physiology. I. Neurophysiology*, Washington (1959).

265. W. A. Shaw, "The relation of muscular action potentials to imaginal weight lifting," *Arch. Psychol.*, New York (1940).
266. A. A. Smirnow, Sprechbewegungen und Retention. Bericht über den sechzehnten Internazionalen Kongress fur Psychologie, Bonn, 1960. *Acta psychologica*, Vol. 19 (1961).
267. A. A. Smith, R. B. Malmo, and C. Shagass, "An electromyographic study of listening and talking," *Canadian J. of Psychol.*, Vol. 8 (4) (1954).
268. R. S. Snider, "Interrelations of cerebellum and brain stem," *Research Publications. Association for Research in Nervous and Mental Disease*, Vol. 30 (1952).
269. A. N. Sokolov, "La parole intéreure dans la pensée concrète," in: *Recherches psychologiques en URSS*, Editions du Progrès, Moscow (1966).
270. H. Steinthal, "Zur Sprachphilosophie," *Zeitschrift von Fichte und Ulrici*, Vol. 32.
271. R. H. Stetson, *Motor Phonetics*, 2nd Ed., North Holland Publ. Co., Amsterdam (1951).
272. S. S. Stricker, *Studien über die Sprachvorstellungen*, Braumüller Wien (1880).
273. C. R. Strother, "Voice Training after Laryngectomy," in: E. Froeschels (ed.), *Twentieth Century Speech and Voice Correction*, Philosophical Library, New York (1948).
274. J. E. Swett, C. M. Bourassa, and S. Inoue, "Effect of cutaneous and muscle sensory nerve volleys in awake cats: a study in perception," *Science*, Vol. 145, No. 3636 (1964).
275. E. B. Titchener, *Lectures on the Experimental Psychology of the Thought Processes*. Macmillan, New York (1909).
276. A. M. Thorson, "The relation of tongue movements to internal speech," *J. of Exper. Psychol.*, Vol. 8 (1925).
277. B. L. Van der Waerden, "Denken ohne Sprache," *Acta psychologica*, Vol. 10, No. 1-2 (1954).
278. H. Wallerstein, "An electromyographic study of attentive listening," *Canadian J. of Psychol.*, Vol. 8 (4) (1954).
279. J. B. Watson, "Is thinking merely the action of language mechanisms?", *Brit. J. of Psychol.*, Vol. 11 (1920).
280. M. Wertheimer, *Productive Thinking*. Harper, New York (1954).
281. R. S. Woodworth, "A revision of imageless thought," *Psychol. Rev.*, Vol. 22 (1915).
282. R. S. Woodworth and H. Schlosberg, *Experimental Psychology* (Revised Edition), Holt, Rinehart & Winston, New York (1962).
283. A. Wyczoikowska, "Theoretical and experimental studies in the mechanism of speech," *Psychol. Rev.*, Vol. 20 (1913).
284. N. I. Žinkin, *Mechanisms of Speech*. Mouton, The Hague-Paris (1968).

Author Index

Subject Index